T0121941

BERNICE:

A fiery story of love and family

In her daughter's pen

Bernice Haney and Janet C. Thomas

BALBOA.
PRESS
A DIVISION OF HAY HOUSE

Balboa Press books may be ordered through booksellers or by contacting:

Balboa Press
A Division of Hay House
1663 Liberty Drive
Bloomington, IN 47403
www.balboapress.com
1 (877) 407-4847

Because of the dynamic nature of the Internet, any web addresses or links contained in this book may have changed since publication and may no longer be valid. The views expressed in this work are solely those of the author and do not necessarily reflect the views of the publisher, and the publisher hereby disclaims any responsibility for them.

The author of this book does not dispense medical advice or prescribe the use of any technique as a form of treatment for physical, emotional, or medical problems without the advice of a physician, either directly or indirectly. The intent of the author is only to offer information of a general nature to help you in your quest for emotional and spiritual well-being. In the event you use any of the information in this book for yourself, which is your constitutional right, the author and the publisher assume no responsibility for your actions.

Any people depicted in stock imagery provided by Thinkstock are models, and such images are being used for illustrative purposes only.
Certain stock imagery © Thinkstock.

Printed in the United States of America.

ISBN: 978-1-4525-1581-6 (sc)
ISBN: 978-1-4525-1583-0 (hc)
ISBN: 978-1-4525-1582-3 (e)

Library of Congress Control Number: 2014909679

Balboa Press rev. date: 06/19/2014

Dedicated to Bobby

PREFACE

My daughter wanted to write this book, and after a lot of encouragement from her, I agreed. I enjoyed talking about my childhood and the good times I had. It was even nice to let some things out that I'd never told anyone before. But I didn't realize how many memories I would have to recall after blocking them from my mind for so many years. At times the questioning and prying was upsetting. It was as if I was reliving all that I went through years ago. I realize now that sometimes looking back is the only way to become aware of how lucky we are that things can change for the better and how blessed we are to have unconditional love.

This story starts in the 1930s when I was a child and ends in the '70s when I was in my forties. Attitudes and beliefs were so much different when I was being raised and changed dramatically in the '50s and '60s. There was a lot to reckon with. I know the younger generations might find some of my story hard to believe, but it is all true as best as I can remember it.

Now that the book is done, I'm glad my daughter wrote it. I hope it inspires you to find strength and courage in your life.

—*Bernice*

* * * * *

I asked my mom years ago if I could write her life story for her. I knew that she had gone through a lot, because I was there for some of it. I also knew that she had put the past behind her and didn't talk about it. I felt compelled to know what it was that she wasn't saying. I also wanted to know what motivated this woman, what kept her going, how she was able to become the pillar that she now is in so many people's lives.

Some readers might think she did what she did because she is a stubborn redhead; some might see the strong heart and soul that carried her through life. You might even find it comical, but after hearing her stories, I think everything she did was backed by love in one way or another.

Her story, her life, is an example for me, as I hope it will be for other women who struggle. The morals, ethics, and laws were different then for women than they are now. Yet, without the support of any laws, she trusted herself, relied on the church, and had faith and trust in the unconditional love she got from her family. She did what she thought was right at the time. She never got down on herself, and she was willing to make mistakes and handle everything that was set in her path with immense courage, determination, and the guts and tenacity to take it all in stride.

I did my best to write this story as it was told to me—in my mom's plainspoken voice. The no-nonsense tone carries her story through drama and suspense as she ricochets from one challenge to another on this unsentimental journey. I am proud to call this indomitable woman my mother.

Built upon the trials of those who came before me and bestowed, with respect, to my mother's love.

—Janet

ACKNOWLEDGEMENTS

First and foremost, my deepest thanks to my mother, Bernice Elvira Smith (Haney), for supporting the idea of the book and for the hundreds of hours she spent answering my endless questions about things she never talked about before, for revealing feelings she never let show, and for having the courage to share personal information that she kept to herself, until now.

I would also like to express my gratitude to my writing group—John Andrews, Laura Rankin, Amy Scott, Ludmila Shebeko, Jim Tracy, and Marion Kee. Their early and constant support, encouragement, feedback, and editing were instrumental in the successful completion of this book. A special thanks also to Carlene Cross, who got me going in the right direction in my first memoir writing class.

Finally, this book would not have been possible without all the moral support of our family, who answered questions, told us stories, and helped us recall old memories.

CHARACTER LIST

Throughout my life and my story, my family plays big and small parts in helping me navigate through my journey. There were twelve of us Smith kids, and I was an aunt as soon as I was born. I figured I might as well tell you a little bit about my brothers and sisters so you know who they are as you read along and they come in and out of my life.

Rosella Pearl, born January 6, 1913

Pearl was the eldest of all us kids—about twenty years older than me. She was the cornerstone, solid, stable, and reliable. For the most part she was a housewife and mother. She always kept her hair neat and short—off her shoulders—and carried herself with confidence and certainty. She was married to Sam Baker, who was a car mechanic with his own garage, appropriately called Baker's. They had five kids: Donald, CE (Charles Edwin), Sammy, Phyllis, and Harold.

Ellis Ulysses, born June 18, 1914

Ellis was a tall, thin man who favored Daddy in looks and had Mama's sensitive and caring nature. He married Edna and lived in Texas. I remember him as a gentle, kind, and caring brother who would put his arm around me or maybe touch my arm while he was talking to me, just to let me know he cared or to remind me that he was there for me.

Sarah Elizabeth, born March 1, 1916

Sarah was a redhead, like me. But her hair was a darker reddish brown, not as bright as mine. She was average height and had a little heavier frame, maybe because she was a diabetic and had to eat regularly and take insulin to control it. She was strong in her will but had an undeniable soft spot for babies.

As long as I can remember, Sarah was married to Alden Cates and lived in Randle, Washington. Her husband was in the Merchant Marines and provided for their family. They owned a home and always had Shetland ponies in the back pasture. She came home every couple of years to visit and usually brought her three girls with her: Myrtle, Marjorie, and Marie. Myrtle was two years younger than me, and her sisters were younger than her. Sarah decided to become a nurse after Marjorie's first baby was born. But she also ran a yarn store from their home before, during, and after her nursing career.

Aubrey Uriah, born February 8, 1918

Aubrey looked like Daddy more than any of the other boys—with a tall, strong body and square jaw—although all the boys had Daddy's bigger-than-normal ears. The only difference between Daddy and Aubrey was that Aubrey had some red in his hair and Daddy didn't. I didn't see Aubrey much while I was growing up. I think he was closer to Ellis than his other brothers and sisters.

He changed his name to Scott Ericson and was a bit of a nomad, but he stayed in California longer than anywhere else. But no matter what he called himself, or where he lived, he was known as Stormy to many of us, all through his life.

As far back as I can remember, he was married to Gladys (we called her Renee—I'm not sure why). Renee and Scott had a daughter, Gay, another child who died due to crib death, and then umpteen years later they had a son, Reo, whom Scott fondly called Rebel.

Zelma Climena, born November 5, 1919

Zelma was a redhead, like Sarah and me—but again, not the bright-red hair that I had. She was also a nurse and a very family-oriented wife and mother with a smile ready to bring out the cheer in you. She was my older sister by about fourteen years, but she was more like a friend than anything else.

Zelma was a very loving, caring person. She enjoyed life and laughter and liked to travel and camp out. But she could also be too serious and very sensitive and could cry over watching the news. She was married to Bill Yalotz, a retired boxer. Daddy used to say he was punch-happy. I don't think I ever heard him laugh, and I never knew Bill to hit anyone, but he was different than anyone I've ever known. It could be that he brought Zelma's seriousness out.

Zelma and Bill had four kids: Babes, Bill, John, and Kitty.

Edwin Earl Jr., "Sonny," born July 17, 1921

Sonny was named after Daddy, but I never heard anyone call him anything other than Sonny. You know how parents sometimes use a kid's full name when they are in trouble—well I never knew him to be in trouble either.

Sonny used to tell me that I was pretty. But I thought Sonny was dashingly handsome. I don't know if it was his soft features and big smile that made him so nice looking or if it was the fact that he was confident, always in a good mood, and easy to be around. He was either singing, whistling, or laughing, no matter what he was doing.

Charles J., born April 18, 1923

I don't feel like I really knew Charles. He probably moved out when I was pretty young. I think he came home for a short visit once when I was a teenager. When I was older, we had more of a business relationship than anything. He was married to a woman with a couple of teenage kids. I never met any of the kids, but I vaguely remember meeting his wife once, before they moved to Indiana. I didn't see him again after he moved, but I would have known him if I did see him. He definitely looked like a Smith—same dark hair, brown eyes, and similar features, although a little reserved. And I think he was just a little shorter than my other brothers, except David.

David Grant, born June 4, 1927

David lived at home with us until I was about 10. He was an average kid as I remember. Maybe a little quieter than most. He liked working on the farm and the normal boy stuff like hunting and fishing.

He had a bald spot in the middle of a crown of dark hair, which, along with his glasses, made him look older. David never married.

Agnes Sophia, born September 13, 1929

Beautiful Agnes. She used to have dark-brown hair with a light red cast, like highlights. But later on she started dyeing it, and it kept getting darker and darker—so dark it was almost black. When she smiled, deep dimples poked the middle of each rounded cheek. On one side, between her dimple and her jawline, was a dark mole about the size of an eraser on the end of a pencil. She could flash her toothy smile and make you like her in an instant. Everyone loved her, especially the guys.

She was married several times and had three girls: Kathy, Myrtle (we called her Pud, and later others called her Kitty), and Johanna (who always went by Jody). They all had different fathers. But I'm not saying that as a bad thing. Agnes loved men and having a good time. She also dearly loved her girls and all her brothers and sisters.

Agnes was the first one of us girls to go into nursing, even before our older sisters Zelma and Pearl. And from what I know, she was damn good at it. She was a true people person.

Arthur Eugene, born August 21, 1931

Arthur was Mama's boy, very coddled and adored. I think I was in the fourth grade before he quit sucking his thumb and twisting his hair. He had pretty, dark-brown, naturally curly hair—and dimples. He was the only one of the boys who had curls. The girls all thought he was cute. So did I.

Arthur instigated fun. He was very charming and could talk me into most anything. He was a lot like Sonny. He liked to play the guitar and sing and have fun. He was a happy-go-lucky guy, but if something was bothering him, I could tell, and probably anyone who was close to him could tell. But he could bluff others. I think he was the type of person who tried to hold his feelings back and smile through it. Arthur never married.

Elva Ruth, born February 9, 1935

Elva was my only younger sibling. She was the baby, and she was Daddy's girl.

Growing up, she was always skinnier than me, with dark hair, darker brown eyes, and a darker complexion than me. She was fourteen when I moved out. She married Frank Bensik when she was eighteen years old.

Elva was always a tender-hearted, thoughtful person. Even if you didn't know that about her, you could see it in her eyes. She kept her tall, thin frame, and dark, shoulder-length hair throughout her life, but her weight did fluctuate some over the years as she and Frank raised six kids. She enjoyed being a housewife and mother. But I do remember her working a little too.

Bernice Elvira, born May 2, 1933

And there's me. This is my story. Read on, and I'll introduce you to my husband and kids and help you get to know my mother and father as well.

1

___

I wasn't more than ten years old the first time I realized that life was tricky. Some people live a charmed life, and for others, like me, there's trouble around every corner. I don't even know if trouble is the right word for it. It's more like stuff that gets in your way and moves everything in your life around so that nothing is as expected. When it all started out, everything in my life seemed to be going along just fine. Then, out of nowhere, the sheriff and his men came into our home in the middle of the night and took my brother. That one moment changed my whole life. It also prepped me for the next turn and the next... I learned the hard way that no matter what gets in your way, call it trouble or call it what you will, you just keep your feelings to yourself, trust yourself, and keep on going—no matter what.

I'll just start at the beginning and let you decide if trouble is what you would call it.

I was born in 1933 in Monument, Kansas, in a two-room house that had been an old schoolhouse before we moved in. My parents named me Bernice Elvira after one of my aunts. I was the eleventh of twelve Smith children. Out of the twelve of us kids, I was the only one born in Monument. For some reason we tended to move a lot. Consequently, every one of us twelve kids was born in a different place.

My mama was twenty when she had her first child. My eldest sister, Pearl, was born in 1913. Mama and Daddy kept the kids a-coming just about every two years for the next twenty-two years. The last child was my little sister, Elva, who was born in 1935. Mama had a Bible that she recorded all our birth dates in. It was the very first page of the Bible, and it said "Family Record." Mama wrote down all the birth dates and names but not where everyone was born.

I think all my brothers and sisters before me were born in either Arkansas or Kansas. But my little sister, Elva, was born in Colorado. She was the only one of the twelve of us that was actually born in a hospital. I'm not sure how Mama did it. I wonder if she had a midwife, but I don't really know. In those days, birth wasn't talked about much, so I don't really know much about how she went about having twelve kids. In fact, anything having to do with sex was pretty much taboo. We just didn't talk about such things.

Mama was a schoolteacher before she got married. At that time school only went through to the ninth grade. While she was teaching, Daddy went back to school just so they could keep the school open— and so he could see Mama, I bet. In December 1911, when Mama was eighteen, she married my daddy, and soon thereafter she stopped teaching. Back then, I don't think women were allowed to work after they were married. A woman was expected to stay home to be a wife and a mother.

I was just a baby when we moved to Colorado, so I was pretty much raised there. My little sister was born just before I turned two. I told Mama that I remembered when Arthur was born and came home from the hospital. She gently corrected me—it was Elva, not Arthur, because Arthur was older than me. I guess I think of Elva as just always being there.

We landed in Vineland, Colorado, by the Arkansas River, at the eastern foothills of the Rocky Mountains. We were still living there when I started school. I ended up living near there again after I was married. But I'm getting ahead of myself.

All twelve of us kids didn't live at home at the same time. There were too many years between us. By the time Elva and I were born, most of my brothers and sisters had already moved out on their own. Back then kids tended to move out on their own when they were younger—well before they were eighteen. The five youngest kids—David, Agnes, Arthur, Elva, and I—were the only ones home with Mama and Daddy while I was growing up. We all went to the same school. I can place myself each year from my earliest memories pretty much by which school I was attending that year. In first grade, we lived in Vineland. In second grade, I went to Riverview Grade School, and we lived in an area called St. Charles Mesa. We called the house we lived in "the tar paper house" because the outside was just tar paper and it never did get painted. Daddy was a carpenter, and most of the time he would fix up the houses we lived in for part of the rent. I remember us girls slept upstairs in the attic. There was a ladder that went down from the attic to Mama and Daddy's room. All three of us girls slept in one bed. I think Agnes, Elva, and I always slept together all the time we were growing up.

In the third grade we moved to Rock Creek. I went to a school there that had a total of thirteen kids. It was also a two-room schoolhouse, and the kids were all ages from the first grade to the eighth grade. Our entire school (all thirteen of us) were in a picture in the local newspaper that year.

Our house in Rock Creek actually had eleven rooms, but I still slept with my sisters. It was a fun time when we lived there. We were always having parties with singing and dancing. Coy Baker was a good friend of my daddy's, and he and his younger brother Sam would come over and play music for us to sing and dance to. Everyone who came over brought their kids. It seemed as if we always moved to the same place as Coy and his family around the same time that they moved. Coy's younger brother Sam was married to my older sister Pearl when she was just sixteen. So I ended up having nieces and nephews that were older than me. Their eldest boys, Donald and CE, always called me auntie because they were bigger and older than me. CE was always ready to have a little fun, up to something, or trying to find his way out of trouble. Sammy was cute, with curly, blondish-red hair. Phyllis was a year younger than me and more like a sister than a niece.

In the fourth grade we moved to Rye where Daddy did share farming. The ranch in Rye was different than the farms we lived on before because it was hundreds of acres. Before this we had always been on farms that were just a few acres. The ranch was located in what Daddy called a box canyon.

From the main road you had to go down a hill, over a bridge, and past the cornfield, about three miles, to get to where you could turn into the ranch. I know because Agnes, Arthur, Elva, and I had to ride our horses to the main road to catch the bus to school. But it wasn't bad; it was kind of fun. Daddy built a shed for us to park the horses in while we were in school. The neighbor, from about a mile away, parked their horses there too. Then, when we got off the bus after school, the horses were still there, and we rode them home.

The house we lived in had to be the smallest part of the ranch. It had four rooms: the kitchen, Mama and Daddy's room, the boy's bedroom, and a bedroom for us girls. Mama and Daddy's room was supposed to be the front room. The front door opened into their room. The back door opened into the back porch and then the kitchen. There was no indoor plumbing. We had an outhouse just the other side of the chicken coop.

Agnes, Arthur, Elva, and I used to sneak Daddy's cigarette butts out of the ashtray or find them out in the yard and then go out to the outhouse and smoke them. The outhouse was big enough that three of us could be inside at once, while someone kept watch on the outside.

4

Mama had a match holder that hung on the wall by the stove. So it was pretty easy to grab a stick match when we needed one. We all learned at a pretty young age how to strike a match on a board and light a smoke.

We didn't like going out to the outhouse in the dark at night to go to the bathroom, though. So Mama and Daddy would let us bring a bucket in at night to pee in. We all got a bath once a week in a big tub in the middle of the kitchen floor. There was a wood range in the kitchen that we would heat bathwater on. All of us took turns and used the same bathwater—oldest to youngest—and never gave it a second thought. This was all just normal stuff we did as we were growing up.

There was a creek that ran through the middle of the ranch behind the house. We loved swimming in the creek. Every once in a while Arthur would talk me into going fishing with him down at the creek. Elva wouldn't go with us because she didn't like hurting animals (fish in this case). I didn't really like fishing, but Arthur could talk me into doing things. He was handsome and always cheerful. He was just fun to be around—always singing or whistling a tune. There were also wild fruit trees and berries along the creek. I remember picking the chokecherries that grew wild out there. We would pick them for Mama to make jelly with. You sure didn't want to eat them right off the tree, unless you really wanted to pucker. They were really sour. But Mama made good jelly out of them and the currants that grew wild out there.

If you followed the creek far enough, it turned a corner and ran alongside an old log cabin that old lady Colvin would come and stay in during the summer months. Even farther down the creek was what we called Rock Mountain. It was about three-quarters of a mile up one side. There were trees on top of the mountain and down the other side, but by the creek, it was all rocks. Us kids would spend hours playing there—except for Agnes, she thought she was too old to play with us.

Across the creek from Rock Mountain were a couple of grave markers. We figured it was the Colvin family members buried out there.

The best part of being out there on the ranch was sleeping in the trailer in the summertime, outside. It was an open trailer, with wooden sides, and you could see the entire sky full of stars, clear and bright. It was the same wagon that we hooked the team of horses up to when we would go to town. It was great being a kid out there, but there was a lot of hard work to be done too, and all us kids were expected to pitch in and do chores as well. David had turned sixteen, had a girlfriend in town, and started spending most of his time in town. He was staying at our sister Pearl's house and worked a couple of days a week at the broom factory and a couple of days a week at the Pueblo newspaper. So it was just Agnes, Elva, Arthur, and me at home now.

We had cows, pigs, and of course we had our horses. We always had a milk cow, and we always had chickens too. We all had to learn to milk the cow, and we all had to go feed the animals. Most of the time Daddy would do the morning milking and chores, but like I said, we all had to pitch in.

Daddy planted field corn, or what they call maize, and we had to shuck the corn for animals and then stack the stalks like a teepee. We fed the animals the stalks in the winter. Mama and Daddy kept us busy. We just did our chores—there was no taking turns and all that nonsense. Things just had to be done, and if one person was taking care of one thing, you just went and took care of a different chore. We never fought about it. Of course, we had squabbles and spats, but we always did it where Daddy couldn't hear us. Daddy just didn't believe in fussing and fighting. You had to stick to business. It was an important responsibility to raise kids, and he believed there was a certain way to do it right. Don't get me wrong, he really wasn't that bad. In fact, he was a wonderful dad.

Our home life was pretty happy. In all my life I never heard or saw my mama and daddy fight—except for one time. That was when Mama thought Daddy hit Arthur too hard with the razor strop for skipping school. The razor strop kept us kids in line.

I got the razor strop once when I was being stubborn. I'm a redhead, and you know what they say, redheads are stubborn. I was sitting at the kitchen table with Arthur doing homework. It was a good-sized, round kitchen table. The kitchen was lit by oil lamps, and Daddy's razor strop hung by the kitchen sink. He used the strop for two things—to sharpen the razor he shaved with and to keep us kids in line.

While we were doing our homework, Arthur asked to use my eraser. For some reason I didn't want him to and just flat out refused to let him use it. Daddy heard what was going on and got down the razor strop and spanked me with it—just one spank. He really didn't hit me too hard. I think he just wanted me to know that he would use it on me if he had to. I sure didn't want him to have to. I knew if he did it once, he would do it again. Once I realized this, I simply behaved myself around Daddy. This was pretty much the consensus of all us kids—behave.

Mama was always busy too. She had a garden that she took care of, and she did canning, cooking, cleaning, and made all our clothes. She was very easygoing and easy to get along with (the redheads in our family came from Daddy's side of the family). We used to buy flour in hundred-pound sacks because she made all our bread and biscuits from scratch. The flour sacks were printed with flowers or stripes or other various patterns. Some of them were actually quite pretty. Mama made our dresses out of them. She also made shirts for the boys. When we were a little older, we told Mama that all the other girls at school were wearing jeans. So she even made pants for us.

When it got dark outside, we would all come in for the day, and the whole family would sit around the radio and listen to shows like the

Grand Ole Opry or news about the war. This was in the 1940s during World War II. I was around ten years old. It was before television was invented.

The radio sat in the corner of Mama and Daddy's room. Mama kept a green felt scarf on the top of it. The scarf was pretty, and it made the radio look nice. The radio was battery operated—we didn't have electricity. The radio stood about as high as the kitchen counter and was about the width of a chair. There was a fairly good-sized battery that went into the back. Mama and Daddy's room was the biggest room, so it was also like our family room. Sometimes while we listened to the radio, we would sit on the floor and play checkers, dominoes, or Chinese checkers. I enjoyed playing games together at night. When bedtime rolled around, we would crawl into bed and get warm under the quilts that Mama made for our beds.

During this time my older brothers Sonny and Ellis went into the service. I'm not sure where Sonny and Ellis were living at that time, because I was still young. But they managed to make it home for one last Sunday dinner before they went off to war. Every Sunday us kids would have to pluck chickens, and every Sunday night we had a fried chicken dinner. They came home to tell us good-bye. Sonny went into the army and Ellis went into the marines. I remember Sonny saying that he may never see us again. I wish he wouldn't have said that, because he didn't come home. We never saw him again. He was killed in action in 1945 in Manila one day before Americans recaptured the area. Ellis didn't say anything like that, and he came back home and got married while he was stationed in Texas. Everyone loved Sonny. He was Junior, named after Daddy, and despite the age difference, he and Arthur were just alike—great disposition, always cheerful, handsome, and just fun to be around.

Before Sonny died, sometime after the war started, Daddy started working at the army depot, building things for the war department—as well as doing his carpentry and other work on the ranch. On Sunday night he would head out for work and wouldn't come back until Friday night or Saturday morning. Every once in a while Daddy would pick David up in town and bring him home for the weekend. David had gotten his girlfriend pregnant, and her family had totally cut David out of her life and refused to acknowledge him as the baby's father.

One weekend when David was home, on a Saturday, to be exact, I remember being wakened by men's voices and bright lights flashing through the room. There were no doors on our bedrooms. You walked from the back door through the kitchen, then through a door to the right to Mama and Daddy's room, and then you walked through Mama and Daddy's bedroom to get to our room or the boys' room. Our room was on the left, and the boys' room was on the right. When I got up to see what was happening, I saw two sheriffs carrying big bright lights and walking through Mama and Daddy's room to the boys' room. Daddy told me to go back to bed. I could tell from the sound of his voice that I needed to do exactly that, without asking any questions. The sheriff took my brother David with them that night. I didn't know exactly why until later in life. All I knew was that he had done something bad. We didn't talk about it much, but it definitely changed me and life as I knew it.

Earlier that day Arthur and David had gone up to the Hutchinson farm with the Hutchinson's grandson, Carl, to get an old sword and some other things for a play at school. The Hutchinsons lived about two miles from us across the foothills, as the crow flies. On their way up to the farmhouse Carl told Arthur and David that his grandmother might not be at home because it was about time for the pension check to come in and she might be in town. David was sixteen at the time, and there was a car in town that he wanted to buy for twenty-five dollars. The guy in town told David that he would hold the car for him for two weeks. David thought if he had the Hutchinsons' pension money he could buy that car. Twenty-five dollars was a lot of money to come by back then.

While they walked, David thought about how he could get that money. Mama said that since he got jumped in the alley that one time, he wasn't really himself. I know David had a big scar and a bald spot on his head from it. But I don't really know what actually happened to him. He was a nice brother. He did his chores and even had a job. He went hunting a lot, and he loved animals. I guess it just came into his mind that day to kill the Hutchinsons and take their money.

The Hutchinsons were home when the boys arrived. But David didn't do anything except go with Arthur and Carl to get the things for the play and then leave with them. When David got home, he got his gun and told us he was going hunting. Nobody thought anything of it. David was always hunting. But instead of going hunting he went back up to the Hutchinsons'. This time when he got up to the farmhouse they weren't there. But he saw them in the field with the hayrack. David went into the house and took Mr. Hutchinson's rifle off the wall in the kitchen because his own gun was only a single-shot .22. Mr. Hutchinson's gun held eighteen rounds. He went to the barn with both guns and waited for them to return. The repeater was already loaded, and he had two full boxes of shells.

He sat there waiting for at least a half hour before he heard the wagon coming up by the barn. It was pulled by two horses and loaded full of corn fodder. Mr. Hutchinson was driving the wagon, and Mrs. Hutchinson was following behind on foot carrying three bundles that had been lost from the load. When the wagon pulled up in front of the barn, David took his first shot. It hit Mr. Hutchinson in the hand. The horses bolted and started down a steep grade. David kept shooting. David knew he hit him when Mr. Hutchinson fell off the wagon about a hundred feet from the corral while the horses and the wagon plunged on across the creek.

He started up the road to where Mrs. Hutchinson was. He had two shots left. She started yelling and pleading with David.

"David, please he's hurt. We need to help him."

"I shot him. He's dead," David said. "And you're next."

"Are you going crazy!" she screamed.

"I think I am," David replied as he raised the gun and fired his last two rounds.

Mrs. Hutchinson fell to the ground. David didn't have any more bullets in the gun. He approached her. One bullet had grazed her scalp; the other hit her in the shoulder. He struck her with the butt of the rifle. She raised her arm up to block a blow to the head, and he could hear the crack just as loud and clear as the gunfire before it. It broke her arm and also the butt of the gun.

"Please, David, don't!" she cried as David stood poised to strike again. Her voice softened. "Help me. Help me to the house," she said, finding her voice and thinking quickly. "It's going to be okay. We'll say that I was hurt by the runaway team."

He looked down on her there on the ground. The gun, broken and empty. Mrs. Hutchinson, broken. He himself, broken but not empty. Quietly, a moment passed. She was sobbing and hurt pretty bad. He let his gun fall to the ground, and he bent down to help her.

"You have to say that you were hurt by a runaway team."

"Yes, I promise," she said.

He lifted her to her feet. Slowly they walked up to the house.

"I can't find my keys," she said, breaking the silence as they approached the back door.

Without hesitation David kicked the back door in, breaking the lock. As she walked in the door, she turned and asked him to go get

11

help. She promised that she would not contradict his story that both she and her husband had been hurt by a runaway team. He turned and walked away. She watched him as he went to the barn and got his single-shot .22 and headed down the road. She then filled a basin with water and washed the blood off and inspected her wounds. She wasn't sure if she could trust David to return with help. So she gathered herself together and headed down the road to Jess Kent's place. She didn't know if she would make it, but she had to try.

At the foot of the hill David noticed the team of horses tangled in their harnesses. He thought they were in pain. So he shot them with his .22 to try to put them out of their misery. About a half mile up the road he hid his gun in the brush. The closest neighbor was still another mile up the road. When he reached the farm, he found Jess Kent and told him that Mr. Hutchinson had been killed and Mrs. Hutchinson had been hurt by a runaway team of horses. Jess had a car that they took to go to two other houses looking for some more help. But no one was home at either place. Finally they found Bus Caple working in the field and told him about it. The Caples had a phone, so his wife called the mortuary. Jess and David headed back to Jess's house. As they drove back, they saw Mrs. Hutchinson coming up behind Jess's barn on foot. They drove around to where she was and put her in the car.

Jess drove Mrs. Hutchinson to the hospital, and David got out of the car when they passed Caple's place. David went with Mr. Caple back to the Hutchinsons'. He acted like everything was normal. The people from the mortuary were there, and David showed them where the body was. After they loaded up the body and left, David shut up the cows and walked home. He just went about his business like it was all going to be okay. Mama said he kind of had episodes when he wouldn't remember what he was doing, and then he would snap back to himself. Fact is, no one really knows what was going on inside of David.

12

When he got home, Mama asked him where he had been. He told her that he had been to the Hutchinsons' and that Mr. Hutchinson had been killed and Mrs. Hutchinson had been hurt by a runaway team. David ate his supper with us and went to bed. It is strange in retrospect. But at the time, everything seemed normal until the sheriff knocked on the door that night.

Sunday morning seemed like any other morning too—except the air we breathed was somehow different.

There was an old woodstove in the kitchen, and Mama built a fire early in the morning so that she could cook us breakfast, just like she always did. Breakfast was pretty much the same as every other morning. Breakfast was my favorite meal of the day. We would have either ham or bacon with some homemade biscuits. Mama would make sugar syrup on the stove by adding sugar to some water and boiling it. Then, we would pour hot sugar syrup on top of heavily buttered biscuits. To top it all off, we would have hot cocoa every morning. There was coffee for Mama and Daddy, as usual. No one talked about the sheriff coming to take David away the night before.

My mama was a very happy lady. She would sing while she did her work. It seemed as if she was always singing. But that morning it was quiet.

We did our chores after breakfast, and then just before lunch, the silence was broken. Mama took Arthur, Elva, and me out by the woodshed and had a talk with us. She said that David had been accused of something bad and that the kids at school might say something about it to us. But that didn't matter. We needed to go to school on Monday, and we needed to try not to let what anybody said bother us. Everything would be okay, she said. And I believed her. But when we didn't have fried chicken for dinner that Sunday night, it started feeling like everything wasn't okay.

When I walked into the schoolroom on Monday morning, it was still early, before the morning bell. There were a couple of kids up at the front of the room at the teacher's desk. I walked to my desk to put my book away, and I heard the teacher tell the kids that they needed to play with Bernice today because of what happened this weekend. I'm not sure why, but that made me cry. A couple of girls came over and took me by the arms and walked me outside to the school yard. When we got outside, Agnes asked me what was wrong. I said nothing was wrong. I remembered what Mama had said. I controlled the crying and went to play. But it didn't seem real. These girls had never played with me before.

The news about what had happened was in the papers, and everyone in school knew. Simply everyone knew, and everyone treated us different. I watched Arthur. He was confident and outgoing. I thought it must be easier for boys. The kids didn't seem to hold it against him like they did us girls. But it wasn't something we talked about. For me it was just a quiet cloud that hung overhead. I wouldn't learn the full story about what David had done until many years later.

Fifth grade was a bad year. Just a short while after the thing with David happened, we found out that Sonny was killed in the war. Mama just didn't seem the same. It was different for me too. I didn't have any friends after the thing with David. It was a very lonely time.

It was my first lesson in how to keep my feelings to myself, and my first lesson in how to keep on going no matter what.

We lived in Rye Colorado for about four years. It was the longest I remember ever living in one place. At times, it seemed like an eternity.

Bernice, Arthur, Agnes, Elva, and David around 1935–36

2

In the eighth grade, we moved away from the ranch in Rye back to St. Charles Mesa, between Baxter Road and Thirtieth Lane, an area in Pueblo County. I started in at a school called Pleasant View. What a breath of fresh air that was.

St. Charles Mesa was an area outside the city limits of Pueblo. It was all farms out there. For the most part, they were run by Italians that did truck farming. They would grow vegetables and load them up by the bushel in their trucks and then go sell them in town at the markets. Some people also had fruit and vegetable stands right there at their farms and sold to anyone who would stop by. We rented a house on the Cozzolino farm. Old man Cozzolino and his son farmed the land. Daddy worked in town (Pueblo) at Westland Oil Company.

Elva, Arthur, and I walked about three miles to Pleasant View School because there were no school buses. This was the first time we were ever able to walk to school; before we always lived too far from school to walk. This was also the first time we didn't have horses. Daddy had to sell them when we left Rye.

Even though it was a three-mile walk to school, everything seemed a little bit closer here. Lots of the kids in the area walked to school. I remember three of the girls I used to walk to school with: Helen Cozzolino, who lived in the main house on the farm; Helen Plant; and another girl, I think her name was Hazel. Elva was younger and two years behind me in school. I was a typical teenager that didn't want to walk to school with my little sister now that I had girls my own age to walk to school with. This was when I made my first really good friends, like Helen Plant.

No one here knew about the incident with David. If they did, they didn't let on. Boy, what a difference that made. All of a sudden the whole family had friends. We actually had neighbors close enough that they would come over and visit. People would actually talk to us. Helen Plant and I would hang out at each other's house all the time. She lived with her aunt and uncle; her parents were divorced. Mama and Daddy really liked her. People weren't like that in Rye. The only people that came over to visit us out there were my older brothers and sisters.

The school was a little bigger, but the class sizes were still about the same. The school grounds consisted of a big, long building off to one side that was the high school, for the ninth through twelfth graders, and a separate building for grade school, which was first through eighth grade. There was a fence around the school grounds, but it wasn't really a fence like you would imagine. It was simply two iron bars parallel to the ground that you could climb through or over. The gate wasn't really a gate either; it was just a couple of upright bars. The grade school was all gravel in the front. Behind the grade school was a dirt yard where we would play baseball. The only grass was in front of the high school.

Even though I was the new kid at school, the kids were friendly. In Rye, no one wanted to play with me at school. I basically spent my recesses just standing out in the school yard watching all the other kids play. Now, recesses were fun—like they should be. I played jacks with the other girls or drew squares in the dirt with a stick and played hopscotch. When it got colder and snowed, we made snowmen or drew a big circle in the snow and played a game called fox and geese. If nothing else, we played kick the can. It was so different, like nothing bad had ever happened. I had a clean slate.

I don't remember going to church before, but we certainly were going now. First we tried a Baptist church, but I don't think Mama liked it. Then we tried a Nazarene church, or I guess you call it "the Church of the Nazarene." Daddy didn't go to church. He would drive us there in the old coupe car and then pick us up afterward. The old coupe had a rumble seat in back that us kids would sit in. That was fun until one of my friends said he knew it was us coming down the road as soon as he saw my red hair perched up on top of the car like a ball of fire.

My hair was fire red. It was so red I just used to hate it, especially when people made jokes about it. It made me so mad and embarrassed when people teased me about my hair and my freckles. I was very self-conscious about it. I'll never forget the day I was standing out by a tree at school in Rye, just watching the other girls play, when this new girl, Jo Heibert, looked over at me out of the blue and said, "If you didn't have so many freckles, you would be pretty." I acted as if it didn't bother me, but I'll never forget those words or who said them. It made me feel that I was ugly because I had freckles. I would never show my real emotions to people who talked to me like that. I had learned that it was easier to get by if you didn't let people know how much things bothered you. The only thing that ever really got me riled up was knives. I couldn't make them stop bothering me.

It started when I was little. Mama and Daddy would tell us stories occasionally when there was nothing on the radio in the evening. Not fairy-tale stories, but real stories about things they had experienced or family news and such. Mama told us a story once, when I was six years old, about two women that she knew who lived together. They were doing their housework one morning when one of them noticed a man under the bed with a butcher knife. She turned to the other woman and told her to come help her gather some eggs for breakfast. Once they got outside, they went for help. I don't remember all the details or the outcome, but I remember that they both left for fear of what the man with the knife might do. After hearing the story, I always checked under my bed at night. From then on, knives were the one thing my brothers Arthur and David (and their friends) knew they could tease me about. It could be the smallest little pocketknife and them saying "I'm gonna getcha," and I would yell and scream and run to Mama. She didn't mean to scare me with her story; like many of her stories, I think it was meant to teach us something—other than the fear of knives.

Mama enjoyed church. Some Sunday nights we would go back to church again for special services in the evenings. I guess we needed an extra dose of God at that time. And we were sure getting it. The Nazarene church had some pretty strict rules. They didn't believe in women wearing makeup or nail polish. My mother never did anyway, but Elva and I were getting older, and I know it interested me.

Another church rule was that we couldn't stand in front of a tavern, not even if it was just to catch the bus. They also didn't believe we should go to picture shows, which was the greatest thing to do—when we could. We liked going to church, but thank God Mama and Daddy weren't real sticklers for all the church rules. Every once in a while they would take us into town and drop us at our sister Pearl's or our sister Zelma's house where we could catch a bus to town to go to a picture show. Daddy would pick us up after the show. That was really a treat. They would also let us take the bus to town to shop at the dime stores. I loved shopping. We didn't have a lot of money, but that didn't seem to stop us. There was Kress's, Woolworths, and Newberry's. With twenty-five cents in those days you could buy a lot of little things. Suckers for a penny, jawbreakers for a couple of pennies, or caramel suckers for a nickel. You could treat everybody to a piece of candy and still have money left over.

Sometime, during eighth or ninth grade, a new girl came to school and started walking part of the way to school with Helen Plant and me. Her name was Donna Rogers. She lived on the opposite side of the highway from us. She had crooked teeth—you know, some teeth in front of the others—brown, stringy, medium-long hair, and she was thin but not what you would call skinny. I think what attracted us to her was that her folks let her wear makeup and do stuff that our folks wouldn't let us do. I think she was older than Helen and me. The best thing was that her folks didn't care if she went out. She could come and go as she pleased.

My folks didn't like her. They thought she was kind of a wild gal.

Donna seemed to hit it off with the boys right away. She liked to have boys pick her up in a car after school. She got me my first date, but I had to sneak out to go on it.

She invited me to spend the night at her house and told me we would call a couple of guys and go out. I knew my folks wouldn't have approved. So as far as they knew, I was just spending the night at Donna's house. I guess I was kind of naive. She knew more about life than I did—let's just put it that way.

It was a double date with guys I didn't know. In fact, they were men, not boys our age. My date was twelve years older than me and had already been in and out of the service. His name was Butch. Well, that wasn't his real name, but that was what everyone called him.

He was very handsome. Every feature on his face was perfectly proportioned and positioned. I could tell he was an Italian. His skin was an even tone, not too dark and not too light, and his hair was dark like Mama's. He had a buzz cut like most of the guys. The guys wore short-sleeved, western shirts with snaps up the front and jeans. Butch's shirt and jeans were a snug fit that made him look strong and muscular. I could see that he had a tattoo on his forearm.

We didn't have much money then, so I just wore one of my regular dresses with silk stockings that hooked onto a garter belt. They had a seam down the back that you had to get lined up perfect down the back of your leg, or they didn't look right. They were a light tan but darker than my skin. I tried to fix my hair up. But regardless of what I wanted to do with my hair it just did its own thing. My hair was about shoulder length, and the curls and waves separated and went in whatever direction they chose. I had no control over it despite the curlers and time in front of the mirror trying to make a wave curl the way I wanted it to. I generally gave up and just wore it down and parted on the side. I knew we weren't going anyplace fancy anyway. We just went driving around.

The guy Donna was with drove. There was a little place in Blende (not too far away) that we went to for coffee and pop. Of course, Donna was always all lovey-dovey with all the guys. But I wasn't like that at all. This was my first date, and I didn't even know this guy. We had just met. I didn't feel comfortable cuddling up and being too close to him. But just to fit in, I tried.

After having coffee and pop at the little place in Blende, the guys took us back to Donna's house. When the car was parked and the headlights turned off, I could see that Donna was kissing her guy. I looked over at Butch, and he was looking at me.

"Can I kiss you good night?" he asked.

I fidgeted a little. I didn't think that I should be getting that friendly with a guy I just met. I didn't really even feel like I knew him yet. But he was confident and handsome, so I said okay. I thought he might be a good person to give me my first kiss, since he was older and probably knew what he was doing. Turns out it was perfect for a first kiss. It wasn't just a peck, but it wasn't a big, sloppy, uncomfortable, wet kiss either. I gave him my phone number.

Butch didn't call me for a long time after that. Usually us girls would call the guys anyway. They never called us. So I didn't think much of it. I went out a few other times after that with Donna. Always with different guys. But I really didn't consider it dating either. It was sneak dating. Something to giggle about with my girlfriends.

At first, I wasn't sure why my folks didn't like Donna. I had fun with her. But later on, I pretty much figured out that she was sleeping with a lot of the guys she was going out with. Eventually, Daddy told me that he didn't like the people Donna ran around with, and he banned me from seeing her. Maybe she quit school around that same time. I'm not really sure what happened to her. I heard rumors that she was in a scandalous interracial relationship with a guy who beat her up. But I'm not sure—she just kind of disappeared.

Helen Plant and I were still friends, though. We hung around together for years and years. I graduated from eighth grade at Pleasant View Junior High School in 1947 and then went on to high school there until Daddy built a house in Pueblo and we moved again. Actually, we (Mama, Elva, and I) helped Daddy build the house in Pueblo.

We started on the house the summer after I got out of school in the ninth grade. My sister Pearl and her husband, Sam Baker, owned some property in Pueblo. I remember Sam talking to Daddy about selling some of the land to him, and I remember them closing the deal. They agreed that if my daddy ever sold the land he had to sell it back to Sam. I knew we were going to be building a house of our own. I was excited because we always rented and moved almost every year. If we had a house of our own, we would never have to move again. But in a way, I also wanted to stay where we were.

We were still living out on Cozzolino's farm, and Daddy was now a manager of Westland Oil Company. Every day he had off we were out on our new property building that house. We would all go—Mama, Daddy, Arthur, Elva, and I. We would go first thing in the morning and have lunch at my sister Pearl's house. Sometimes we would spend the entire day there, and she would bring dinner to us.

It was all dry land, with weeds growing and tumbleweeds blowing between Sam's house and where our house would be built. Not a tree in site. There wasn't even a street going to the place where we were building. We used to go to Sam and Pearl's house and then drive up the side of their property to get to our place. We had to make our own driveway. When we first got there, all I could see was a big square hole dug out in the middle of some dry, dusty land.

If Sam wasn't busy, he would come up and help us. Basically Sam and Daddy did all the construction work. But they found plenty for the rest of us to do as well.

Daddy was a strong man who was used to hard work. He never slouched. I know he wasn't quite six feet tall, but he stood tall. And he was handsome in my eyes. He had black, straight hair, parted on the side and combed back. His soft brown eyes were friendly and safe to look into. All us kids had his eyes. He was normally clean shaven, but on his days off when we were out working on the house we could see his whiskers and the start of some grays.

The first thing Sam and Daddy did when we got there was build an outhouse. I think they had done it before because they put it together in the first few hours. They dug a hole in the ground and hammered some wood together and it was done. Usually when the hole got full, you just buried it and dug another hole and picked the outhouse up and moved it. But we didn't have to do that here—it would be the first house we would live where we didn't have to rely on an outhouse. But we needed one for temporary use while we were working. It was no-nonsense time while we working on that house. No horsing around. It was a family project, and we were on a mission.

That summer we poured a cement floor for the basement and covered all four sides of that big square hole with cinderblocks. There was a pump over at Sam's house that we got water from. We carried it over by the bucketful so Daddy could mix up cement. He mixed the cement in a wheelbarrow, and then we hauled the cement in little buckets over to him so he could smear it on the cement blocks. When the floor and walls were done, they made the basement ceiling with boards and put tar paper on top of it. The top of it was only about a foot above ground level. It was just high enough for a small window between the ground and the tar paper top, which would be the floor for the upstairs.

The door and the stairs were the last things to go on. The stairs protruded out of the ground. The door was totally above ground, with the bottom of the door at ground level. There was a three-foot-square entryway between the door and the stairs. Daddy actually bought a door rather than building one. Actually he was pretty meticulous about the whole thing. Everything had to be just so. I can still see him working away with a hand-rolled cigarette hanging from one side of his straight lips, the ember on the end black and ashen, having extinguished itself hours ago. He wouldn't stop to light it again and wouldn't toss it aside until he came to a good stopping spot where he had to step back and inspect his finished work.

It seemed as though we worked on that house forever and ever. I was a teenager, and having to do all that work just made it seem a lot longer than it was. We would get so exhausted. It was dry and hot and dusty. I can't say that I hated helping with the house, but I can surely say that by the end of the day I was just as tired as the day was long and hot.

Mama helped carry cement and blocks and helped with everything too. She never complained once about it. As far as I know, this was the first and only house my parents ever owned, and Daddy built it himself from the bottom up. We could see the pride in his eyes. Both Mama and Daddy were happy with the fact that they were doing something for themselves. They weren't working for someone else. The end product was theirs, and at long last, they wouldn't have to move again.

When I started tenth grade at Pleasant View High School, Daddy was still working on the house in Pueblo. He put petitions up to divide the big square cement underground structure into three rooms. Two of the rooms were small bedrooms, and there was one larger main room. The larger room had plaster board on the walls, but in the bedrooms you could still see the two-by-fours that made up that side of the wall. He bought a coal heater and put it in to keep the place warm for the fall and winter that were upon us. And of course he put in the cookstove that we moved with us from Rye. It was a woodstove with a black pipe that he hooked into a hole in the roof.

Just a couple of months into the school year the house was ready for us to move in to. There was still nothing there but the basement, but that was enough. Arthur had decided to join the marines, so it was just Mama, Daddy, Elva, and me now.

We had our same beds. Mama and Daddy had their same dresser that Mama decorated with family photos. She hung the picture of her parents that had followed us from house to house. It was oval shaped, with rounded glass and a metal frame. This picture hung in every home I can remember living in. My grandparents died before I was born, so I never really knew them. But they continually looked in on us in sepia tones. Grandmother was seated and wore a full-length dress with long sleeves and a high collar. My grandfather stood behind her with a jacket and tie, his hand placed gently on her shoulder, straight faced and ever watchful. Mama didn't talk about them much, but I knew her mother was a diabetic and almost all her brothers and sisters were diabetics. Unfortunately, Mama was diagnosed with sugar diabetes (type II diabetes) too that year. It didn't really change anything but what she ate. It didn't change the way she lived or cooked. She stopped eating sweets and a lot of starches. But she still baked. Once in a while I think she cheated a little by eating some of the coconut candy she kept around. She said it was there in case she had an insulin reaction, but I know she liked it too.

I think Mama's favorite wall picture was the one of the sinking *Titanic*. It always seemed to be up on our wall too. It was huge to me. It was about two feet tall, about three feet wide. Part of the ship was sticking up out of the water, and the back part was under dark-blue water with white waves crashing around it. There didn't seem to be any people in the water or on the boat, but I knew from the stories Mama told us that this big, unsinkable ship was full of people—somewhere.

We brought our kitchen table and Mama and Daddy's wooden rocking chairs. Mama did what she could to dress up our new home. She made curtains to cover the windows. They were multicolored with some sort of pattern, probably made out of flour sacks. They were two pieces that you could separate in the middle to look out. She always opened the curtains in the morning and closed them at night. Not like anyone could see in anyway. It was all prairie out there, and the neighbors weren't very close.

From the outside of the house, it looked like there was still nothing there but the basement—but inside it was home. After we moved in, Daddy started working on the upstairs. The kitchen was the first room to be built upstairs. The kitchen was not above the basement, but the rest of the house was (a front room, bedroom, and bathroom). He had someone come in and drill a well for water. We would have running water in our new house and a bathroom, eventually.

Daddy planted some little trees in the yard. I think this was when he finally settled down and stopped moving from house to house. But not me. It wasn't long at all before I started moving on my own.

Arthur and his friend sitting on the fence
in front of Pleasant View School

Bernice outside the front door after the basement was finished

3

I was glad to get moved into our new house, but I sure didn't like the new school.

It only took me a couple of weeks at Central High School—less than a month—to realize that this great big school I had landed in was like a foreign country. All my school years up to this point had been spent in small schools where everybody knows everybody, and even if you were new to the school it didn't take long to get acquainted. This school just wasn't like that. It was a maze of foreign hallways filled with foreign faces. I felt as uncomfortable there as I would have if I were walking the streets of China.

I told Mama that I was going to quit. She told Daddy. Daddy persuaded me to stay put in a way only Daddy could. I went back to appease him, but I didn't last more than another day or two. I just couldn't force myself to continue there—not even for Daddy.

I decided I wasn't going to tell anyone that I was quitting this time. My plan was to find a job. After I found a job, I would tell Mama and Daddy that I quit school. I didn't think that they would try to convince me to stay in school if I was working.

Unfortunately, Mama and I were pretty close, and somehow I ended up talking to her about my plan.

"Daddy'll be mad if he finds out I quit, won't he?"

"Well ya know he's gonna find out," she said.

"Please, Mama, just let me find a job first. Then we can tell Daddy."

"We'll see" was her response. That was what she would say when she didn't want to say yes or no. She didn't say she wouldn't tell him, but she didn't say she would either. With Mama we could get away with most anything. It was different with Daddy. I don't know why it was that way with him. I think he just commanded respect, and I was raised to respect and obey him. Unfortunately, he wanted me to stay in school, and I couldn't make myself do it. But Daddy was reasonable. I was sure that if I had a job he wouldn't mind me quitting school so much. Mama's response was somewhat satisfying. If nothing else I might have bought myself some time for job hunting.

I liked living in town—well, at least I thought of it as living in town. With everything so much closer, it would be easier to find a job. We were out in the prairie, and there was still no street to our house. We still had to go through Pearl's yard, and we had to walk about a block and a half from Pearl's to the mailboxes—but so did most folks. The mailboxes for about eight or ten houses were all together in one long line just up the street and around the corner. Our address was in Pueblo, so I considered it town. I don't remember what our address was at first; we probably just used Pearl's address until the road came through.

I had to walk about ten or twelve blocks to catch the bus to town, but that didn't bother me. Especially when I discovered there was a real cute bus driver that was almost always driving the bus when I came home from town. He was quite a bit older than me and had a good build—a nice, clean-cut-looking guy. He probably never knew it, but I sure liked him. Sometimes, I would be watching him in the big bus mirror that hung in front of him, and he would look up and our eyes would meet in the mirror. As a teenager I thought, *If he's looking at me, I know he likes me.* But I never got up the nerve to speak to him, and he

31

never spoke to me. I never told anybody about it either. I was kind of shy and quiet about things like that. It was just my secret crush.

I found a job pretty quickly. I started babysitting and cleaning house for a lawyer who had two little girls. When I went to talk to him about the job he had advertised, I told him that I was sixteen, when actually I was only fifteen. He hired me on the spot and agreed to pay me fifteen dollars a week plus room and board.

That afternoon when I got home, I told Daddy that I had a job in town working for a lawyer. Only after that did I tell him that I had also quit school again. I think I kind of expected him to push the issue of me not going to school, but he didn't. I wonder if Mama had already talked to him about me quitting. Something sure seemed to have softened the blow. Even when I told him that I would be moving out because the job included room and board, he seemed okay with it. Mama and Elva seemed okay with me moving out too, although we talked about me coming home on my days off. It's probably because all my brothers and sisters before me moved out when they were young. The girls moved out to get married usually, and the boys to join the service or for a job of some kind. The novelty of a child sprouting wings of their own and learning to fly was probably lost long before the eleventh of twelve kids flew the coop. I excitedly skipped off to pack a bag and prepare myself for what could be considered a fairy-tale dream—living in the middle of town in a big fancy house, working for a rich lawyer.

The lawyer lived in a great big house on the north side of town somewhere around Grand Avenue where all the rich people lived. For the first time in my life I had a bedroom of my own. Like Cinderella's room, it was up on the top floor of the house. It was an attic that had been made into a bedroom. I thought it was grand, but it was really quite simple. There was a full-size bed with white sheets and a blanket, a dresser with a small AM radio on it, and a mirror on the wall. The floor was carpeted. I relished the luxury of getting up in the morning and placing my bare feet on the carpet, as if I had stepped into some imaginary slippers. In fact the entire house was carpeted except for the kitchen and bathrooms. We never had carpets at our house. We couldn't afford it. I don't remember any of my sister's houses having carpet either. We always had good old, tough, washable linoleum or wood.

My workweek started Monday morning and ended Friday evening. The weekends were my own. However, the lawyer and his wife were quite the social couple for having two toddlers at home. I spent quite a few evenings during the week looking after the girls and caring for the house while they went out. If they went out in the evening, I was expected to stay downstairs until they came home. And I did. They had a big living area and nice furniture—better than we ever had. I really didn't mind it when they were gone and the kids were asleep and the house was all mine.

The house was the picture of neat and tidy. Still I was given a housecleaning routine to follow that included vacuuming, which was totally new to me. I don't remember what the machine looked like, but I figured out how to use it just fine. I also had to scrub the kitchen floor on my hands and knees (nope—no mops), polish the silverware, dust regularly, and of course, clean up after the kids. It wasn't really hard cleaning a house that was already clean. But I couldn't miss a patch of dust, a spot on the floor, or a corner of carpet, or the lawyer's wife would let me know about it. I would also eat the evening meal with the family and help wash, dry, and put away the dishes afterward (nope—no dishwashers either).

The evening meal was always served in the formal dining room. I didn't have to prepare the meal, but I had to help set the table before we ate. There was a certain set of china that was used for dinner. The plates were larger than necessary. They had an inch around the outer edge that was just wasted space—you didn't eat off of it because that space was reserved for the flowery design that accompanied the meal. There was also more silverware on the table than you could use in one meal. I was taught the proper way to set the table, with the forks, knives, spoons, and napkins carefully positioned like fine jewelry on velvet in a display case. If the placement was off, it was adjusted ever so slightly until a quick glint from the light gave you the wink that said it was just right.

Between the dining room and kitchen there was a room sort of like a pantry, but you couldn't really call it a pantry because it was full of dishes. It was about as big as a good-sized walk-in closet. So I guess you could call it a walk-in closet for dishes. Each wall had shelves buttoned neatly behind glass doors. Looking through the glass, you could see set after set of dishes, just waiting for a chance to come out and serve. It would have to be just the right occasion for a set to be picked. There were some, I was told, that were special enough that they got their own holiday and were guaranteed to be used at least once a year. They had so many sets of dishes you just can't imagine. I don't know why anybody would need that many dishes. Maybe they were wedding presents. I don't know. But we didn't even come close to using them all while I was working there.

Breakfast and lunch were eaten in the kitchen, and it was less formal. I don't remember the lawyer ever being there for breakfast, but he was always there for the evening meal. There was a separate set of dishes in the kitchen for breakfast. Of course.

I learned to cook a bit, just simple things for the girls for breakfast or lunch. The girls really liked peanut butter and bacon sandwiches on toasted bread. I usually ate what they ate, but when they sprung this one on me, I thought it sounded awful. I tried it, just to be nice. Surprisingly it was pretty good. I pretty much got hooked on them while I was there and still eat them to this day.

During the week I spent my free time in my room listening to the radio, reading a book, or writing to my brother Arthur. We wrote letters back and forth all the time he was in the marines. He would tell me about what he was doing, his life away from base, and things he wanted to do. If there was one thing he ever wanted out of life, I think it was just to be happy—have a wife and kids and sing and play music. Arthur's singing voice could send me to a land of wonder. I never wanted anyone to hear me sing, because I didn't feel like I could carry a tune in a bucket. But singing was part of Arthur's nature. He was kind of like Mama in that way. I loved the music they brought to my ears.

When I turned sixteen, Arthur sent me a photo album for my birthday. It was brown leather bound with USMC, a bulldog with a marine helmet, and Semper Fidelis inlayed on the front cover. I learned that Semper Fidelis was Latin for "Always faithful." I held it as close to my heart when I first got it as I do today.

The inside pages were made of black construction paper. On the first page I glued a picture of Arthur, grinning happily as he held our tiny newborn niece Kathy—Agnes's first daughter. That album came to hold many moments captured in time. There were pictures of me, Arthur, Elva, and our friends from Pleasant View School and some of me and my girlfriends goofing around at the house on Cozzolino's farm. It captured happy times when being young and full of spitfire came naturally and could be detected even in the smallest of black-and-white photographs. My first camera took really small pictures, only about three inches square.

Every once in a while Arthur's girlfriend, Deloris Chambers, would come to visit us at Mama and Daddy's even though Arthur was away in the service. I didn't stay away from home more than five days in a row usually. When I got off on Friday nights, I would go home for the weekend and return to the lawyers for work sometime on Sunday after church. Everyone liked Deloris. Unfortunately my nephew liked her a little too much and decided he should have her as a girlfriend instead of Arthur. He kind of broke Arthur and Deloris up. Arthur was very hurt over it. He tried to go back with her for a while after he got out of the service, but it didn't last.

One weekend a gal that I knew from Pleasant View—can't remember her name for the life of me—got ahold of me at my folk's house. We had a rotary phone, and our phone number consisted of four numbers and a letter. There were four other parties on our party line, so we had to listen for our special ring before we picked up the phone. I was happy that she remembered my number and called. She asked me to go out with her and a couple of guys—she needed another girl to go. It was a blind date.

My date was a guy named Bill Patterson. I don't remember anything very distinct about Bill. He was just okay. After our firsts date it kind of became a routine for us to go out on Friday and Saturday nights. No more sneak dating—this is when I started dating for real. Mama and Daddy were pretty lenient with me about dating now that I had a job and had moved out during the week. I was beginning to feel my independence and was coming into my own.

Mama and Daddy never met the guys I went out with because they would never come to the door to pick me up or drop me off. But Mama and Daddy knew that we always double-dated. We usually ended up at the Moose Lodge or out at another country western club by the airport. We didn't drink, but at some places we had to lie about our age so we could get in. I had no problem telling people I was eighteen when I was actually only sixteen. I was never asked for ID. I never saw anybody asked for ID. In those days they just took your word for it. It didn't matter much anyway because I just drank pop, listened to music, and danced the night away. I know it sounds pretty tame and dull compared to the teenage dating stories I hear these days. But you know what? We had fun.

I guess you could say that I had kind of found a boyfriend in Bill Peterson because we were dating on a pretty regular basis. Nonetheless, I was still very self-conscious about my looks. So one day I went down to this place called Merle Norman's. They gave free facials. It wasn't a facial like you get in the big salons. It was more about how to put makeup on. I had tried lipstick before, but that was it. It was red lipstick then, and I've still never worn any other color. Anyway, they taught me how to put my lipstick on and blot it so it wasn't so bright and how to blend foundation and then put powder on. I never wore rouge, and I didn't start wearing eye shadow and mascara until much later. But I soaked up this lesson. To this day I still do it the way they taught me.

I never wore makeup to church, though. I still went to church with Mama and Elva on Sundays, and we were still going to the same Nazarene church. But Mama knew I was wearing makeup. I think Elva started wearing it too shortly after I did.

Unfortunately, my feeling self-conscious didn't stop when I started wearing makeup. It might have gotten worse. Every time I went anyplace from then on, every single hair on my head had to be in place. I think Mama told us that girls were supposed to part their hair on the right and boys on the left. So naturally I wore my hair parted on the right. I religiously washed my hair once a week and curled it. Since I was working, I was able to buy store-bought clothes. My dresses had to be clean, pressed, and coordinated with my shoes (I wore a sort of platform shoe with a one-and-a-half-inch heel that was connected to the front of the shoe); the seam on my stockings had to be perfectly straight; and of course the outfit had to look good on me. And last but not least, my makeup had to be perfect. I enjoyed fashion, wearing nice clothes and dressing up. Being a teenager was fun.

One day I happened to stumble on an ad in the newspaper for a job working at the K&O malt shop. I had been working for the lawyer for a while, and the family was nice and treated me well. But the malt shop sounded too fun to pass up. I went down that weekend to apply, and I got the job. It didn't seem hard at all to find a job if you wanted one. Of course, now I had to quit the job at the lawyer's, which meant that I would also have to move back home. But I really didn't mind, and I knew Mama and Daddy wouldn't mind either. I knew that I could always come home anytime I wanted to. That's how we were raised. Family was always welcome—no matter what. "If you're family, my home is your home."

Even though I liked living there with the lawyer's family, I never hesitated to go home on the weekends. I think I kind of welcomed the opportunity to go back home. The lawyer's house in town was nice, but I liked my old humdrum poorer way of life. I don't think I was cut out to be one of those high-class people with a lot of fancy stuff, where everything had to be just so. I would just rather have ordinary stuff, and I would rather live in the house that my daddy built with his own two hands than their big fancy house any day. That might not make sense to some, but it does to me. If you asked me today to tell you where all the silverware is supposed to be placed when setting a formal dining table, I couldn't tell you. That sort of thing just doesn't seem important to me.

I've always preferred old houses to new fancy ones anyway. It's probably because of the old haunted house that I fell in love with when we lived out in Rye. We used to go hiking out in the hills in Rye. We would walk for miles and think nothing of it. There were old abandoned houses up the hills that we used to go in and explore. There was this one we used to call the haunted house. It had linens, dishes, furniture, and everything in it just like the people had just up and left in the middle of everything. Every time we went hiking we would end up at the old haunted house. We enjoyed going there and having the run of the house and rummaging through whatever we wanted to. One time we brought some knives home for Mama. I was still deathly afraid of knives. They still gave me this fear that grabbed ahold of my stomach and wouldn't let go.

Anyway, I went to work at K&O's and moved back home. K&O's was just a small malt shop. There was a bar there as you came in the door and four booths over to one side. There was also a long counter with all different flavors of Francis ice cream. My favorite was the lemon custard ice cream. We had bulk ice cream, and we had soft ice cream for milk shakes. We also served sandwiches. Two brothers ran the place. One of them cooked, and it was busy enough that there were always two girls taking orders and serving the meals.

I was still seeing Bill Patterson then, but at some point while I was working at the malt shop I ran into Butch again. He came in to get something to eat and drink. I was surprised to see him. I hadn't seen him or thought about him since our sneak date about a year ago.

He gave me a friendly greeting and sat down at the counter. I lingered at the counter a little so we could talk. He wasn't working. He was living with his parents, helping them on their farm. He told me a little bit about what he did out on the farm. They lived just a block or two from Pleasant View School. When he finished his sandwich, he hung around for a few minutes longer, just talking.

"Can I pick you up after work and give you a ride home?" he asked.

"I usually work until closing time. We close at 10 p.m."

"That's okay."

"After we lock up, I still have to clean up, so it's usually around ten thirty when I get out of here to go catch the bus."

"I can wait for you. You don't have to catch the bus if you want a ride."

It didn't bother me to walk from where I got off the bus up the street to my house at night. But there weren't many streetlights back then, let alone sidewalks out where we lived, so a ride would be nice. "Okay," I said with a smile.

I thought it was kind of neat that an older guy was interested in me. Then he started calling about once a week and asking if I needed a ride home, and I would let him give me a ride again.

He drove a black '32 Chevy sedan. It was a huge car with plenty of space for four people or more to sit in the front seat if it weren't for the gearshift in the middle. But eventually I began to scoot over and sit next to him while he drove me home. I also started telling Bill Patterson that I was busy, and eventually he stopped calling.

One night when Butch brought me home, we sat parked in the car in front of Pearl's house for a while before I went in. Butch had turned the car off and went to start it to let it warm up before he left. In those days you always started the car and let it run a bit before you drove it. You couldn't drive the car while it was cold. But the car wouldn't start.

"The battery must've died. We'll need to push start it."

"Wow! You really think we can do that?" I knew the big old Chevy that we were sitting in was extremely heavy.

"Yeah, but we'll need another car."

"It's kinda late. I know my folks go to bed early, like around eight thirty. You want me to go get Sam?" I said apologetically.

"How about if we just borrow your dad's car without waking him up?"

"I don't know." I wasn't sure this was such a bright idea, but I didn't say as much.

"What choice do we have?"

I shrugged. I really didn't want to wake up Daddy in the middle of the night.

"Do you have any idea where they might keep the keys?" Butch was convinced his idea was the only solution.

"Daddy's the only one that drives. He usually just throws them on the table I think."

"I'll walk you up to the house. Try not to wake them up and just bring me the keys."

I agreed. It sounded simple enough. I went into the house being quieter than I usually would have been. I found the keys quickly and easily right inside the front room on the table and quietly sneaked back out. I dangled the keys in front of Butch, and we smiled at each other and then walked together over to Daddy's car. Without saying anything to each other, we got in and Butch pulled the car right up to the back bumper of his car. Then he opened the car door and got out.

"Okay. You have to drive this one while I start mine," he said, looking at me still sitting in the passenger seat.

"I don't know how to drive."

"It's easy. Just push on the gas when I give you the signal."

I'm not sure what I was thinking, but I got behind the wheel. Daddy's car was an automatic. It was a Cadillac and newer and nicer than Butch's car. I had been in this car numerous times and even posed for a picture once while sitting behind the wheel. In the picture, the driver-side door was open, and I had a skirt on. My legs were swung out the open door and my torso twisted slightly toward the front of the car. His car had what we now call suicide doors that opened from the front of the car instead of the back. This was nothing like posing for a picture. I was nervous and a little anxious as I gripped the wheel with sweaty palms, eyes forward.

Butch gave me the signal, and I pushed on the gas. The car jerked forward, and then both cars started moving. Everything was fine for about a minute. Then the unthinkable happened, and Butch's car started and pulled away from me. That was what was supposed to happen. The problem was I had no idea what I was supposed to do now. I panicked. I think I let off the gas, but the car just kept going and headed straight for a barbed wire fence. I watched the hood of the car fit neatly underneath one piece of barbed wire and heard the chilling sound of it scraping across the hood of Daddy's car before the car stopped. I don't know if I stopped the car or the fence did. It scared me to death. Butch must have seen me in the rearview mirror because he came back. It's kind of funny now, but at the time I was too scared to laugh or cry. I didn't holler. I had to be quiet because I didn't want to wake anyone. I'm not sure what I did at that point. I know that I didn't park the car. Butch did it for me. I was done. I went in the house even more quietly than the first time, sure Daddy was going to hear me. I placed the keys back where I had found them and got straight into bed as fast as I could.

I was still scared in the morning. I lay in bed listening until I was sure that Daddy had left for work. Only then would I get out of bed. I even stayed scared for a few more days. I just knew I scratched Daddy's car, but I was afraid to look during daylight hours for fear Daddy would see me and know I did it. I'm sure that barbed wire had to leave scratches, but Daddy never said anything. I think I was scared for more than a few days, because I've never told anyone that story before.

All the time I was dating Butch I didn't introduce him to my parents. In fact, I think I lied to Mama and Daddy when they asked me about him.

"I don't want you running around with a bunch of wops," Daddy said for some reason I wasn't sure of at the time.

"Oh, he's not Italian," I told Daddy, even though I knew that he didn't call them Italians. Apparently there were two different kinds of Italians, Sicilians and the others. The Sicilians were dagos, and the lighter ones were wops, or the other way around. I can't remember. They can call each other wop and dago, but if you weren't Italian you were not supposed to. My family was a duke's mixture as were most of the other families around us. That's just a mixture of more than one European nationality. I guess Mama and Daddy didn't believe in different races marrying. Italians were considered a different race in their eyes.

It was pretty easy to go out with Butch without ever introducing him to my family since he would just beep the horn and I would come running out. That's the way everyone did it in those days. And the guys never walked you to the door after a date either—we said good night to each other in the car.

Butch had brought me into his circle of friends. There was a whole group of us that would meet up at the nightclubs in Pueblo. There would be Saudi and Patty, Gene and Sharon, Imogene and Jim, Gene Solvo and Chris, Tony and Marge, and Georgia and Joe. All the guys were Italians from the farms on St. Charles Mesa. I think Chris was the only girl that was Italian. All the guys were in their late twenties and older than us girls. I was around sixteen years old and Butch was twenty-eight.

We spent a lot of time at the Moose Lodge as well as a couple of other nightclubs, but I still didn't drink. None of the girls drank—just the guys drank. I smoked cigarettes, though, off and on. I started that when I was about fifteen, and then I would quit for a while and then start back up.

The live music was definitely the highlight when we went out. It was always a country western band. There were mostly local bands, but every once in a while they would bring in big names. There was always a cover charge for the big-name bands, and we would pay the dollar so we could see them. Actually, the guys would pay for us. Butch wouldn't dance much, so mostly we would just sit and listen to the music. I don't remember the guys getting drunk—they were gentlemen.

Occasionally we went to a picture show. We went to drive-ins more than we went to inside shows. But the drive-ins were just opened in the summertime if I remember correctly. There was a drive-in out at Blende called Mesa Drive-In and one in Pueblo on the north side of town.

Butch and I were seeing each other more and more now. It was almost every night for a long time. We started talking about getting married. He told me he had been married before. I wanted to marry him, but it was just talk. We never set any dates or anything. I think this was also when we started having sex in the backseat of his car.

Bernice sitting in her daddy's car

4

I moved up from my job at the malt shop to a full-time job at Walgreens, serving shakes at the fountain, and I was seeing Butch almost every night. So I thought it might be a good idea if I moved out of Mama and Daddy's house. I had saved up some money and found an affordable studio apartment in town, not too far from work. It felt pretty good to earn a living on my own, have my own place, and be independent.

I still loved shopping, but I was careful with my money. One day after work I was shopping at Crews-Beggs department store, in the basement where all the bargain deals were, and I ran into a former classmate from Pleasant View. It had been at least a couple of years since I saw her last, and we started chatting to catch up.

"Hey, I'm heading down to the Bluebird to have a soda with my boyfriend. Want to come along?" she asked.

"Sure. I've got all night. I just have to make sure I'm home by eleven. My boyfriend is coming over after he gets off work."

When she and her boyfriend dropped me off in front of my apartment, it was just a little after eleven. Butch was sitting in his car out front. He got out of the car and walked with me up to the apartment building.

"Hi." I smiled, happy to see him.

"Where were you?"

"I was down at Crews-Beggs and ran into an old friend that I went to school with at Pleasant View. I went with her and her boyfriend down to the Bluebird for a while."

"You knew I was gonna be here."

"Yeah, I planned on being back before you got here, but I guess we lost track of time. Sorry," I said as we started the climb up a long flight of wooden stairs that led to the door of my apartment.

"So you just leave me sitting here waiting in the car?"

His voice was getting a little loud, so I tried to talk a little more softly. "It's only a little after eleven. When did you get here?"

"You're not supposed to be going out with other people."

I didn't understand why he was getting so upset. I tried to explain, "I wasn't out with a guy. I was just with a girlfriend from school. We were just out talking," I said, stepping into my apartment and turning to face him.

Suddenly he slapped me hard across the face. I was frozen, stunned and frightened. He began cussing in Italian and slapped me again. I couldn't even speak. I simply stood there and held my stinging cheek in my hands. I watched his face change. He wasn't looking at me the way he usually did, and I didn't recognize the look in his eyes. I tried to reach out to touch his arm, to calm him and try to make him stop yelling. He rejected me with another slap and then another sending me flying onto the bed. As I sat up, I noticed that we had left the door open and there were a couple of the neighbors in the hallway. Butch saw me look past him and turned to see them too. He made one last hard glance in my direction and walked out the door, slamming it hard behind him.

I sat there alone for one silent second before I fell back onto the bed in tears. I was sure that it was the end of our relationship and that I would never see him again. I cried myself to sleep feeling awful, yet not quite understanding why Butch had gotten so angry with me.

The next night, as I lay on the bed around the time that Butch would usually show up after work, I studied the small table, two chairs, small stove, and four walls that accompanied me. I knew I would be spending the night alone. Then to my surprise I heard footsteps coming up the stairs and a knock on the door. I jumped up and flung the door open. There stood Butch. He gave me a kiss, hugged me, and then came in like nothing had ever happened. I think I was in shock. He acted like he had never been mad at me. He acted like he was supposed to be there. He didn't apologize. In fact, he didn't say one word about what had happened the night before. So neither did I. It seemed to me like everything was okay again. Maybe I thought his anger was a fluke.

I can't imagine how different my life would have been if our relationship would have ended the first time he hit me. But at the time, I didn't want to leave him. However, I did become uncomfortable around my neighbors down the hall. They looked at me different and acted different after they heard Butch yelling at me and saw him hitting me. It made me want to move away from their disapproving glares.

Within a couple of weeks I found another studio apartment that was even closer to work. As I was moving out, one of the neighbors came up to me, looked me right in the face, and said, "I'm glad you're moving out. That man that comes here and hurts you, I don't like him." I couldn't believe it. I watched my neighbor walk away, and a bad feeling washed over me. Maybe I should have taken it as a warning, but instead my teenage reasoning told me that I didn't care much for these neighbors. I was in love and happy to be moving away from them. What did they know anyway?

After I moved, Butch and I happily spent every night together. But as luck would have it, I missed my period. My cycle was as regular as a clock. I didn't need to see a doctor or take a test (there weren't any home pregnancy tests back then). I just knew it—and I just blurted it out.

"Butch, I'm pregnant."

"What? Are you sure?"

"Yes."

"We're not ready to have kids."

"Well, I can't help that. I guess we better get ready."

"Oh no. You're gonna have to get an abortion."

My happy tone suddenly turned serious. "I'm not gonna do that."

"You're too young to have a baby, Red."

"Seventeen is not too young, and I'm certainly not going to get an abortion. I don't believe in it."

Not only did I think it was wrong, but I had heard so many horror stories about women going to see a doctor in some dark alley office where the doctor would cut the baby out and the woman would bleed to death. I never heard one good thing about abortions. I wasn't about to do that to myself or to an innocent baby. I liked the idea of having a baby.

For the next couple of weeks Butch kept trying to push me into abortion. When I explained my fears, he tried to tell me there was nothing to be afraid of. He said he knew a doctor who did this type of thing all the time and said it would be all right. We had talked about getting married before, so I brought it up again. I wanted to get married and start a family. He told me he wasn't ready for marriage. We just couldn't get on the same page. Still I knew in my mind and in my heart that I would not get an abortion. I knew it wasn't the right thing for me to do, even if we weren't going to get married. I think the discussions ended when I flatly refused. I just told him an abortion wasn't going to happen.

Still, he seemed as determined to get rid of the baby as I was to keep it. But he softened a little. One night he brought over some miscarriage tea.

"It's not like getting an abortion, Red. Nobody is going to cut the baby out of you. You just drink a couple cups of tea each day for about a week and you miscarry."

I studied him like a puzzle. What was so wrong with having a baby? "I don't know," I said.

"You'll just start your period again, and that will be it."

"That's it?" He made it sound like there wasn't a baby to think about. Instead, we just needed to restart my period.

"Yeah, you might get some cramps, but that's it."

I set it aside and told him I'd sleep on it. I was still a little naive. I thought that I could accept a miscarriage as he described it, but not an abortion. The next morning, I boiled some water and made a cup of tea to appease Butch before he left.

When I took a sip, it was the most awful thing I had ever tasted. It was like drinking dirty, rotten water. I left it sit there on the kitchen counter and poured myself a cup of coffee to drink while I got ready for work. When I passed by the cup of tea next, I tried it again to see if it was any different if it was cold. But I couldn't get more than the tiniest sip down. Think about drinking the worst thing you can imagine, and that was what it was like. I haven't tasted anything in my life that tastes as bad as that tea did. Before I left for work, I tried one more sip, spit it out, and rinsed the rest down the sink.

Of course Butch asked about it that night. I told him I drank a cup. He urged me to drink two cups tomorrow. So, for him, I made another cup of tea the next morning, and I actually tried it again, but one sip was it. After Butch left I dumped it down the sink. I decided I wasn't going to put myself through it, not only because the tea was awful, but also because I didn't really want to get rid of the baby. So for the next week I just let Butch believe that I was drinking two cups a day, when actually I was just throwing it away.

"Did you get your period?"

"I think it's supposed to happen slowly." I acted like I knew all about this stuff now.

"So you drank all that tea?"

"Yes, I drank it all," I lied. "Maybe it just doesn't work."

"I'll get some more."

"No, I don't want any more. I've never tasted anything so awful. I think we're just going to have a baby."

"For Christ's sake, what are you gonna do, quit your job, move back in with your mom and dad?"

I was crushed. "If I have to, I will."

His posture softened just a little. "Ah, Red, I just can't get married right now."

"I don't understand you. If you're not going to marry me, I'm gonna leave town."

"What the hell you wanna do that for? You just wanna leave me like that?"

"What do you want me to do? I can't go home to Mama and Daddy's."

"Geez, Red, I don't know what the hell... I'm just not ready for this."

I was near tears but didn't want him to know it. "I think my sister Agnes would let me stay with her for a while in Washington." I swallowed hard, straightened my posture, and worked it all out in my head. He was twenty-nine years old, he had a good job, and he could provide for us. I knew he could. That's one thing Mama and Daddy would like about him. I couldn't tell them that I was pregnant if we weren't going to get married. Maybe getting away until after the baby was born was a good idea. But I didn't have a plan for anything beyond that.

"Ah, what the hell. Go stay with your sister for a couple months. I'll come and get you as soon as I can."

That was all I needed to hear. I gave him a big hug, and life was good again. I was going to be a mom.

I quit my job, gave up my apartment, and told Mama and Daddy that I was going to spend the summer with Agnes to help her out with her two little babies. The next thing I knew I was on a bus heading to Washington State.

I figured I would go up there and stay until Butch came to get me and we got married. That way I wouldn't have to tell Mama and Daddy anything until after we were already married. Maybe then it would be okay that I was pregnant.

I hadn't been to Washington before. It was springtime, and there was so much green. The air was clean, fresh, and cool. Agnes lived in the small town of Morton where you could see the snowcapped mountain ridges from almost anywhere you stood. She had recently had her second child. For some reason we called her Puddy (like pudding with an "ee" on the end instead of an "ing"). Maybe I was oversensitive because I was pregnant, but I just thought that Puddy was so precious. I realized that I thought all babies were precious. You could just be yourself around a baby, and there was so much carefree love. I felt happy that I was going to have a child of my own. I felt like maybe everything would be all right.

Then I realized that springtime might be beautiful and full of new beginnings and all that, but you needed to watch out for bumblebees while you were smelling the flowers.

As it turned out, Agnes told our sister Sarah, who was also living in Washington that I was up there because I was pregnant. Sarah told Mama. Then Sarah came back and told me that Mama didn't believe her. Mama said I couldn't be because there was blood in my underwear that I had left there. I figured it was okay to just let Mama believe what she wanted to. But the truth was I would bleed a little bit all the time I was pregnant. Nothing serious—just a little and then stop. Maybe it was the stress or the few sips of tea I had. I never saw a doctor until I was about six months along, and if he told me why I was bleeding a little I don't remember what he said, but it never worried me.

My sisters both wanted me to go to a home for unwed mothers. But there was absolutely no way I would ever agree to that. I tried to tell them that Butch was coming up to get me and that we were going to get married. They tried to convince me that if Butch didn't show up I needed to go to the home for unwed mothers. I still said no. I can be as stubborn as all get-out if I want to be. It just wasn't going to happen, and I knew it. Besides, Butch was writing letters to me all the time I was there. Love letters. So I knew he loved me and wouldn't let me down. When he finally wrote that he was on his way, I was relieved. He said that he had to stop in California on his way up. So it wouldn't be that much longer.

When he finally got there, the mild Pacific Northwest summer was upon us. The sun shone softly in the sky, and things began to warm up. Together, Butch and I told Sarah and Agnes that we were going back to Colorado and that on our way home we were going to stop in Raton, New Mexico, and get married. We told them that everyone went to Raton to get married. It was easy. You just signed some papers and paid for a license and you were married. Everyone was doing it. Why couldn't we just do the same?

5

When we got back to Pueblo, Butch gave me some money and told me to go house hunting for an apartment. He didn't care what kind of apartment it was or how big. It just had to be something we could afford. Since he was working and I wasn't, I would have to find it.

I discovered a nice little furnished place that had everything we needed. It was small. It had only two rooms—a kitchen and a bedroom. The bathroom was in the hall, and we would have to share it with the apartment next to us. The kitchen had a square dark wood table with matching chairs, a nice clean white stove and fridge, a sink and cabinets, and a wooden rocking chair that I hoped would provide welcomed relaxation for me and the baby that would be here in about three more months. The bedroom contained a naked bed and a lone dresser. The walls were draped in drab beige wallpaper that had some indistinct design penciled on it. There was a window in each room with frail curtains trying hard not to block the little light that tried to shine in on us. We brought ourselves, some bedding, our clothes, and some dishes and made it our first home together.

Mama gave me a couple of quilts that she had made, a green one and another one that was mostly yellow—my favorite colors. I placed them both on the bed, and it seemed to bring a slight smile to the otherwise stark room. I went out and bought a Pyrex coffee percolator just like Mama's and placed it on the stove in the kitchen to warm the air with the smell of coffee each morning. Best of all, I had brand new dishes to fill the cupboards. While I was working at the malt shop I had placed two sets of dishes on layaway—one set of four white plates, cups, and saucers with gold trim and another set with silver trim and silver flowers that included a matching sugar bowl, creamer, and serving bowl.

The cycle of weekend dating with our little group of friends had come to end so that each of us could start our families. It turned out that I wasn't the only one who was pregnant. When we got back to Pueblo we found out that every one of the couples that we used to hang out with at the Moose Lodge was also pregnant, except for Gene Solvo and Chris. Don't ask me how this bizarre group pregnancy happened, because I have no idea. Us girls never talked about sex among ourselves. I don't know if the guys did. But it was common knowledge that every one of us went down to Raton, New Mexico, and got married. And that was no surprise. If you were pregnant, you had to get married. That was just the way it was.

Butch was now working at the steel mill on the south side of town— Colorado Fuel and Iron, or CF&I as we called it. He would regularly go out after work with a couple of the guys from our little group, who were also working there. But none of us girls went out anymore. I didn't drive a car, so I usually stayed home the better part of the week. Sharon (one of the gals who used to go out with us) and her husband didn't live too far from our new apartment. She came to visit once in a while or would pick me up to go to her house for coffee.

I knew the state fair was getting ready to start up, and I thought it would be fun for all of us to get together and go. Butch didn't think it was such a good idea, because I was pregnant. Funny thing is, Sharon's husband told her the same thing. I really didn't understand this. I don't think it was because he was concerned about my health. I was getting around the same as before. I didn't have morning sickness or any of that.

In fact, I had two maternity outfits and didn't even really need to wear them. I could still wear most of my normal clothes. Regardless, I ended up staying home while Butch went to the fair. This was the outline of a pattern that would define our roles as husband and wife. Like the pages in a pattern book with small, gray-dotted lines sketched on very thin paper, I could see the shape that would take form if we followed the pattern. But I could not imagine the color or texture of the cloth.

I was raised during a time when the expectations set for a girl were simply to become a woman, a wife, and a mother. That was what my grandmother, my mother, and my sisters did. They were my examples in life. I knew this was what I was going to do too. So I tried as best I could to settle into my new role.

One thing I wished that I had learned more about from the women in my family was how to cook. I seemed to do okay with baking, but other food preparation didn't come that naturally to me. Mama had a knack for it. I used to watch her and help in the kitchen some, but Mama never used a recipe, and when I would ask about how something was made, it was always "a little bit of this and a little bit of that." This left a lot of guesswork for me. My first mashed potatoes turned out more like lumpy, thick white gravy than mashed potatoes. With Butch being from an Italian family, I knew preparing and eating an evening meal was supposed to be more of a festive, artful celebration than just a necessary chore. I knew I would need to go out to Butch's folks and learn how to can spaghetti sauce and cook chili peppers and Italian meals like his mother made. But since his mother spoke only Italian, I wasn't in any hurry to take on that challenge. The funny thing is, he didn't want to go visit his family either. I know he was passionate about his family ties, yet things were different for him; he didn't seem close to his family in the same way I was with mine. I treasured the times when Mama, Daddy, and Elva would come over and visit me while

Butch was at work. There seemed to be a mysterious divide between Butch and his family.

I quickly realized that I had lost contact with most of our friends, except Sharon and Gene. We saw Imogene and Jim every once in a while too. But I spent a lot of time alone, and I didn't like being idle. So one day I decided to call up my friend Helen Plant (from my Pleasant View School days) and have her over for coffee. Helen and I had known each other for years, and our friendship seemed to grow stronger as the years passed. She never went out with us when I was dating Butch, so maybe he didn't know her very well, but I was kind of surprised at how much he really didn't like it when she came over for coffee. He just wanted me to stay home alone. I just couldn't be isolated like that. Once I realized how Butch felt, each time Helen came to visit I would know that he was going to get mad, and I would just let him. And that was how it was going to be.

I guess you could say that I didn't know all that much about negotiating your way through a marriage. Mama and Daddy never got mad at each other. At least not in front of us kids. They made it all look so easy. I didn't know much about being pregnant either and the effect it has on a woman physically and mentally. I was still pretty young and had a lot to learn. But I knew deep down in that place where you just know stuff that it wasn't right for Butch to try to stop me from seeing my friends. At times he would try to tell me what I could and couldn't do. It made me think that he saw me as a possession, like something he owned and just wanted to control. Mama and Daddy's marriage didn't seem to hold that dynamic. I thought that maybe it just took time. I was taught that marriage was forever, and we were just starting out.

Maybe I needed a wedding ring. Butch didn't have the money to buy one at first, but I knew Mama's meant so much to her. I wanted something like that. Maybe it would make a difference.

I remember one time when Mama lost her wedding ring. We had a dishpan that we did dishes in. Since we didn't have indoor plumbing, when Mama was done doing dishes, she took the dishpan full of dirty water out the back door and threw the water in the yard. About an hour or so after she had thrown the dishwater out she realized her wedding ring was gone. She knew it had been thrown out with the dirty dishwater.

Mama was very upset. She wanted that ring found. It was a simple gold band, kind of wide for a woman's ring. She had worn it every minute since it was placed on her hand. We looked for days for that ring and didn't find it. It probably just rolled somewhere out of sight. Years later Daddy found it in the yard while he was out hoeing weeds. If he offered to buy her another one while it was missing, I know she would have said no. For some reason another ring wouldn't have meant as much to her as that one meant.

I talked to Butch about wanting a wedding ring. So one day after he got paid, we went down to Bullock Jewelers on Seventh Street. It was just a tiny jewelry store. He told me how much he could afford to spend. It was a lot of money for us. I don't remember exactly how much it was, but I know it wouldn't be considered very much at all today. I helped him pick out one that I liked that was in our budget. It was a set that included a thin gold band that fit together with an engagement ring that had one small diamond in it. At that moment, I suppose the shine of it captivated and motivated me in some way.

I worked myself into a little routine of doing laundry on Mondays and ironing clothes on Tuesday. I taught myself to crochet, kept house, and did my best to prepare meals for us when Butch was home for dinner. I felt as if I was doing a pretty good job of being a homemaker and a wife.

6

O ur apartment didn't have a washer or dryer. So every Monday Butch took me and the laundry to my sister Zelma's house. I was eighteen years old, pregnant, didn't work, and hadn't learned to drive a car yet. Going to Zelma's was something I looked forward to. It got me out of the house and gave me a chance to visit with my sister, as well as get the laundry done.

On Monday, September 17, 1951, Butch dropped me and the laundry off at Zelma's house just before seven o'clock in the morning and came to pick me up around three in the afternoon, just like always. I was well past my due date, so when Butch came to pick me up, he came in for a few minutes to see how I was doing. Everything seemed fine. There was absolutely no sign that the baby was coming yet.

It was harvest time, and Butch needed to go help his folks with the vegetables. He didn't want me staying home alone. So he asked me to stay put until he could come and get me later that night. I didn't mind, and neither did Zelma. So off he went.

It wasn't more than five minutes after he left that my labor pains started. I was sitting at the kitchen table, and Zelma was fiddling around in the kitchen when I got a real bad stomachache. I got up from the chair slowly, but as quick as I could with a full term baby protruding from my waistline. I waddled toward the bathroom holding my stomach as if it might fall onto the floor if I let go. By the time I got to the bathroom and sat down on the toilet, my stomachache had subsided, and it didn't feel like I had to go any more. I sat there for a minute or two just to make sure. Yep, it had passed.

I gathered myself together and went back out to the kitchen. I don't think Zelma even noticed that I was gone. She was still fiddling around in the kitchen getting it cleaned up so she could start supper and mess it up again. Then my stomachache hit me again.

"You all right?" Zelma asked.

"Oh, I've got a stomachache." I grunted the words out as if they were stuck in my throat.

I got up, stopped in my tracks, and held my stomach. It was as hard as a basketball. I slowly waddled back to the bathroom.

As I sat there in the bathroom on the toilet, I thought to myself, *This could be it.* But I really didn't know for sure. I thought I would just see if it passed. It's kind of funny how I went a full nine months knowing that I was going to have my first baby and never really realized what that meant until the baby actually started coming. It's an eerie feeling when you don't exactly know what to expect and you have absolutely no control over what happens next. It kind of scared me to think this could be it.

I went back to the kitchen as if everything was okay. But it wasn't. There was that stomachache again. But this time I knew it wasn't a stomachache.

"Zelma?" I called in as normal a voice as I could muster.

"Yes?" she said, turning to look at me.

"I think I'm having labor pains."

Now Zelma is fourteen years older than me and had already had three kids, so she didn't seem rattled at all. She set down her dish towel, walked over and put her arm around me, and walked me to the chair to sit down.

"How many have you had, and how far apart are they?"

"Just two or three in the last few minutes—maybe fifteen minutes," I said kind of pathetically.

"Okay, well let me call the doctor. You just sit here and tell me every time you have another contraction."

Besides being my sister and experienced, I trusted her and felt safe in her care. Over the next few minutes, or half hour, or whatever it was, I lost track of time, I focused on my stomach and the pain that it brought as I listened to Zelma on the phone with the doctor, then trying to reach Butch, and then on the phone with the nurse, and then trying to reach Butch again.

"They're not answering the phone at his folk's house. They must all be out in the fields," she reported.

It wasn't anything like today when everyone and their brother have cell phones on them at all times.

"Well," she said, "we're gonna have to take you to the hospital, so I guess I'll call a cab."

Zelma didn't drive either. Her husband was at work until around suppertime, and he couldn't be reached at work. So a cab was our only option.

The cab ride was perfectly miserable. I could feel every single bump in the road regardless of how big or small it was. Other than that, everything else was kind of a blur when I got to the hospital. They got me in and situated in a room. The labor pains got worse, as expected. Then they gave me something to help me relax and help with the pain, and that's when it got blurry.

Zelma finally got ahold of someone at Butch's folks' house, and they got a message to him that I was having the baby. He didn't believe them at first because he had just left us not too long ago and everything was fine. Zelma finally convinced him that this was the real thing and he should come to the hospital.

Labor only lasted about four hours. I don't remember much of it. But I do remember the doctor looking in on me after the baby was born and asking me if my throat hurt. I was kind of confused by his question. My throat didn't hurt. I told him no and asked him why he was asking.

"Because of all the screaming and hollering you did," he huffed with a grin.

That was news to me. But I do remember the beautiful baby boy they placed in my arms and the pure awe I felt in my heart.

I named him after his father—the same first, middle, and last names. For some reason I just knew it was going to be a boy. I didn't even have a girl's name picked out. I think Butch was glad we had a son. Our relationship was pretty good, and we got along well. Having a child together somehow strengthened us and our relationship. Everything seemed perfect. Except for one tiny detail… we were lying to everyone about being married.

Butch, Tony, and I standing outside Zelma's
house when Tony was about a year old

7

The truth is we couldn't get married. I never told a single soul about this until now. Butch and I didn't get married on our way back from Washington, but we told everyone that we had. Less than a handful of Butch's relatives knew the truth, and it wasn't because of anything that came from my mouth.

When Butch came to pick me up at my sister's in Washington, there was a lot going on. My sisters hovered over me, trying to protect me from the rainstorm they had predicted. I didn't think I needed their protection, and I saw no sign of rain, until I finally got a private moment alone with Butch, away from Sarah and Agnes.

"I didn't want to tell you this," he reached out to me nervously, "but I'm still married."

I knew he was married before, but I didn't know he was *still* married. What could I say? I was devastated. I searched for strength. I didn't find it in the eyes of the man who stood before me. I looked away from him. I knew I wouldn't find it in my sisters and the home for unwed mothers that they wanted me to go to. I thought about what Mama and Daddy might think. I lowered my head and focused on the green grass that grew beneath my feet. Daddy would have looked at me with all sorts of love in his eyes and said, "You made your bed, and now you gotta lay in it," and I would know instinctively that he was right.

I didn't say anything. I looked straight into his eyes. My eyes must have spoken for me.

"I'm sorry, Red." He hesitated, looking at me carefully.

I knew he wanted me to say something, but for all the thoughts that were swimming around in my head, I couldn't say a thing.

"I went to California on my way up here to file for divorce."

The weight of the blow was lessoned ever so slightly. Somehow I found the strength I was looking for. It was there inside me. I knew how to not let things bother me. I had practiced it well while I was growing up in Rye. I had taken hurtful comments before, and no matter how hard they were thrown, I never flinched. *You gotta take it as it comes*, I told myself. *You gotta make the best of it.* I yielded, resigned to accept it for what it was.

He continued to tell me that there was also a child. I don't remember if he told me he had a little girl when I was dating him. I felt like he hadn't been completely honest with me while we were dating. Now it was too late. I too was going to have his child. I took the strength I found within and projected it like a shield in front of me. At least he was willing to start the divorce proceedings.

"I gave her enough money to pay for all the fees that are involved, and she will do the actual filing. She's in California. Nothing's gonna be in the Pueblo papers. No one even needs to know about any of this," he explained.

It was after this conversation that the story of our marriage was initiated on my sisters Agnes and Sarah. After that it became a little easier to tell everyone else that we went down to Raton, New Mexico, and got married on our way back from Washington. It was a real common thing to do. Since so many of our friends got married this way, it was easy to let everyone think that we had done the same.

It took about a year for Butch's divorce to become final. He wanted to go out and celebrate, but Tony was just a baby. So we couldn't really go out. Instead I talked him into bringing the baby with us to Kansas to see my grandma Smith and visit with her. It was our first family outing. Unfortunately, it was also one of the only outings we would ever have as a family.

Not long after that, we moved out of our first apartment and into another one. We had to move. There was barely enough room in that cracker-box apartment for the two of us let alone one more, even if he was just a tiny little baby.

We moved into a furnished apartment off of Lake Avenue that had bigger rooms, but it was a dump. It was crawling with cockroaches, and I hated it. The only thing good about it was the location. It was between Daddy's work and his home. Every once in a while he would drive by on his way home for lunch. Usually he wanted to see his new grandson and take him home with him so that Mama could spend some time with him too. Then I would get him back whenever Mama and Daddy decided to bring him back. I didn't mind. My folks were wonderful with kids. They had a plethora of grandchildren. It was wonderful to watch Daddy with little Tony. He loved babies in general, but to me it seemed as if he thought the sun rose and set in my little boy. In his eyes, Tony could do no wrong. It seemed as if Mama and Daddy had the baby just as much as we did.

Some of the grandkids were favored more than others, and sometimes it was obvious. At one time, all my brothers and sisters were mad at me because Daddy bought a combo stroller/walker for Tony. None of the other kids or grandkids had ever gotten a present like that. It made me feel as if Tony was special. He was a cute little baby—everyone told us so. And in all this mess, I felt as if I had done something right.

When Tony was about eight months old, I happened to notice an advertisement in the *Pueblo Chieftain* newspaper. It was for a baby beauty contest that was being conducted at Crews Beggs department store. I think they called it a baby festival. Since everyone was always telling me that Tony was a really cute baby, I decided to take him down to the department store and enter him in the contest. They took his picture, and I filled out some paperwork. There were quite a few babies there. The next thing I knew, we were back there lined up with a handful of other baby festival finalists and their mothers. Tony came away with a blue ribbon and a certificate that said Baby Festival Royal Winner. He scored a 99 percent on beauty and 100 percent on health. There weren't really any other prizes besides the ribbons and the certificates. Butch didn't know that I entered his son in the beauty contest, but he sure was proud that his son won, and he coveted that certificate for years to come.

After Butch's divorce was final, we decided we should probably go ahead and get married. But by the time the conversation came up, I was pregnant with my second child. I didn't really want to get married while I was pregnant; at least that was what I told myself. But I think some of Butch's behavior was starting to worry me. He was beginning to be cruel at times.

When I told him we were going to have another baby, he said that he wanted me to go lift up on the back of the car to see if I could lose it. I don't know what he was thinking. I gave him an emphatic no. I didn't even consider it for a second. I couldn't understand it either. Where was the man I had dated and fallen in love with? The man I had wanted to marry was receding from my vision. I guess it didn't matter if we waited anyway, because everyone thought we were already married—except for Butch's family. They knew the real story.

I didn't meet his folks until just before Tony was born. Butch warned me that they didn't speak English very well. They were full-blooded Italians from the old country. I had seen them before because we used to walk right by their farm when I was going to school at Pleasant View. I remember them out working in the yard or the garden in the afternoons. He was a little old man, with a small frame and only a few strands of hair on his head. She was just as short as he was but stout and ever clad in a flowered dress and an apron that covered her front, from neckline to hem line.

Our visits with them were short and our conversations bumpy. I had a hard time understanding them when they spoke. Quite often I would find myself just starting to follow along, and then they would speed up and start speaking Italian and I was lost again. Butch understood them when they spoke Italian but didn't always offer up a translation. Consequently I was a little uncomfortable and didn't do much talking myself.

They never had coffee on, but there was always wine. His dad made the wine himself. They would offer it to me, but I didn't drink and wasn't interested in what seemed to be his dad's pride and joy. Once, his mother told me I had to at least taste the wine. Beside the fact that I didn't drink, I was pregnant with Tony. But she insisted repeatedly in broken English, "You try it. You no want da baby ta be marked, eh." When I finally understood what she was saying, I pictured my baby being born with some big black blotch on his face because I didn't try the wine. I was only a little over eighteen. I had no idea why this might happen to my baby, but I didn't want it to. So I tasted the wine. It was awful. I know now that it was just a silly superstition they had. They thought a pregnant woman should taste any kind of food or drink she saw, or the baby would be "marked"—whatever "marked" meant. There were other superstitions as well. Like don't hang clothes out on the clothesline while you're pregnant, or the baby could end up getting strangled by the umbilical cord. I think my family held that superstition too. So just in case, I never hung the clothes out to dry while I was pregnant—I had someone else do it for me.

When I first met his folks, they knew that he was still married to another woman and that she and Butch had a child together. Once in a while, I would pick up on something that they were saying about Butch's first wife. They didn't call her by name. They simply called her his wife. I'm not sure if it was because they couldn't speak English very well or for some other reason, but they continued to call her his wife even after they knew he was getting a divorce. This didn't sit well with me, but apparently that's just how they saw her—as his wife.

I guess Butch had married her because she was pregnant, and then they had moved into his parents' house together. So they got to know her a little bit. It only lasted about a month. And then, to hear Butch's side of the story, he kicked her out. He said he couldn't stand her. And I believed him. He used to call her all kinds of names, and then he would go off on an Italian rant spouting out what I'm sure was some healthy Italian cursing.

When she moved out, she moved to California. His parents never got to see the baby girl she had. But I got to see a picture of her. Butch's sister Helen brought over a picture for him after returning from a trip to California. She gave it to me to give to him, but when I tried, he said he didn't want it. For some odd reason I kept it and put it in my photo album. I wonder if Butch's mother ever knew that the baby was named after both her grandmothers—Lucille Annette.

Butch told me our second child was going to be as close to his folks as Tony was to my folks.

The night our second child was born we went to see a movie and left Tony with Mama and Daddy for the night. I started having contractions in the middle of the night. Butch finally took me to St. Mary's hospital at four in the morning. They admitted me and sent Butch to the waiting room. I was in labor for about three hours before the baby was born. It didn't even enter my mind that he should be in there with me because it just wasn't allowed back then. Even though I imagine my dad helped deliver most of us kids.

Normally you might picture a father being a little impatient or on edge waiting for a baby to be born. Not Butch. One of the hospital staff had to wake him up to tell him that we had a daughter. He came in to see me for a few minutes and then told me he was going home to go back to bed. It seemed a little odd to me because I remembered Zelma telling me that when our son was born she had been so surprised at Butch's reaction. He had been uncharacteristically excited and genuinely proud to be a father.

With Tony I stayed in the hospital for about nine days. (There was only one time in my life that I was in the hospital longer than that.) With my daughter, the stay was shorter. I was only in the hospital for about five or six days. Butch came to visit most every day.

Our daughter's name was decided before she was born. We were going to name the baby after the grandfathers, Edwin Joseph, if we had a boy. But a girl's name didn't come so easily.

All of his family had a fit about the girl's name that I picked out. I really had my heart set on naming her Janet Charlene. Butch's family raised holy hell about it because there was already a baby girl in the family named Janet. In his family, they believed if someone else had a kid about the same age—like a cousin—then you shouldn't take the name because someone else had already used it and it would be too confusing. Butch sided with his family rather than me. He just wouldn't have it. It seemed a little excessive to me. I was peeved, disgusted with the whole control thing, and didn't feel like fighting with him about it.

I gave in. Unfortunately, we ended up picking names out of a hat until we came across one we could both agree on. Butch has a sister named Helen, and his family would be okay with us naming our daughter after his sister. I had a good friend named Helen. I let my friend think I named my daughter after her, and Butch let his sister think she was named after her. In reality it was neither really. We were just getting into a habit of leaving out the story and just letting people think what they wanted.

We took our new baby girl home to our modest two-room house. Fortunately we had moved out of the cockroach dump. Before Helen was born we had moved into a quaint white house with a small front lawn, positioned only a few hundred feet from Butch's folks' house. It was on their farm. It had an outhouse rather than a bathroom, but there was running hot water in the house. The house was pretty small with only a kitchen with an eating space and the bedroom. For the first time we had to buy some furniture, because this one wasn't furnished. We bought a double bed, a chest of drawers, some nightstands, and a table and chairs. Someone gave us a crib for Tony, and we had the bassinet for Helen. We got our first black-and-white television while we lived there. We positioned it proudly on a stand in the bedroom.

Helen was born in January 1953. Soon afterward Butch and I finally got married. I don't even remember the exact date. In fact, in the years to come we never celebrated an anniversary. The wedding ceremony wasn't really a ceremony; it was just us and our witnesses—Butch's sister Helen and her husband. We got married down in Raton, New Mexico, just like we had let everybody believe we had done four years ago.

When we went to get married, we left the kids with Butch's folks, which was rare. They hardly ever watched the kids. Considering they were the only ones that knew we weren't married yet, we thought it was our best option. But it was just a day trip. We left early in the morning and came back that night. From Pueblo it was a shorter drive to Raton than it was to Denver. It was uneventful and unmemorable. Nothing romantic and no honeymoon that followed. As far as I know, most people didn't go on honeymoons in the early 1950s. If you didn't have the money to do it, it just wasn't something you did. I guess we just didn't have the money. Of course, I don't really know if we did or not, because Butch was the only one working at the time and he kept all the money as well as the knowledge of how much he earned to himself.

Butch was still working at CF&I. He worked in the wire mill making galvanized wire. It was hot and dirty work. He never told me how much he made, but my understanding was that the pay there was outstanding. Generally it was an hourly wage plus a bonus if the crew you worked with made quota, and with a good crew, he could have been making bonuses every shift—but I will never know for sure. The only money I saw was when he would take me to the grocery store. We were always able to get what we needed, but he would never give me any money to shop with alone. I never really knew what our financial standing was as a family. We could have been in debt up to our eyeballs or had thousands in the bank, but I was never privy to that information.

In my opinion, he was kind of stingy with his money. In all the years we were married he only bought me one gift. It was a little red radio for the kitchen. It was a birthday present. I would have to ask for money to buy birthday gifts and Christmas gifts. I remember asking him for some money to go Christmas shopping once, and he reached into his pocket and handed me some cash. I'm pretty sure it was just what happened to be in his pocket at the time, but he told me that it was all he had. I had to take it or leave it. I couldn't believe that it was all he had because I knew he had enough to also go out, drink beer, and gamble several nights a week.

It irritated me to no end when he went out and played poker after work. He wasn't playing for the fun of it; he played for money. Because it was illegal to gamble back then, the gambling spot was kept secret, even from me. Sometimes he would be out all night, but he would swear he was just playing poker. I had a hard time believing him. And I didn't understand why he could be out all night, but I wasn't allowed to go out and do anything. I began to wonder if Butch didn't have other things that he was keeping from me. We argued about his gambling and staying out all night quite a bit.

Once, after being out all night, he came home the next day with a washing machine to try to soften the blow. But he didn't really give it as a gift.

"I won some money, so I bought a washing machine. Now you can wash clothes at home."

What I think he meant was now he wouldn't have to haul me over to Zelma's to wash clothes every Monday. I could spend more time at home—where I belonged.

So there I was, home with the kids, no transportation and no phone—isolated really, except for the fact that his folks lived a couple hundred feet from us.

One day, when Helen was less than a year old, she stood up in her high chair and fell out. We were in the kitchen, and I was at the sink. I had just given her a snack. I glanced over at her, and she was sitting there contently slurping in as much finger as snack—the way babies do. She was in a wooden high chair with a metal tray on it. Back then they didn't come with seat belts. I turned just in time to see her trying to climb out of the chair, but I couldn't reach her before she fell to the floor. I heard a thud as she landed square on her head. I picked her up as fast as I could and realized she wasn't responding. I thought she was dead. I didn't know what to do. I grabbed Tony and ran out of the door as fast as I could. The cool air shocked my maternal instincts as I thought for a brief moment that Tony didn't have a coat and Helen didn't have a blanket. I knew there was a phone at Butch's folks' house, and that was all that mattered at that moment. I navigated through the small yard, two driveways, and across a ditch with a limp baby in one arm and a toddler hanging onto my other hand trying to keep up.

Helen started crying just as I got to their door, and her small body took shape again. She wasn't dead. The relief was enormous, but somehow the fear inside me still lingered. Normally I would have knocked, but I just burst in the kitchen door. Butch's mother was in the dining room. I blurted out my story to Butch's mother telling her what had happened. I wasn't really sure if she understood me or not, but I'm sure she could tell I was upset. Helen was still crying, and Butch's mother came over and took her out of my arms. I kept on with my story. I began to think that she understood at least parts of what I was saying. She started talking softly to the baby and petting her head. As I quieted down, I could pick up some of what she was saying to the baby.

"You stay with Granma, dissa no happen."

Did she think I wasn't taking good care of my baby? I had never been all that comfortable around her. Now I was feeling a little wall go up. She didn't say a word to me. I watched her with my child for a few minutes and noticed that Helen was settling down. My senses came back to me, and I realized that the fall must have just knocked her out. The cool air outside must have helped to bring her to. I swear I thought she was dead. I vowed that the next time I put her in that high chair she would be tied in with a diaper around her waist.

I knew Butch's mother could understand some English, but she couldn't speak it well enough to give me any advice about what to do next. It was comforting at least to know she were there. But it was frustrating as hell not to be able to talk to my baby's grandmother about what happened. It was even more frustrating not being able to get somewhere when there was an emergency. A great sigh that held relief, frustration, and resignation escaped me. I took Helen from her grandmother's arms and went home.

8

I decided that I was going to find a job.

I tried to go back to work once before when Butch and I were still living in town and I could catch the bus. It was at Walgreens. I worked one, maybe two shifts before Butch called the manager and fed him a line of bull about how my working there was causing problems in our marriage. His phone call got me fired. But it wasn't me working that was causing problems in our marriage. Ever since we got that damn marriage license, we had been squabbling. He started dictating what I could do and whom I could have as friends. I didn't like being told what I could and couldn't do. He was becoming mean and controlling. I was stubborn and becoming rebellious and withdrawn from him.

He didn't like my girlfriends coming over to the house, especially Helen Plant, and he wasn't afraid to let her know it. I think he had me where he wanted me. I couldn't drive. I had no money or access to our checking account. And I had two small children at home to take care of. I was nearing my twenty-first birthday, and I felt caged.

I had one reprieve—for some reason he didn't mind too much if Sharon came over or if I went somewhere with her. Probably because he didn't want to make his drinking buddy mad. Butch and Gene (Sharon's husband) used to go out after work. They both worked three to eleven at CF&I. Sometimes it was one or two in the morning before they would make it home. Whenever we asked about why they were getting home so late, they always said, "We just stopped for a beer." After a while Sharon and I started wondering about where their watering hole was. Sharon could drive a car, so one night we tried following them. We put the kids to sleep in the back of the car, and we waited until they were off work. We thought we knew where they were headed, but we lost them. And when they didn't go where we expected them to go, we couldn't find them. But I couldn't confront Butch about this because I knew he would be furious if he knew we had followed them.

CF&I was the main industry in Pueblo. The other major employer in Pueblo was the Colorado State Hospital for the insane. After I ran into an old friend of mine, Georgia, and found out she was working at the hospital, something told me that I was going to find my next job there.

Georgia was one of the Firestone girls. The Firestones were a family that lived by us back when I was too young to remember. They had a big family of kids like we did, and Georgia was only a couple of years older than me. She dated my brother Charles for a little while. Later on, while I was dating Butch, she was dating Butch's cousin Joe, and they would go nightclubbing with us. We had stayed in touch off and on throughout the years. She was married to Butch's cousin now. But marriage didn't seem to have the same hold on her that it did me. She was still as outgoing as ever and still liked to have a good time, and her husband didn't care if she worked. We chatted for quite a while about her job out at the hospital. She had nothing bad to say about it. It sounded like a pretty good job, and she made it sound so easy to get hired on there. They hired people right off the street. You didn't have to have any special training. Georgia gave me the names of the people I needed to talk to for an application.

When I told Butch I was going to try to get a job out at the state hospital, I think he didn't take me seriously. He told me to go ahead and try because they wouldn't hire me. I expected him to tell me no or say that I didn't need to work, like he did when I tried to go to work for Walgreens. The fact was, I needed to work. If we needed groceries, I had to wait until he was ready to take me grocery shopping. If I wanted to buy something for the kids, I had to ask permission. It was irritating. I was a grown woman, not a child. I had started working when I was fifteen years old. I had been working while we dated. I missed not being able to shop or buy what I needed when I needed it.

I had to talk him into driving me out to the state hospital to fill out an application. Since he didn't think they would ever hire me, it was easier than I thought. I didn't tell him that I talked to Georgia and had a door in. I just let him think what he wanted. In the weeks that followed I made up every excuse I could think of to have him take me into town to visit one of my sisters. Then I would catch the bus out to the hospital and check on my application. If I couldn't get into town, I would give them a call and see how thing were coming along with the open positions. I was determined.

I think they finally hired me simply because they were tired of me bugging them. I had no experience in nursing. But I was hoping to get a job taking care of patients, and that's what I got. Mama was the first person I told. She was a little concerned about me working there because she thought I might get hurt. But it was a good-paying job, and I was ecstatic.

Butch was furious. Our marriage was never like a partnership or anything like that. He didn't want me working, and I was supposed to do what he said. We did nothing but fight about it. Helen was little more than a year old, and she would go in the bedroom and cover her ears because she didn't like to hear Butch and me screaming at each other.

His anger toward me began to manifest with both fists doubled up shaking at me while he cursed in Italian: "You goddamn, no good...

[curse words in Italian]." I took his fury and hoped that I wouldn't get hit. But he did start hitting me. When he did, it was only one or two punches at a time. Our fighting would end at that. But he was always careful not to leave any visible cuts or bruises.

I began to think that maybe he didn't really care about me. Maybe he didn't know how to care about anybody. His father sure wasn't any kind of example for him. I remember Butch showing me the scars that he had on his head from his dad beating him up when he was just a boy. Maybe Butch was just living what he had learned. But what didn't make sense to me was that it seemed as if his mother had the say-so in the family. She was the one who wore the pants. Whatever she said to do, her husband did. That had never worked for me with Butch. But I'm not sure I wanted it to, because Butch's dad would do what his wife said, but then he would take out his frustration on the kids—probably just the boys, but I don't know. At least Butch wasn't like his dad in that respect. I had no say in things, and although he didn't pay much attention to the kids, he wasn't taking his anger out on them either. What made it even more confusing was that I thought that Butch was a mama's boy. I think his mother thought that he could do no wrong. I think she knew he was hitting me. We did live only a few hundred feet from her. But she never stepped in to make it stop—neither did his dad. I never really expected them to. I had seen their reaction when Butch beat up his brother-in-law right in front of them.

We were all standing just outside his folks' house when his sister Christine drove up with Chuck and their kids. The instant Butch saw Chuck he came at him swinging. With just a couple of swings Butch had knocked Chuck to the ground. Christine ran around the car and begged him to stop. Butch seemed unaware of anyone else around him. He was screaming and cussing. His fists continued to strike even after

Chuck was on the ground. I think I heard him call him a two-timing SOB, but most of what came out of his mouth was Italian. I don't think Chuck spoke Italian, but the rest of Butch's family understood what Butch was saying. All the while his folks just stood there and didn't say a word. I knew better than to try to tell him to stop, so I stayed out of it too. Finally Butch's brother came out and pulled him off.

Chuck struggled to collect himself, pulling everything together except the blood that had gathered on the ground. Butch continued to cuss and scream while his brother restrained him. With Christine's help Chuck walked back to the car wiping the thick red mixture of blood and dust from his face. They got in their car and left.

Butch said he did it because Chuck was running around on his sister. Butch and his sister never talked much after that incident. In fact, he wouldn't have anything to do with her after that, nor she with him. I can understand Christine's standoffishness, but Butch… that's a mystery. I'm not sure why he felt the need to step in like that. He did something similarly weird with his other sister Helen when she left her husband. She left him and went and got a room at the Y. Butch made me go with him to sit for hours in the car parked outside the Y. He had to make sure she didn't leave there and go out with some other guy. Because after all, she was his sister, and she was married. She belonged to her husband only. It became more and more apparent that in Butch's way of thinking, the kids and I were his possessions. We belonged to him, and he wanted to control us.

Possession or not, after he started hitting me, I wish I could have left him. I can't remember what all our fights were about—the significance is lost. Although, I do remember the trauma. Once he hit me in the head so hard that it broke my eardrum. It hurt like hell, and my ear wouldn't stop ringing. Luckily my brother Arthur happened to show up at our house shortly after the fight, so he took me to the doctor.

"You can't go back to that house, Bernice."

I don't know why I went back, but I gave Arthur the only explanation I could think of. "Yes, I can. I'm married. Marriage is for life, for better or worse."

"But you can't let him hit you like that. It's not right."

"You can't just quit a marriage, Arthur."

"Well, he could really hurt you. You need to do something."

"Oh, believe me, he's gonna hear about it."

The next day I told the son of a bitch that he broke my eardrum and impaired my hearing. He said, "I didn't hit you that hard." Basically, he called me a liar. I don't think it ever came up again. Quietly, I started asserting myself in other ways. I went months sometimes without speaking to him. When I did speak to him, it was only out of necessity. I really didn't tell him much of anything.

I hated that Arthur had to know about Butch hitting me, but I was so glad that he was out of the service and could come see me. I had missed my big brother. He had a way of cheering up the gloomiest of my days. One night he stopped by while Butch was at work. He was accompanied by his new girlfriend, a bottle of vodka, and a jug of orange juice. The kids were still babies and were tucked in early and fast asleep when he introduced me to my first drink.

"Come on, have one little drink with us."

"I don't think so. I don't really like the taste of alcohol."

"Oh, you'll like this. It'll be just like drinking a big glass of orange juice." He already had three glasses out and was opening the bottles. He splashed a little vodka in the bottom of one glass and lifted it toward me. "I'll mix it really light, and you won't even taste the alcohol."

"If Butch finds out, he'll have a fit," I said, feeling a little nervous at just the thought of this.

"He's not gonna find out. Vodka is different than most liquor. You can't even smell it on your breath." He topped the glass off with orange juice and handed it to me.

I was reluctant at first. I hadn't drunk alcohol before, except for that one little taste of wine that had been pushed on me. I looked into Arthur's charming face, and I believed him. He wouldn't purposely put me in harm's way. I saw nothing but good in him.

I sipped away at one drink and then another. It was a fun, relaxing evening. We sat around and talked until about time for Butch to come home, and then they left. I went to bed, and Butch didn't come home until much later. Arthur was right. He never suspected a thing. And he would never know either, considering how little we talked.

Later, Arthur would move away to California to work on his music.

9

Getting a job was a step in the right direction for me. Unfortunately, I hadn't thought it through enough. I still needed Butch to take me to work. He never thought I would get hired in the first place, so whenever I asked him for a ride to work, it almost always became an argument. To say the least, it was a rough start. But I felt as if I was standing my ground with Butch despite his attempts to control my entire life.

The day I started work at the state hospital, I checked in with the director of nurses, Rose Chorney. I had met Chorney and her assistant many times before while I was applying for the job. Chorney was short like me, yet just a little more heavyset. She greeted me with a familiar smile, and we talked as she walked me to the ward where I would begin working. As we walked across the lawn, I realized that the hospital itself was no less than a self-contained city. It covered about three hundred acres of land on the northwest side of Pueblo between Thirteen and Twenty-Fourth Street. The buildings housed thousands of patients. There was also a bowling alley and a swimming pool and housing for nurses and the administrator.

Chorney's manner was very pleasant, yet her voice was a little stern as she explained some of the basic rules that I should follow.

"You will be caring for people who are mentally sick. They are not responsible for what they say and do."

I nodded to indicate I understood and stepped a little more quickly to keep up.

"If anything happens that you can't handle, you need to send for me or the nurse in charge. But no matter what happens, you never let a patient think you are afraid of them. Ever."

Interesting. *Maybe I should try that with Butch,* I thought.

She didn't look at me to see if I understood. She just walked on in front of me reaching out to unlock a heavy door with a key that hung with several others on a key ring attached to a cord around her waist. I watched her intently as she quickly and easily found the right key on the first try and pulled the door open. She explained that all the doors were locked, and if I was given a key, it wouldn't be until I got into the ward. If I accidentally took a key home, I must immediately return it. Taking keys home was grounds for termination. Once inside the ward, the medicine room, the clothes room, and the shower room were locked. And they all had to stay locked. Even the door to the laundry chute was locked. The director of nurses (DNS) had keys to get into the buildings, but even the supervisor had to pass on the keys to the next shift.

"For the time being, you can ring the bell to have someone let you into the ward." She looked at me as she held the door. "And you'll need to get one of these so that the keys are always attached to you and in your pocket out of sight." She put her thumb through the plastic cord around her waist and then shoved the keys down into her pocket out of sight.

"Never carry the keys loose or where a patient can see them. The keys and the meds are counted at the end of every shift."

We walked into a hallway, up a set of stairs, and through a set of double doors (that were also locked) into ward 12. A nervous chill went through my body, and her words echoed in my head. "Never let a patient know you are afraid of them." I made a conscious effort to relax and remember that this was what I wanted. I wasn't going to be afraid—of anything.

I quickly realized that ward 12 was a bed-patient ward. *No need to be afraid of patients who stay in bed all day and all night*, I thought. But I let her words of caution play over and over in my mind as I thought of the consequences of showing fear. The words just stuck with me.

My responsibility during my eight-hour shift was to see that the patients' sheets were changed every two hours if they were wet or soiled. They had thick white rubber sheets on the bottom, then a white pad in the middle, and a white drawsheet that the patient lay on. Everything was white. Changing sheets didn't sound too bad at first, but as the week progressed, I found myself checking a patient's sheets and hoping that he or she hadn't gone so much that it went down to the bottom, which meant I had to change the bed all the way to the rubber. If the person was too big for me to roll them by myself, it would take two of us. So it wasn't always as easy as I initially thought it might be.

There were bedpans in the ward, but the people in the beds didn't know to ask for them. So they just went in the bed. I discovered that some of them wouldn't have even known what a bedpan was. Besides, the bedpans were metal, and most of the patients were nothing but skin and bones with lots of bedsores, so a bedpan would have been pretty hard on them. Some of their sores were so bad you could see clear down to the bone.

The beds were lined up like dominoes on a glossy wooden floor, three rows of beds in each dorm room. The patients didn't get out of bed to go to the bathroom. They didn't get out of bed when we changed the sheets. They just didn't get out of bed period. I think, out of about a hundred patients, there might have been a half dozen of them who could walk. But so many of them looked like they had just curled up in a fetal position and lay there for so long that their legs wouldn't straighten out anymore. Still, for some odd reason, there were no doorknobs inside the rooms. The doorknob and the locks were on the outside of the door.

I learned how to put these rubber rings up under a patient's hips to keep the pressure off and help prevent bedsores. I also learned how to use maggots to eat out the rotten skin on the real bad bedsores. I learned that a bedsore was dead, rotted skin.

I learned that even though the patients were in bed all day and night, they weren't always asleep. There was one patient who we could hear screaming at any hour of the day or night because of the excruciating pain she was in. She had skin cancer on her face, and it wasn't bandaged. The only thing we put dressings on were the bedsores. Most of her nose was gone, and there were actual holes eaten into half of her face. I wondered if it was the pain that made her insane. In those days doctors weren't as generous with pain medication as they are today.

Another patient had skin cancer all across her stomach and under her breast. It was like crusty oozing sores. She was in a room with a gal who thought she was Jesus Christ. This gal would yell at the top of her lungs, "I am Jesus Christ!" and go on and on about being the savior. If I had to speak to her, she would tell me, "You know I'm Jesus Christ," as if that should make a difference in how I spoke to her or what I said.

For the most part there was very little communication with the patients. Most of them just lay there wasting away. Nor was there much movement among the patients, with one exception: a woman who was younger than I was and had Huntington's chorea. She had short, red hair and was kind of pretty. It seemed to me that her mind was okay—it was just her body. She was skin and bones, but it wasn't because she was wasting away like the other patients; it was because the disease made every part of her body move constantly. When meals came out, instead of one tray she got two. She ate it all, and it never put one bit of meat on her bones.

There was another patient that I knew was plenty capable of movement, but I didn't want to see her move. She was in a straitjacket, four cuff restraints, plus sheet restraint tied at all four corners. I learned that she had to be tied down like that because she put out her own eye. So it was to protect her from herself—and hopefully to protect the people that worked there too.

To be honest, I was kind of afraid of some of the patients, but I did everything in my power to never let them know it. I had never done any kind of nursing before. I was turning twenty-one years old and seeing a lot of things that I had never seen before. It's hard to describe the various emotional responses I had that first week. To see the people in the shape they were in… for me, mostly, it was just kind of hard to believe.

I found out that they offered a psych tech class for people like me who had no training. Psychology sounded fascinating: the study of the soul—*psych* (soul) and *ology* (study of). However, I knew that what I was seeing at the hospital seemed worlds away from this. We were caring for bodies not souls. Wondering where that treatment idea came from, I found that in the late 1800s when German psychologist Wilhelm Wundt established the first "experimental psychology" laboratory, he officially rejected the existence of the soul and declared that man was merely a product of his genes. In his words, "If one assumes that there is nothing there to begin with but a body, a brain and a nervous system, then one must try to educate by inducing sensations in that nervous system."

In a Wundt textbook, he declared, "The soul can no longer exist in the face of our present day physiological knowledge." This promoted the idea that one's mental health depended upon an adjustment to the world rather than a conquest of the world. It also promoted the idea that behaviors were entirely the product of the functions or malfunctions of the brain. This was what led to such treatments as electroshock therapy and the prefrontal lobotomy.

I didn't realize it at the time, but I was on the cusp of great changes in the medical treatment of the mentally ill. In 1954, just before I started working at the hospital, chlorpromazine was introduced into the US market and would soon be administered to patients at the state hospital under the name Thorazine—the first wonder drug. It was a little pill that hindered brain function in the same manner that lobotomy did. Our drug-based paradigm of care for mental illness was born right before my eyes.

Eventually I became a little more relaxed and got to know some of the gals I worked with. There was a big laundry chute that we threw large bags of dirty laundry down. It shot the laundry out the side of the building that housed wards 10 and 12, and laundry trucks came to pick it up at different times during the day.

One day a bunch of us were standing around talking (in between bed changes), and someone commented that the laundry chute reminded them of a big slide. It was maybe three feet wide. It went straight for a while and then curved a little and went out of sight. We knew it had a regular door at the end of the chute that lifted up from the bottom and gave way when a laundry bag hit it. We were on the second floor, but it was still a fairly gradual slope. Everyone agreed that it looked pretty much like a slide at a playground from where we stood.

All of the nurses I worked with were around my age—probably in their twenties—still young enough to dare to have a little fun. The chute looked big enough. So we thought we would give our newfound slide a try.

Once we tried it, we didn't stop. We weren't supposed to leave the ward until the shift was over. We were expected to take our breaks and lunches right there on the ward. But once we discovered the laundry chute as an escape route, we would slide out of the building just for something to do and every once in a while to run and get something to eat. We had to make sure we had our keys with us if we wanted back in, but if we forgot them, we could usually buzz the ward from outside, and someone would let us back in. Thank God we never got caught. We probably would have been fired. But it was a fun way to break up the monotony of changing bedsheets for eight hours.

I was learning so much at my new job. I loved it. It was fascinating in so many ways. Plus I was making friends and having a little fun too.

10

As I became more confident in myself, I started leaving when Butch would hit me.

I think the first time might have been when his fists shaking in my face were replaced by a waving gun. Thank God I managed to get out of that house with the kids. I remember the journey to the neighbor's house across the street was something like a dream—or nightmare—where you had the feeling that you needed to move but it didn't feel like you were getting anywhere.

Butch kept several guns around. He had a .22, a pistol, and a rifle for hunting. God only knows what we were arguing about this time. It didn't take much to set him off. His temper was explosive. In the heat of the argument he reached over and grabbed the pistol out of the dresser drawer and pointed it at me. I thought he was going to shoot me. Without thinking, I grabbed up the kids and ran out of the bedroom door into the yard. I couldn't go to his folks' house, so I set my sights on the first neighboring house I could see. He came out right behind me. I was running, and he stood there at the door screaming at me. I guess he could have shot me in the back, but I didn't even think of that at the time. I made it to the edge of the driveway before he stopped screaming. As I crossed the street, the hair on the back of my neck bristled in the quietness. He carried his anger like a force field around him. It penetrated the air in every direction. I knew he was still there, but I was so scared I couldn't look back. I could hear myself breathing harder. I wanted to run faster, but I had the kids with me. Unrelentingly I tried to keep both feet in motion. It was only three or four hundred more feet to the first house I could see. Then behind me I heard the car door slam and the car start. The urgency intensified as I expected him to try to run us down with the car. He backed the car up, spraying gravel hard and fast. As I entered the neighbor's yard, I turned to see the car was facing us and fast approaching. He still had the gun in his hand. I banged on the neighbor's door with hard, rapid, urgent beats that hurt my knuckles as he pulled into their driveway. The front door swung open, and I edged forward, blurting out that my husband was chasing us with a gun. We all looked to see him getting out of the car. Thank God they let us in and shut the door vigorously behind us. As we huddled there just inside the door, Butch began pounding on the door. My heart pounded even louder, and my whole body shook. I had met the neighbor before, but I didn't know him very well. Yet he protected us. He wouldn't let him in. They yelled at each other through the door. I don't remember exactly what was said. I assume he told Butch to go home and cool off. Finally, we pulled the curtains back from the windows, and we all watched as he drove off. I hid out there until I could calm down enough to call my sister Agnes to come and get us. We went to stay with Mama and Daddy for a while.

After finding out what had happened, Daddy took me to see an attorney. He offered to help me get a divorce. He said he would pay for the attorney and everything. We did some initial paperwork. But you know what? I couldn't go through with it. I know Daddy meant well. He wanted to protect me, but I refused to get the divorce. I think he might have thought I was being stubborn, like I was the day he had to spank me with the razor strop when I was a child. After Butch cooled off, we returned home.

We separated several times in the year and a half after we got our marriage license. I would call one of my sisters to come and get me and the kids, and usually we ended up staying a night or two at my folks' house. There, I would get a taste of what a real marriage was like, how two people who loved each other acted and treated each other. Then I would go back to Butch. Maybe I hoped things would be different when I returned home. I guess when I got away I got a different perspective. From far away, with my eyes kind of squinted, I could see a blurry version of us trying to get along. We ate together occasionally, and we slept together occasionally. But if I opened my eyes, I couldn't see much more than that. Nothing ever really changed. There was little to no communication, and I was continuously nervous around Butch. Whenever I sensed the anger in him flaring up, I would get that same feeling in my stomach that I got when my brothers used to tease me with knives.

All the while he told me that I would never leave him (or stay gone for long). He told me that I could never make it on my own. Maybe I heard it so much that I started to believe it. But after working at the hospital for a while, my thinking shifted. Maybe I could take care of myself.

Once I changed the way I thought about things, things changed— ever so slightly.

One day when I asked Butch for a ride to work, he flat out refused. Rather than arguing and fighting with him about it, I took the kids by the hand and started walking down the road toward town. Luck was with me that day because someone I knew came down the road, pulled over, and offered us a ride. I took the kids to Pearl's, caught the bus to work, and this time I was in no hurry to go home.

I had to find a way to let him know that he couldn't continue to control me like that. Of course, after a few days he wanted me to come home. He thought that home was where the kids and I belonged. But I wasn't simply going to do what he said. This time, I was going to try a little negotiation. I told him I would go back when he bought us a real house with enough room for us and the kids. I was tired of living in the two-room jail cell next to his parents.

His negotiation tactics included trying to sabotage my job again. He tried to pull the same stunt that he had pulled when I worked at Walgreens. He called the administrator at the hospital.

After Mr. Barkley, the administrator, got the call from Butch, he actually asked me about it rather than just firing me like the manager at Walgreens did. Mr. Barkley was older than I was and was a single man who was having an affair with the assistant director of nurses. They actually got married later on—but that's beside the point. There were so many juicy stories there at the hospital. I didn't want to become another one. He told me that Butch said we were separated because of my job and that I needed to be fired so that we could get back together. I told my Mr. Barkley that yes, we were separated, but it wasn't the first time we had been separated. Without going into too much detail I told him we were not separated because of my job. Thank God he didn't fire me.

After that, Butch took my ultimatum seriously. He came over to Pearl's to visit on my days off and was apparently doing some house hunting. It wasn't more than a month or so before he came over and told me he had found one. I remember being in Pearl's small front room, seated on the edge of a small flowered sofa with a cup of coffee in my hand. Butch was seated about a foot from me, also on the edge of the sofa, leaning forward with his elbows on his knees. Sam and Pearl were across the room from us in armchairs.

"It's a brand-new three-bedroom house for Christ's sake. What more do you want? All you gotta do is sign the papers with me, Red. I'll put up the goddamn money."

"Well, ya can't beat that," Sam interjected.

"I think it'd be good for the kids to grow up in a nice neighborhood like that Bernice," encouraged Pearl.

I looked over at Pearl. I knew Mama and Daddy raised her the same way they did me—to think marriage was forever. But I really didn't know if I wanted to live with this man again after all we had been through. I don't care how close you are to any of your family or friends—nobody really knows what goes on in your home. I couldn't look at Butch. I thought of the kids.

"Well, I suppose" was all I could muster up. If he wasn't buying a house, I probably would have told him I wasn't going back.

Our new home was located in a development called Belmont, which was divided up into two sections. The first section had street after street of fancy new homes. The section we moved into was the second phase of the development, and the houses were a little cheaper built. The streets all had Indian names. Our street was called Kickapoo. It meant "one who moves about" or "wanderer." It seemed to fit my pattern in life so far.

It was fall when we moved in, and the colors of the season adorned the streets. Kickapoo contained rows of similarly built houses in various pastel colors, neatly positioned so that each front lawn was divided by a driveway. I would just call it a regular 1955 working-class neighborhood. All the houses on our street had three bedrooms and one bathroom. I don't remember exactly, but I think they sold for around $10,000.

When I opened the front door, it was obvious that this house had never been lived in before. I took a deep breath, let all the new smells fill my lungs, and then let out a sigh. When I walked in the door, I was greeted by the echoing sound of my heels clacking on the hardwood floors. My first thought was that I would need to get some front room furniture. We hadn't really lived in a house with a front room before. I was immediately drawn to the doorway across the room that led to the kitchen—the heart of the home. Everything was new from the Formica countertops and matching linoleum floors to the shiny appliances. There was a utility room off the kitchen that contained a new wringer washing machine and a fenced backyard with a clothesline and plenty of room for the kids to play. It was perfect actually. The best I'd ever had.

Butch came through the door with his arms full of boxes. The sleeves on his shirt were rolled up just enough so that I could see his bulging biceps. I got that nervous feeling in my stomach. The same feeling I got when I knew he was mad and might hit me. I'm not sure why my stomach cramped with fear. He wasn't mad. He seemed to be in a rather good mood. I told myself not to let the fear show.

"It ain't bad, huh, Red?" he said without looking at me.

"It's all right." I turned and went down the hall to check out the bedrooms.

One by one, the women in the neighborhood came over and introduced themselves and welcomed us with a pie or cookies or some such homemade treat. I discovered that a lot of the other couples in the neighborhood also had toddlers. It seemed as if all the husbands worked at CF&I, which was no surprise since it was the main source of work for men in Pueblo.

One of the women asked if I would like to bring the kids over in the morning to play, and have a cup of coffee with her after the men went to work. A couple of the other women joined us. Soon we were meeting regularly at one another's houses, sitting around a kitchen table drinking coffee, talking about our kids and our homes.

My sister had given me some hand-me-down furniture for the front room. One of the women mentioned that she could make me some curtains to dress the room up a bit. Everyone agreed that she was a wonderful seamstress. I picked out a sturdy polyester fabric with a pattern that had a cabin and some trees and mountains on it. It was mostly green, which has always been my favorite color. They were full length and hung from the top of the front room window to the floor. Butch didn't mention them, but I know he noticed. He probably would have said something if he had to pay for them, but I had my own money now, so it wasn't an issue.

Butch worked days at the steel mill, and I worked afternoons (three to eleven) at the hospital. This meant that there were three to four hours in the afternoon when we needed someone to watch the kids. I found a grandmotherly English woman whom I hired as a live-in babysitter. Unfortunately, that only lasted about three months. She was nice enough, but she didn't like the food we ate. We always had to buy her prunes and weird foods that we wouldn't normally buy for ourselves. Plus she had to go to the doctor a lot. I didn't really want to tell her that it wasn't working out, so I told her that someone in the family was going to start watching the kids. Actually I had made friends with the other women in the neighborhood, and none of them worked outside the home, so it wasn't hard finding a replacement right next door.

When I got off work at eleven, I would quietly go in and check on the kids before I went to bed. Their peaceful little faces poking out from under the covers would ease my mind. Butch was usually asleep by the time I went to bed. By six in the morning the kids were climbing into our bed, eager to start a new day. So I would get up and get into my routine. I'd make a pot of coffee, pour myself a cup, pour the rest into a thermos, and put it into Butch's lunch pail with a couple of sandwiches. By the time the second pot of coffee was done, Butch would come out and grab a cup.

"Are you going to pick up the kids before dinner tonight?" I asked, looking down at the stove where I was frying up some eggs for the kids.

"I'll take 'em out to see my mom, if I get home in time. If I don't, I'll pick 'em up around seven or eight."

"I'll leave a meatloaf and some potatoes in the oven." I'm not sure why I bothered fixing dinner. I knew this meant he would probably be stopping for a beer after work and the kids would eat with the babysitter. I was tempted to pick up some of the TV dinners that Swanson had just come out with, but I didn't. I always made sure there was something ready to be warmed up for dinner.

He finished his coffee and left without another word before the kids sat down to breakfast. Generally, this was the most I would see of Butch on days that we both worked.

After I fed the kids breakfast and bathed them, I let them play for a while so I could get some housework done before the neighbor ladies and I met for coffee. After lunch I would put the kids down for a nap and get ready for work.

One day I was riding to work with a friend and looked over at her poised behind the steering wheel of the car, eyes forward, but carrying on a conversation like driving was second nature and required no concentration at all. I was twenty-one years old. I felt like it was about time I learned to drive. The next morning, when Butch came into the kitchen for his coffee, I decided to mention it to him.

"I think I should learn to drive."

"Pshh, you can't drive a car."

"I could learn. It doesn't look that hard. You could teach me."

"I'm not gonna teach you to drive a goddamn car. What's the matter with you?"

"Well, I guess I'll get someone else to teach me then."

"You're not gonna find anyone to teach you, and you're not gonna use my car. So don't even think about it."

"Why not? You can put the car in my name, but you can't let me use it?"

"I use that car to get to work for Christ's sake. What the hell do you want me to do?"

There was no sense in making him any madder. After he left for work, I took out the phone book and found a Chevy plant listed under driving lessons. It was perfect. They provided the car and came out and picked you up. I wouldn't need Butch's help.

For an hour a day, five days a week, I drove around in a brand-new Chevy learning to drive while Butch was at work. When I was a kid, we rode horses; we didn't even have a tractor. I remember trying to drive a couple of times while I was dating. But this was different. The teacher was great. She told me every little detail about driving a standard shift, the rules of the road, and how to be safe. She made it seem easy. She talked incessantly, telling me that this was a necessary tactic for teaching me to deal with passengers. Before I knew it, I was driving in downtown Pueblo. Back then it was relatively small, especially compared to what it is now. There were no one-way streets or rush hour traffic and all that. Still, I felt pretty good about driving downtown after just one week. After a couple of weeks, I took my driving test and passed on the first try.

I couldn't wait to tell Butch that I got my license. I stopped him as soon as he walked in the door.

"Guess what I did today."

He turned and walked into the kitchen and placed his lunch pail on the counter. "What?"

"I went down and got my driver's license." I presented it proudly a few inches in front of his face so he could see it. He just shook his head and walked back into the front room and sat down and started pulling his boots off. So I tried again.

"Don't you want to see it?"

After he got his boots off, he finally took it out of my hand and looked at it.

"Huh," he said as he handed it back to me, got up, and walked back to the bedroom.

I was disappointed at his lack of interest, but at least I knew that it registered with him.

A couple of days later Butch finally brought it up again. We were going out to his folks' for a while on Easter day before I went to work. When we got to the car, he handed me the keys.

"Let me see if you really can drive."

I took the keys and got behind the wheel and drove out to the farm like I had been doing it all my life.

After that, I asked him several time if I could use the car. He'd always reply, "No, you can't drive my car." I think he finally got tired of me asking because it wasn't too long before he went out and bought himself a brand-new pickup truck. He had always wanted a pickup truck. I'm not sure how he could afford it. It must have cost him at least $1,700. He still never let me know how much money he made. Apparently he was doing pretty well. I guess we both were. We were the only couple on the block with two vehicles.

After he bought his new truck, he told me I could have the car so he wouldn't have to run me around to the store and whatnot. It was a two-door, gray Chevy—nothing special, but I liked it. Technically, it was my car anyway. He had put it in my name when his ex-wife sued him for $10,000 in back child support. He never got in that car again. He always drove the pickup after that.

For us, things were going along pretty smoothly. At least we weren't fighting.

Maybe it was because we didn't see that much of each other. Maybe it was because we had someone else living with us for the first few months that we were back together. But I think maybe Butch didn't want me to leave him again. I know he really wanted a family. So did I. But I have to admit, more often than not, I was nervous around him, and I lived with a fear in the pit of my stomach. It wasn't what I expected a marriage would be like. I thought that husbands and wives generally asked each other about how their days were, had conversations about the news and the kids, and complimented each other on things they each contributed to building a home. I think I just adjusted to the fact that our marriage wasn't like that. But at least we had a nice home, and we both had good jobs. I loved my job, I loved being able to drive, and I loved having a little more self-sufficiency and having the neighbors to visit with. I didn't feel so cut off from the rest of the world anymore.

11

Although I liked the house in Belmont, we only lived there for a couple of years. Butch wanted to move out to the country. He was born and raised in the country and wanted to farm like his folks did, but I refused to move back onto his folks' land again. So we agreed that we would look for a farm of our own. He talked me into putting our home up for sale before we found a farm to buy. When our house sold, we had to pack our stuff into the back of his pickup truck and move into an apartment out on the mesa. The apartments we moved into used to be chicken coops—if you can imagine that. They cleaned them out and made apartments out of them. Ours was a real long one, and it had about three or four rooms. The kids had one bedroom, and Butch and I had one. Luckily we were only there a couple of months before we found our farm.

I was excited to move. When I wasn't working, I helped Butch pack everything up. But he did most of the moving himself. We were both excited.

It was an older home, built in the 1930s, on ten acres of land ready to be farmed. There was also a big barn and a corral behind the house. We were still in Pueblo but out in the country on Everett Road not too far from his folks' house. We moved in 1957, just before Tony was old enough to start school. It gave me a sense of belonging to know that he would start school at the same elementary school that I attended in the second grade—Riverview Elementary, although they changed the name to North Mesa Elementary just before he started.

Again I found myself preferring old houses to the newer ones. I loved the porch swing on the big covered front porch, the coal furnace, and the big enclosed back porch. And it didn't have hardwood floors. I hated cleaning the hardwood floors in our house on Belmont.

Butch planted the fields and started truck farming. We both kept our jobs, and when we weren't working, sleeping, or taking care of the kids, we were working the land. There was a lot to do. We planted in the spring. Butch decided what to plant. Tomatoes were a big crop, I think because of all the Italians that lived out on the mesa who canned their own tomato sauce. I know Elva and I canned bushels and bushels of tomatoes and tomato sauce, enough to stock up both our houses with enough sauce to have spaghetti twice a week for a year.

Butch planted about fifteen rows of tomato plants, another fifteen rows of chili peppers, six rows of cucumbers, some sweet corn, and some bell peppers. The irrigation ditch had to be run on a schedule—on and off at certain times. Once the vegetables started to get ripe, we had to pick every day. We would get up early in the morning and then spend time in the field in the afternoon or evening as well. We sold vegetables by the bushel to the grocers, restaurants, and vegetable stands in town. Occasionally one of the other farms would get an order that they couldn't fill and would give us a call to help them fill it or to fill it for them. We would do the same if we got a big order that we couldn't fill. It was a lot of work. Once in a while Butch would bring in some Mexicans to help pick a crop or fill an order. When fall came, we picked the green tomatoes and put them in newspaper in the basement and had fresh tomatoes through Christmas every year. There was nothing as sweet as the taste of a cucumber or a tomato picked right off the vine, especially when it was the fruit of our own labors.

Although we sold a lot of our vegetables in town, we also had people who would just stop by our house to buy something. We didn't have a sign out front or a stand; it was just word of mouth. In those days people would just stop by when they drove by a farm, and they would walk right up to the house and ask you what you had for sale. If Butch wasn't around, I would sell them what they wanted. I was instructed to drop everything if someone came by, because it was money and he couldn't get enough of it. Butch was always very concerned about how much I sold. Sometimes I would keep the money. He really didn't like that too much. He thought the money that we made off the farm was his money—not ours. He would always question me about it. He'd ask, "Are you sure that's all you sold? You didn't sell anything else?" He was very controlling when it came to money. In those days, it was common for husbands to control the household money. The husband was expected to be the breadwinner of the family and provide all the necessities and pay all the bills. The wife was expected to take care of the home and the children. The problem was that we weren't the normal husband-and-wife family. Butch wouldn't provide money for everything we needed. He paid the mortgage and utilities, but I had to buy food and clothes for the kids, plus any household items that we needed. Over time, I think I bought almost everything that was in our house, including a new washing machine, a chrome kitchen table with chairs, and a new sectional couch for the front room. I think I was providing for us just as much as he was.

I asked him once about combining our money in a joint checking account, but he said he didn't want to have a bank account with anyone else's name on it. There was no discussion. That was just it—end of sentence. It was fine with me. I went down to the bank where he had an account and opened a separate account of my own.

Eventually I fell into a routine of helping out with the farm, taking care of the kids and the house, and working at the hospital five days a week. While I was at work, the kids were at the babysitters. I would drop them off on my way to work, and Butch was supposed to get them at night when he got off, but he wouldn't always. I found it so aggravating to get a phone call at work from the babysitter because the kids hadn't been picked up. The babysitter never put up a fuss because she was getting paid by the hour. But I was usually pretty mad when I had to go over there at eleven o'clock at night and get the kids. Of course Butch always had some excuse about getting busy out in the field or being held up out of town at a livestock sale. It would have been nice to know what he was doing beforehand, instead of after the fact. But that's not how it played out, and anytime I spoke up about it, he got mad at me.

I know he still thought I might leave him again, because if we fought, he still made it a point to tell me that I could never leave him because I could never make it on my own. Daddy's advice about getting a divorce still popped into my head periodically, but divorce was a pretty uncommon thing in the fifties. Most people I knew held onto the belief that marriage was forever. Even if there were problems, families stayed together and worked it out or stayed together and remained unhappy. Our marriage was no exception.

It wasn't long before I started feeling isolated again. It wasn't like living in Belmont where the neighbors were right next door. The houses out in the country were spread out across the land. The closest neighbor was about a quarter mile up the road. I hadn't met them yet or started visiting with them the way I did with the neighbors in Belmont. I guess I could have gone over and introduced myself, but I didn't really have time for that, and Butch wanted me at home. If I was going somewhere, he wanted to know where I was going and why. He didn't trust me. At times, I felt as if he was purposely trying to isolate me from everyone.

One day my sister Sarah called and said she was coming down from Washington for a visit. She said she would like to spend a day with me while she was in town. I was so happy to have her visit. I invited her to stay with us on my night off. I told her she was welcome in my home anytime. But when I told Butch she was coming over, he had the opposite reaction.

"I don't know why she has to come here and stay."

"She just wants to come and visit while she's in town."

"Go and visit her at your dad's house."

"I've already invited her out. She's my sister, and she's going to be here whether you like it or not."

"Why the hell does she have to stay the night? Let her stay somewhere else."

"She's my family. I won't even consider it."

It was as if a family member needed some kind of special reason to visit or as if I would even consider not inviting my sister to stay the night when she was in town. His reasoning made no sense to me. He continued to complain the entire night. Even though I was nervous and scared, I wouldn't let him see it, and there were times when I just wouldn't back down—unless he hit me. This was one of those times. That's the stubbornness in me, I guess. I know it caused us to fight.

Sarah showed up in the early afternoon while Butch was still at work. When Butch came home, he was very cordial. We all had dinner together, and I don't think Sarah had any idea how he really felt about her being there. I know I certainly didn't mention it to her. I wanted her to feel comfortable.

I gave Sarah one of the kids' beds for the night. As soon as Butch knew we were out of earshot (hopefully Sarah was sleeping), he started in on me again.

"She doesn't belong here. She doesn't live here. Don't let it happen again. You don't let people spend the night here. This is my house."

As much as he disapproved, he didn't say anything to her, just to me. It was always like this. That way he wouldn't have to take the blame. I would have to be the one to make up some excuse as to why someone couldn't come to our house. We went to bed fighting, which wasn't all that unusual. I know he thought that I belonged to him and that I was supposed to do what he said. If I didn't, I knew he would get mad and wouldn't let it go.

I felt nervous all the time because I knew by now that I shouldn't do anything that he wouldn't like. Sometimes I just reacted and did what I thought was right. Other times I would play it out in my head to try to figure out if what I was going to do would make him mad. This became the story of my life. If I did something that I thought would make him mad, fear would grab hold of the pit of my stomach and twist and turn. It was impossible to relax. I was as afraid of him as I was of knives. In fact, every night before I went to bed, I would make sure that every knife in the house was hidden away. As much as I tried not to show it, maybe he knew I was afraid, and maybe he wanted to keep me that way—I don't know. But by this time, I wasn't just afraid for myself; I was afraid for my kids too, especially Tony. When I knew Butch was going to be mad at Tony, I got that same sickening fear in the pit of my stomach, the same fear I felt when he was mad at me and I thought he might hit me.

Butch was always a little rough on Tony, even when he was just a toddler. The very first time he hurt Tony it might have been an accident. Tony and I were over at Zelma's visiting. Tony was probably about a year old. He was playing contentedly with a toy in Zelma's living room when Butch came to pick us up to go home. Butch must have had a hard day at work and just wanted to get home. Tony just wanted to play and didn't want to leave. Kids are like that some times. Butch had absolutely no patience with him. He grabbed Tony by the arm and yanked him up and carried him out of the house screaming and crying. I could hardly believe it.

In the car I held Tony on my lap because he was crying so hard. His little arm hurt, and he couldn't move it or hold anything. He wasn't old enough to say more than just a few words, but it was obvious that he was hurt. I told Butch that he needed to drive us to the emergency room. He was reluctant at first, but he took us to Corwin Hospital—it was the closest. It was a small hospital. One long, two-story building with a small waiting room. We didn't have to wait because the emergency room wasn't busy. I don't think people ran to the emergency room back then like they do now. Most things you just took care of at home if you could.

Butch parked the car and stayed in the waiting room. I told the doctor that my husband had picked him up by the arm. He didn't really question me any further, but he did tell me that Tony's arm was out of the socket. He said it would really hurt when he put it back in place, but then it would stop hurting almost immediately. Tony was sitting on the examination table. I had to hold him still while the doctor took his arm and moved it straight up and got it back in the socket. We were only there a few minutes, and Tony was feeling better in no time.

Once we got back out to the car, I told Butch what he had done. "You pulled his arm out of the socket."

"Is he all right?"

"Yes, but you can't pick him up by his arm like that. He's just a baby."

"Well, then teach him to listen when I tell him something. When it's time to go, it's time to go."

The argument ensued. It was my fault because I wasn't raising Tony right. We probably wouldn't have fought about it if I wouldn't have spoken up. But I did, and we argued most of the way home. Then we both just shut up about it. Sometimes we would go for days without talking to each other after an argument. It wasn't hard, because most of the time we didn't see each other that much anyway. But I think I made my point, because he never picked Tony up like that again.

By the time Tony started school, he had chores around the farm. I would try to make sure he did everything, but there were times he would get distracted, like a normal kid, by things that were more fun than chores.

There were lots of interesting things to explore on the farm, like the house jack that Tony got his hand caught in. The doctor told him he was really lucky. He waved his three-fingered hand in front of Tony's face and told him he lost two fingers doing the same thing. That's when Tony decided he was going to be a doctor. He was a creative and adventurous little boy. I remember when he tried to catch a squirrel. Don't ask me how he did it, but he actually managed to get close enough to the skittish little creature that it bit him. Another trip to the doctor's office and one tetanus shot later, he was all right. In no time at all, the doctor was Tony's friend and hero. Yet his father was someone he feared and ran from.

One evening Tony bolted through the back door. I was standing at the stove. It was a straight shot from the back door, through the porch, to the kitchen stove. As I turned around, he quickly squeezed between me and the stove. Butch came in right behind him fuming about something Tony was supposed to do but didn't. My stomach wrenched down tightly as I reached my hands behind me to hold Tony's little arms. Without hesitation Butch grabbed him and jerked him out from behind me and started hitting him wherever his fists landed. Tony put his hands up and tried to block the blows and hide his face. I yelled at Butch to stop, but I doubt he heard me over his own yelling. It all happened so fast. By the third or fourth blow Tony was knocked to the floor crying. Butch stopped and looked down at him and told him to act like a man, then turned and went back outside.

Tony tried so hard to be tough, but he was just a kid. I made sure he was okay. He ended up with some bruises but no other physical injuries.

Eventually Tony stopped running from his dad because it only made things worse. But I never stopped trying to protect him. No matter how nervous and scared I was, I still tried to get between them if I had half a chance. I would rather he hit me than Tony. Sometimes I could get between them, and Butch would turn away and say something like "That's all right. I'll get him later." Other times he would threaten me and tell me I was making a sissy out of Tony by trying to protect him. Most of the time, he would just grab him away from me and start hitting him. I wish I could have stopped Butch, but he was physically stronger than I was.

I got my shift at the hospital changed when Tony started school. I figured that if I worked the graveyard shift it would be easier for me to keep a closer eye on the kids. I could take Tony to school and be there when he got out of school. He did great in school. The teachers told me that he was adorable. I think they favored him a little.

I was also able to stay home with Helen during the day. I took catnaps on the floor in the front room with my cold feet propped up on the heater vent, while Helen played beside me. I didn't go to bed because I was afraid I wouldn't wake up. But I also slept while she napped and then got up in time for my soap operas. I was home to put the kids to bed at night and still get a couple of hours sleep after they were in bed, before I went to work. We no longer needed a babysitter because Butch would be home while I worked and the kids slept.

I enjoyed the graveyard shift. The ladies I worked with taught me to play canasta—a card game with multiple decks of cards, a fair amount of complexity, and unforgiving scoring rules. We each usually brought a thermos of coffee and chatted over the card game as the night flew by.

I had been working at the state hospital for four years now and was able to get my LPN license through a waiver. All I had to do to get my LPN license was to have two doctors and two nurses sign some papers. In those days they could give you an LPN license based on your work experience. All you really needed was two years of experience, so I had more than enough. I didn't have to go through any training other than what I got on the job. But it really didn't make that much difference to my job at the hospital. I didn't get a raise or a promotion or get recognized in any other way after receiving my license. But it was a huge achievement for me. Being a licensed nurse was a well-respected profession for women. Several of my sisters also became nurses. In fact, Zelma got her license around the same time I did, but she went to school to get hers.

While working the graveyard shift, I met one of the dearest women I have ever known—Mary Walsh. She was a very devout Catholic who never missed a Sunday Mass. She was a little older than me and had such a sweet demeanor. I found it very easy to talk to her. She constantly wanted to talk about church. She seemed to get so much out of it. I hadn't been to church since before Tony was born, and I had never been to a church that I was really satisfied with. I knew Butch was raised Catholic. In fact, I don't know an Italian who isn't Catholic. But he never went to church either or even brought it up. However, he did always make the sign of the cross whenever we passed a church. He would lightly touch his forehead, chest, and both shoulders, and then bring his hand up and kiss the tips of his finger and thumb. I wasn't sure exactly what that meant. I was curious about Catholicism, as well as what I really believed.

Mary's belief was so strong and my questions so continuous that she eventually convinced me to take a catechism class through St.

Joseph's Church. She wasn't pushy about it, though. Our conversations continued as I took the classes, and she encouraged me to finish the classes before I made a decision about joining the church.

During the off-season for the crops, between work and taking care of the kids, I was able to squeak in an hour a week to sit with Father Murray and the book of catechism in his office. He was an older man, probably between forty-five and fifty years old, nice looking and very friendly. He smiled a lot. He wasn't real serious. In fact he was pretty lighthearted, and I felt comfortable with him right away. For the most part, what he taught me made sense. I couldn't go along with their belief about birth control, though. I thought if you didn't want babies, you should be able to practice birth control. I thought it should be an individual choice not dictated by the church.

But that didn't deter me. After a few weeks of catechism I wanted to go to Mass and see what it was like, but I didn't want to go alone. I thought it might help our marriage if both Butch and I went. It took a little bit of effort to convince him to go with me. He didn't really have any excuse other than he just hadn't been in ages. So when he finally agreed, we all got dressed up and went together as a family. In those days the women wore dresses and had to wear hats to church to cover their heads. The men also dressed up. No one showed up in jeans like they do now. Most of the Mass was recited in Latin—just out of tradition I think. But the prayer book—they called it a missal—that contained the prayers, responses, and hymns used in the Mass was in English, so we could follow along. We made Sunday Mass a family ritual even before I had finished my catechism classes. It was nice, but there wasn't much else we did as a family.

When I had a night off, I tried to do something fun with the kids. If I suggested something that I thought we could do as a family, like a picnic, Butch wouldn't want to join us. A lot of the time the kids and

I would spend time with my parents or one of my sisters. Elva had kids about the same age as Tony and Helen. My sister Elva and I were becoming really close. I knew Butch wanted me at home, but I was from a big family, and I also knew in my heart that he could never really succeed at isolating me from them.

12

Elva and I both arrived at Mama and Daddy's house just after they had returned from a fishing trip up Eleven Mile Canyon on the South Platte River. The kids were outside playing. Mama was putting things away in the kitchen, grinning at Daddy as he showed us his catch and told us his fish stories. When the phone rang, I walked into the front room to answer it.

I breathed in the smell of sweet tobacco tar from Daddy's pipes that rested in the pipe holder on the windowsill. "Hello," I said as I gazed out the window at the kids running through the patches of thirsty yellow grass. I let my eyes follow the dusty trail to Pearl's house. I always felt very relaxed and at home here.

"May I speak to Mrs. Smith please?"

It was a young woman's voice that I didn't recognize. "Mama, it's for you."

She wiped her hands on her apron and took the phone from me asking, "Who is it?" I shrugged and watched as she put the receiver to her ear.

Mama's face was still at first and then started to slowly sadden as she listened intently to the woman on the other end of the line. Suddenly a long wail escaped her. The phone slipped from her fingers and thudded on the floor. She raised her hands to the side of her head and shook them. She continued to cry out as she ran back into the kitchen to Daddy's arms and muffled her cries in his chest.

A mixture of wonder and dread swept over me. I had never seen Mama act like that before. I went over and picked the receiver up off the floor.

"This is Bernice, Mrs. Smith's daughter."

The woman on the other end of the phone told me her name and paused as if I might acknowledge that I knew who she was. But I didn't. "I've been going with Art." She hesitated again. "I was just telling your mother that he's been shot. They found him last night in an orchard here by where we live. I'm afraid he's dead."

At first I didn't believe it. Not Arthur—my dear brother. Arthur had just sent me a record that he had made. His deep rich voice singing his song "Whiskey Runner" echoed in my mind. From his letters he sounded well. He was playing his music and doing what made him happy. I didn't understand how this could happen. I wanted to wail just like Mama did. But I didn't. Instead, I pushed everything I felt down and tried to keep it there.

Images of dead bodies filled my inner vision. But I couldn't picture Arthur this way.

Although I was only twenty-five years old, I had been around numerous patients who had passed away at the hospital and had learned to handle it—a person wasn't his or her body. I remembered the first time I realized this. I replayed it in my head.

It was just a couple of months after I started working at the hospital. A patient had passed away in his sleep, and the charge nurse gathered three of us outside the door to his room. She told us that before the body was sent down to the morgue to be embalmed we had to give him a complete bed bath, clean and clip his nails if necessary, and cover any sores. We would have to close the eyes and the mouth. If the mouth wouldn't stay shut, we would take a piece of gauze and tie it up around the head to hold it in place. We had to put large pads between the legs in case of bowel or bladder drainage. Then, we were to write the name and date of birth on a tag and tie it to his toe and put a shroud over him to cover the head and the body. We had to do this all immediately, before rigor mortis set in, which meant we had about three hours after the time of death before the body would become stiff.

At first I didn't want to touch it. I had never seen, let alone touched and handled, a dead body. The charge nurse was nice about it but very firm. She explained that it was something we all had to do and we had to get used to it—it was part of our job, and this wouldn't be the last time. We would be expected to do it anytime it was necessary. She explained that there would be no show of emotions. She told us that we needed to be professional about this and we needed to keep our emotions to ourselves.

We all went in together. I stood at the foot of the bed and watched at first as one of the other nurses picked up one of his hands. She had no reaction. So I reached out and uncovered his feet to see if his toenails needed clipping. Then I slowly reached down and touched his foot. It wasn't anything like I expected. The body was still warm, so it wasn't as bad as I thought it would be. I did exactly what I was told. I pushed everything I felt down and held it there. It was the thought of handling a dead body that bothered me; the actual act of doing so didn't. It was just a body. There was no one inside of it.

Since that day, I had prepared a number of dead bodies for the morgue, and it was drilled into my head that I wasn't supposed to show any emotion. I was to be professional. I could not become emotionally involved with any patient, regardless of the emotion and regardless of the circumstance. We showed compassion by caring for patients physically—making sure that they were clean, fed, and medically provided for. Our supervisors repeated this over and over. It was what I was taught, and it was what I taught new nurses when they joined the staff. I never had a problem with it.

But I was emotionally involved with Arthur. I loved him dearly. I struggled to hold back my emotions, and I struggled to release them.

Elva walked up behind me and placed her hand on my shoulder. I found myself staring at the name and phone number I had written down. I could hear Mama's and Daddy's voices in the kitchen as though they were muffled in a thick fog.

I could hear myself repeat what the woman on the phone had told me, even though I didn't quite believe the words as I said them. Elva clasped her hands over her mouth, and tears welled up in her eyes. We both turned to see Daddy coming into the room with his arm around Mama. He helped her ease down into her chair. She shook her head as if to say no as she sobbed, and she wiped her eyes and then wrung the handkerchief in her hands. Daddy put his arm around her shoulder and looked over at Elva and me. "I'm going to need your help, girls. We have to let your brothers and sisters know what happened. Can you do that for me?"

I can do this, I told myself, and I gave Daddy a nod.

We alternated calling our brothers and sisters who were in Pueblo. It was numbing repeating the same story over and over. Then, the eerie, unreal feeling in the house was interrupted by a knock on the front room door. I opened it to find the sheriff standing on the steps.

"I need to speak to Mr. and Mrs. Smith. I have some information concerning their son Arthur."

"We already know," I told him. He tipped his hat and backed away.

I went over and put my arm around Mama and held her hand. She was quiet but still wiping her eyes. Thinking about Arthur, I'm sure.

It still didn't seem real. I could only picture Arthur alive. I remembered when Arthur went into the marines. He wanted to go overseas, but Mama didn't want him to. She wrote letter after letter asking the military not to send him overseas. I know it was because

Sonny had died in the war. She said then that she didn't think she could take it if anything happened to Arthur. Arthur and Sonny were so much alike—even the way they looked. But Arthur was also the baby boy of the family.

I'm not sure why he moved to California. He was staying with Mama and Daddy for a little while. He and his previous girlfriend, Doris, had one of the bedrooms downstairs. Then one day Mama thought she heard something in the basement, like someone calling "Mom." When she went downstairs, she found Doris had slit her wrist and was lying there in a pool of her own blood. Doris survived her attempted suicide, but Arthur left for California shortly after that. I thought maybe he was going there to work on recording his music. But maybe he needed to get away from Doris.

When Daddy contacted the authorities in Orange County about Arthur's death, they told him that Arthur shot himself. They were calling it a suicide. Mama and Daddy just couldn't believe that. No one could believe it. I know in my heart that Arthur would never do anything like that. Daddy told us he wanted to look into the story a little more and see what the authorities down there had found.

Arthur died September 3, 1958. Daddy made arrangements for his body to come home for funeral services. Everyone except Aubrey was able to come home for the funeral. We even paid twenty-five dollars for David to come home the day of the funeral, accompanied by a guard, of course.

We all gathered at Mama and Daddy's house early that day. Two long black funeral cars came to pick us up for the services. The immediate family (all eleven of us) rode in one car, followed by our spouses in the second funeral car and individual cars.

The service at the Mortuary Chapel was led by the pastor of the Nazarene church that Mama went to. He was the only one that spoke.

His daughter sang. But I don't remember any of the words from that day. I wept privately with Mama, Daddy, and my brothers and sisters in the family room behind a glass wall, off to the side, hidden from the rest of the people in the chapel. After the service I walked up to the casket and kissed Arthur on the cheek and told him good-bye. The whole family did the same.

I know funerals are a little different these days. But it was normal back then for the family to have a private room, segregated from others who attended the service. It was normal for the pastor to be the only one that spoke. And it was normal to kiss the deceased good-bye.

And even though I was able to tell his body good-bye with a kiss and not break down, I was overcome with emotion as we left the burial site at the cemetery. I remember it very clearly.

It was a warm Indian summer's day. I was dressed in a black, formfitting dress, hemmed just below my knees. We were all dressed in black, except for the men's white shirts peeking out from under their suit coats. The heat didn't faze me. Trying to maneuver in spiked heels that punctured the lawn with every step didn't faze me. But in the end, I could barely see to find my way back to the funeral car through the tears. I leaned on my sister and let her lead me. I couldn't hold it in any longer. When the casket was in the ground and I was walking away from the grave site, I suddenly realized that I would never see my brother again. It was all so final. There was no going back to try to do something differently. Arthur, my brother and friend, was gone.

I have never believed that Arthur would take his own life. He just wasn't the type to do something like that. He was the happy-go-lucky type of person who loved life. Daddy planned to go down to California and gather up Arthur's belongings and see what he could find out about what had happened. There had to be some explanation. Mama was being very quiet. She tried to act normal, but I could tell she was taking it all pretty hard. She would go about her normal everyday activities, like cooking and cleaning, but her song and smile were noticeably missing. She really didn't want to talk about what had happened, but she did tell me that she didn't want Daddy to go to California alone. I told her not to worry, that I would go with him. The hard part would be telling Butch that I was taking a trip to California. I waited for the right moment to bring it up.

"Butch, Daddy's going to California to gather up Arthur's belongings."

"Yeah, that's good."

"Mama doesn't want him to go alone."

"He's a grown man. He can handle it."

"Well, I told Mama that I would drive down with him."

"Like hell you will. What, you got some guy down there you gotta go see?"

I could have guessed he would react like this. He was always so jealous. He didn't even need a reason to be. "No. It's just me and Daddy going to get Arthur's things."

"Well, you're not going that far without me."

Rather than argue with him I just gave in. "Suit yourself, but I'm probably going to stop and see Christine." I thought this might deter him a little. He hadn't spoken to his sister Christine since the day he beat up her husband, which was years ago. She had moved to California shortly after that.

"What do you have to see her for? And that dirty son of a bitch she's married to. What's the matter with you?" He started cussing in Italian.

Still, I knew I wasn't going without him. Daddy and I really wanted to go by ourselves. Daddy didn't like Butch much anymore. He knew how Butch treated me, and he was still upset about the time Butch chased me with the gun. Luckily Daddy was a lot more easygoing than Butch was. I knew he would probably be okay with it if I told him Butch had to come with us. It wasn't going to be a pleasant trip anyway. I just hoped that Butch wouldn't make it any worse.

We made arrangements for the kids and packed up my car. We drove straight through all night and were in California the next day. Butch was extremely civil. He carried on conversations with Daddy and really didn't talk much to me.

Arthur's stuff was at his girlfriend's house. We went straight there to see what she could tell us before we went to the sheriff's office. Arthur's girlfriend didn't think he would have shot himself. She thought someone else must have done it and made it look like he did it, like he was set up and someone wanted it to look like a suicide. But she didn't know who would do such a thing. At least that's what she told us.

The next morning we went to the sheriff's office. Daddy asked for the person in charge. He came out to the counter to talk to us.

"All evidence points to suicide. There was no evidence of anyone else being in the area."

Daddy's voice was calm and low, and he looked him right in the eye. "Well, maybe you could check into it further."

"I'm sorry, Mr. Smith. The case is being closed."

"No one believes that Arthur would do something like this. He wasn't that type of person."

"We found his gun, a gun that he owned, lying next to him."

"There must be some more investigation that you can do. Maybe he was set up."

"I'm sorry, sir; there just isn't anything else to go on."

It felt as if I were watching a scene in a movie. They both just stood there for a solid moment. I could feel the wall going up between them, and I knew Daddy wanted to break it. But instead he looked down, shook his head, and turned away, knowing that nobody would do anything further to find out the truth.

The next day we had lunch with Arthur's girlfriend. We found out that Arthur had just bought a new washer and dryer. Daddy thought it would be nice if he brought it back to Mama. Maybe it would cheer her up a little. But we could tell that Arthur's girlfriend really wanted it.

"Art bought this for me," she said.

Daddy was in no mood to argue over such a thing. "Well, you keep it then" was all he said.

After that he quietly gathered up one small box of Arthur's personal belongings that he thought Mama might like to have, and we left. I had always seen Daddy as such a strong man. Yet it seemed as if he had just had it. It seemed as if he had taken too many blows and wasn't going to fight anymore. Maybe we just needed to let thing rest and keep the peace. It took a strong man to do that too.

Daddy handled Arthur's death a lot better than Mama did. About two weeks after we got back from California, Mama had a stroke. I went to see her in the hospital. It appeared as though the stroke wouldn't have any lasting effects, but her sparkle was gone.

I think this was when Mama started on a downhill slope, and it seemed as if she didn't have the will to keep from sliding. She had been diagnosed with diabetes, but it had been under control up until now. After Arthur's death and the stroke, her eyesight started going. We thought it was caused by the diabetes. The eye doctor told her that he couldn't prescribe glasses because her eyes changed too much from one appointment to the next. After a few examinations he recommended a specialist. It turned out that the retina was detached from her left eye and she needed surgery. I took her and Daddy up to Colorado Springs for the surgery one day while Butch was at work. It didn't improve her eyesight at all, and it kind of disfigured her eye. They finally told us that there was nothing more they could do. Mama would slowly go blind.

13

On my last one-on-one catechism session with Father Murray, I walked to the back of the church to his small office. The door was open, and Father Murray stood up from behind his desk as soon as he saw me. The sound of the wooden legs of his chair scraping against the wood floor filled the small room and echoed out into the corridor. A smile stretched across his broad face. "Hello, Bernice. Come on in," he said gesturing toward three matching wooden chairs that sat in front of his desk. I set my catechism book on his desktop and noticed a slight reflection from the freshly polished blond wood. I wondered if I would miss our meetings.

"How are you?" he said, lowering his robust frame back down into the chair. I could see why everyone seemed to love him. He genuinely seemed to care and to listen as I updated him on the death of my brother and my mother's health. As the silence fell between us, he seemed to be pondering something. Then he looked down and opened the top desk drawer. "I have something for you," he said.

His voice made me feel warm, comfortable, and relaxed. From his drawer, he pulled out a rosary and hung it over the desk between us. "Someone left this in the church some time ago. I want you to have it."

I reached out and let him lay it across my hand. I breathed out a "Thank you" and inspected it closely. It was a true blue that only a strong white light could penetrate. Between each perfectly round bead there was a shiny metal cuff that looked like a fancy lampshade connected to a delicate chain link. At the end was a crucifix of the same metal. It was neither gold, nor silver, nor brass. Upon my palm, just below the INRI at the top of the cross, Jesus lay with his head tilted slightly to one side and downward, his rib cage protruding, his stomach sunken, his waist wrapped, and his limbs nailed. I knew at that moment that I would always cherish it.

When I joined the church, they told me that I could raise Tony and Helen any way I wanted to but that any children I had in the future must be raised Catholic. We didn't plan on having any other children, but we decided to get Tony and Helen baptized. Butch was baptized as a baby. I hadn't been baptized yet, so I decided I would be too. We asked Mary Walsh and her husband, Bob, to be the children's godparents.

They also told me and Butch that we weren't really married until we were married in the church. So Butch and I repeated our wedding vows to God in a church ceremony that made it all official. No one was there except Butch and me and the priest. It wasn't open to the public or a ceremony like you might imagine. It was just us, repeating our vows in a church. Once we were married in the church, they told us that we would have to raise all our kids as Catholics. So when Helen was ready to start school, we enrolled her at St. Joseph's Catholic School, and we moved Tony out of the public school to the Catholic school as well. It was as if we had found a family tie.

I found that I had a little extra time on my hands now that both the kids were in school. I discovered that several of my neighbors went to the same church and also had kids who went to St. Joseph's Catholic School. We would see each other at church and at PTA meetings. It wasn't long before the ladies invited me to join them to play bunco, a dice game. I also had a little more time to help out with Mama.

One day I decided to go with Mama to Canyon City to see David in prison. She went about once a month. The last time I saw him was at the dinner table when I was ten years old, the night before the sheriff stole him away in the darkness. Before now, I hadn't really thought about visiting him. I didn't really know the full story of what he had done. It was all pretty sketchy, but I think I knew he killed someone.

The prison sat just off the highway, corralled by high stone and chain-link fences. When we entered the facility, Mama knew what she was doing since she had been there before. She led me to the registration counter where I entered my name and address as well as the kids' names, since they were visiting too. I copied Mama's entry on the line that indicated who we were visiting: Smith, David G—39794.

When they called our names, we were led into a room the shape of a half moon, cluttered with stiff chairs set in no particular order. It was clean but gray, drab, and dreary. You could tell it was old. The straight side of the room was walled-in by a waist-high countertop and thick, heavy screen that climbed its way from the countertop to the ceiling, reminiscent of the chain-link fence outside. The room gradually filled up with visitors, and the prisoners began to file into the room on the other side of the screen. They wore black-and-white shirts and pants with small stripes—not pinstripes but not wide stripes as you see in the movies either. Each prisoner had a five-digit number on the left breast, like a name tag, and again across the back of their shirt in larger print.

I recognized David immediately. He looked older, taller, and thinner yet still the same, with the familiar scarred bald spot that refused to hide under his dark hair, the same glasses, and quiet demeanor. I was glad to see that he looked as if he was all right. I could tell by the way he looked at me that he recognized me too. It was probably the red hair that gave me away. He smiled as though he was glad to see us. Mama was real comfortable with these types of visits and started right in asking how he was doing.

"I'm okay, Mama. It's good to see you, Bernice. You're all growed up."

It was a little hard to hear him because everyone in the room was speaking at once.

"I'm married now, and these are my babies, Tony and Helen."

He nodded and listened as I told him about the farm Butch and I ran and about working at the state hospital. His occasional reply was "Yeah, Mama told me." As my news waned, Mama jumped in with other family news. It was gradually getting louder in the visiting area. In bits and pieces I picked up that he had made a jewelry box for Mama to take home. He had a deep voice now, but he still spoke kind of quietly. He talked about some tooled leather crafts that he was working on and about making some spurs for Daddy. After a while the guard came up and tapped David on the shoulder. David told us that we had to make room for someone else to visit since it was so crowded. We had been there a couple of hours, but it seemed to go by so fast.

As we said our muffled good-byes, I felt the love I had for my brother, regardless of anything that had happened. It was there, and it was real. I finally knew why Mama had always told us to make sure that if we were going to marry someone and they were going to be part of the family, we needed to tell them about David. It wasn't to air our dirty laundry or see if they would still accept us. It was because he was a part of us, a member of our family, a brother and a son.

Before we left the prison, Mama stopped to pick up the jewelry box that David had made for her. The guard carelessly pushed it toward her and looked past her to see who was next in line. Mama politely vied for his attention again as she dug around in her purse and pulled out a five-dollar bill. "Would you please see that David gets this," she said.

He took the time to write her out a receipt before again anticipating the next person in line.

I started taking Mama to see David once a month. I wanted to do what I could to make it easier for her. I also started giving David money during our visits so Mama wouldn't have to, and I helped her put together Christmas packages for him. It didn't bother me to take the kids there either. I even took a tour of the facilities with her and the kids to see where they worked on their crafts. I had stopped trying to hide it from other people. After our visits I would make sure to tell people that David said hi. That's how we usually wrapped up our visits—David telling me to tell someone hi for him.

When I examined the jewelry box he gave Mama, I knew that it was crafted with love and great care. Each corner was a supported by a curved pedestal. The top was beveled on the edges. There was a picture etched on the top in the center of a decorative oval shape. It was a cabin seated at the foot of the mountains with three evergreen trees carefully placed around it. When I opened it, my reflection met me in a mirror surrounded by lightly hammered, rope-type decorations that indented the wood. The top tray was covered with plush tan felt and the sides covered in red. The tray lifted out to reveal another soft, tan, covered compartment. There were small drawers on the bottom of each side. It was beautiful. Just as nice, or nicer, than the ones I had seen in the stores.

There were also etchings on the front and back of a river that fed from the canyon walls that were recessed in the background. On each side there was an etching of a lone evergreen standing before a canyon wall, below a sky that contained only a single cloud. It reminded me so much of Rye—the last place David had lived before his life in prison started at the age of sixteen. Things seemed so simple back then.

14

To everyone's surprise, I got pregnant again. I had gone almost ten years without getting pregnant. I had been using a diaphragm when I got pregnant with Helen. Obviously that didn't work. I wanted a button (IUD), but the doctor wouldn't give me one because I wasn't perfect on the inside. Birth control pills had just come out the year before, but I hadn't tried them yet. So I hadn't used any other kind of birth control for some time. I knew the Catholic Church didn't believe in birth control, but that's not why I stopped. After we moved out to the farm and the kids were settled in school, I just didn't see much of Butch anymore. He usually came in late, after the kids were asleep, and I was still working the graveyard shift, so I would get ready for work and leave shortly after he came in. Then when he had a day off, he would spend it at the livestock sales, which meant he left early in the morning and got home late at night. If I had a night off, I would stay up late and clean house until I was sure he was asleep, and then I would go to bed. If we did end up in bed together, awake, I felt as if sex was my duty as a wife, but I never really enjoyed it. He never forced me, but I didn't refuse him either.

When I told him I was pregnant, he asked, "Whose baby is it?"

"You're the father of course," I spat. "Who do you think is?" I fought to hold my tongue. I was so angry I couldn't even look at him. I turned and left him standing where he was. I made up my mind on the spot, come hell or high water—I was going to name this child Janet. I didn't care how much he or anyone in his family protested. If it was a boy, I'd name him after my father. If this was how he was going to act, I wasn't even going to ask him what he wanted to name the baby.

Elva was happy for me, and she was pregnant too. We were both a little giddy about it. In December 1961 when we were both about four months along, we decided to throw Mama and Daddy a dinner party for their fiftieth wedding anniversary. We also wanted a picture in the paper. But Mama didn't want her picture taken. So we used one that was taken several years earlier. We were excited about it, but we had a heck of a time trying to convince Mama to even come to the dinner. It was only going to be family—Pearl, Zelma, Agnes, and Elva and me with our husbands and kids—at Frank and Elva's house. But Mama was at a point where she didn't want to go too many places because her vision was getting worse. She could still see a little bit, and she got around her house okay, but she couldn't do things that required focus, like crocheting or reading. She never wanted anybody to do any more for her than they absolutely had to. She was the mother of twelve children and very much used to being the caregiver. What bothered her more than anything was for someone to try to feed her. Sometimes she fumbled a little with her food because she couldn't see it. She didn't like to eat in front of people. Reluctantly, this one last time, she went out for her anniversary dinner. It was the last time we got Mama to go out anyplace. I wanted her to be happy about fifty years of marriage and twelve kids and dozens and dozens of grandkids. I wanted her to get better. She had always been my example of how a woman can just go, and go, and go and never complain. It was so hard to see her body failing her.

It seemed as if after Helen was born and we moved to the farm, all I did was go, go, go. I tried to keep working for as long as I could at the hospital during this pregnancy, but they wouldn't let me work after I got too far along. I got a part-time job at a nursing home, working a few hours a week and when they needed me, which I kept until the day I gave birth.

The day Janet was born Butch wanted to go to a livestock sale in Rocky Ford. I caught him that morning in the kitchen before he left.

"Butch, I think I might have the baby today. I don't want to stay home alone. Do you have to go?"

"Yes, I have to go. Go to your mom's or your sister's."

It seemed so strange to me how important the livestock sales had become to him. He even started calling off work to go to these sales. He seemed to be obsessed with buying cattle and pigs to sell and make more money. I think he must have been making some pretty good money. Yet he still wouldn't give me money for groceries or clothes for the kids or anything else while I was on maternity leave from the hospital. When my car started giving me trouble, he went as far as to agree that we needed to buy a new one, but he wouldn't foot the bill.

I really liked the little two-door cars that started coming out in 1959. I also liked the station wagons. When I told Butch this, he said that he knew a guy at the Ford dealership that would give us a good deal on a new car. He said he didn't want anything but a Ford. When we got there, he started talking to this guy who convinced him that the most economical family car he could get was a Ford Fairlane. He showed us a light-blue one with four doors. I hated it. It was nothing like what I had told Butch I wanted. But he didn't ask me if I liked the car. He just said, "This is what we are getting." He was the head-of-the-household decision maker while we were there, and I knew I wasn't going to change his mind. I really didn't want to make a scene in public, so I just gave in to him. I probably could have argued until doomsday, and he wouldn't have changed his mind. Besides, it would have just made him mad. You know what they say: "You have to pick your battles." This wasn't one of them. We weren't there very long at all. We didn't even take the car for a test drive. Butch did all the talking. He traded in my old car and drove me home in a brand-new 1959 sedan that I hated, but I was stuck with it and the car payments because he put it in my name.

My new car was already a couple of years old by the time Janet was born. So on that particular Monday morning when Butch wouldn't stay home with me, I decided I would drop the car off at Sam Baker's garage for an oil change and go see Mama and Daddy instead of staying home alone.

As I pulled into the garage and got out of the car, I still wasn't feeling right. Sam was there to greet me. "Hey, Bernice, you still haven't had that kid yet? Elva had hers three weeks ago. Whatcha waiting for?"

"Nothing. It's past my due date."

"Well, you certainly don't look that far along. Pearl's in the house. Why don't you just go take it easy, and I'll let you know when I'm done here."

I walked a few feet from the garage to the front porch and labored up four cement stairs to the front door as if I were climbing a mountain. It felt as if I might be bleeding a little more. When I walked into the house I quickly accepted Pearl's offer for a cup of coffee and went to the bathroom. I was right about the bleeding.

"Pearl, I think I'm gonna use your phone to call the doctor. I'm not feeling right, and I'm bleeding a little more than I think I should be."

"Are you all right? Do you want me to run you down to his office?"

I could tell she was concerned. "No, it's probably nothing. I've been bleeding on and off the whole time, and I was just at the doctor's Friday."

When I called the doctor, he told me I was nowhere near being ready to deliver, but I should come in anyway. I told Pearl I was going to borrow Daddy's car and pick mine up later.

"You'll do no such thing. I'll drive you to the doctor's."

"But, Pearl, I'm not having any labor pains or anything. I'll be fine."

"It doesn't matter. You wait right there while I grab my purse."

After the doctor examined me, they admitted me to the hospital, and I delivered a shiny new baby girl without a single labor pain. When Dr. Smith went out to make the big announcement, Butch wasn't there, but Pearl still was. He told her that I had twins, and then he came back in and told me how tickled she was until she found out he was pulling her leg. Dr. Smith was a wonderful doctor who had known the family for years.

I arranged for Tony and Helen to go to the McIntires' house (the neighbors just up the street from our house) after school while I was in the hospital. I didn't see Butch at all that day. Tuesday morning I called Shirley McIntire, and she told me that he picked the kids up around ten o'clock Monday night. The kids knew they had a new baby sister, and I assumed they told their Dad. Tuesday evening after dinner, probably about seven o'clock, he walked into my hospital room as though it was the most natural thing in the world for him to come in when he pleased and leave when he pleased. I was glad to see him but also a little disappointed because I had expected to see him the night before.

Funny thing about Butch was he never usually asked a person how they were doing. So I knew not to expect that. He didn't ask about the baby either. She was in the nursery down the hall. He didn't kiss me, and I don't even remember him saying hi. The heavy heels on his cowboy boots scuffed across the floor as he took three or four steps into the room and removed his hat. I asked him about the kids and where they were. They didn't let little kids on the maternity floors back then. He shuffled his stiff, yellow-straw cowboy hat from hand to hand adjusting the brim. He assured me that they were okay. He didn't come in and sit down. It seemed as if he just wanted to make an appearance so people would know he had been there. Like always, I got a little nervous, and my stomach began to tighten and agitate. Then, out of nowhere he announced, "I quit my job today."

I couldn't believe it. There I was lying in a hospital bed, after just bringing another child into our family, and he made this kind of announcement. I could have spit. I wasn't about to support him. What's more, I couldn't go back to work yet. The only thing I could think to say was "Well, then I'm quitting my job too." I figured if I told him I was going to quit working, maybe he wouldn't. In the back of my mind I knew that he probably planned on continuing with the livestock sales since he was so obsessed with that.

That was pretty much the extent of his visit. He just turned and walked out in the same manner he had walked in. I don't even know if he stopped to see the baby while he was there.

I stayed in the hospital for a few more days and finally convinced the doctor to let me go home on Friday. I couldn't reach Butch, so Zelma came and got me.

When I got home, I had no more than walked in the door when the phone started ringing. It was the school. Tony had gotten mad and hit the wall with his fist. Then, after he realized that his behavior was going to get him in trouble, he played it up. He started crying and telling the teachers that his mom was in the hospital and his dad wasn't home. I had to explain to the school that it was all true but wasn't as serious as Tony made it sound. I knew that it was just his way of getting some extra sympathy. He was about to turn eleven and had been getting into trouble at school more and more often as the years progressed.

I had to take him out of the Catholic school his third year there. I really liked the school, and Tony did too, at first. When he started there in second grade, all the nuns thought he was so cute and so precious. Then when he passed on to third grade and had a new nun for a teacher, they just didn't get along. She was pretty strict. The nuns before her were always bubbly and happy. He just couldn't adjust to a strict nun. She said he didn't like to study, didn't like to learn, and wasn't getting good grades. Tony said that she was too mean and that he just didn't like her. Up until then he had always been this special little cute boy in the class. Now he wasn't being catered to, and he wanted to be.

They were allowed to swat the kids with rulers and spank them on the bottom with a paddle. If the kids didn't play by the rules, they got hit. Tony was getting his share. Looking back now, I don't think it was right, but it was just the way things were done. I also think that some teachers did it more than others.

I talked to the nun repeatedly that year about Tony and then just took him out. When I put him in public school, he got along fine with the teachers, but his grades never came back up.

The day I came home from the hospital with Janet, Tony came home with a busted-up hand that needed medical attention. I called my friend Helen Plant. She came over and saw the new baby and went with us right back to the hospital that I had just left. The doctor told me, "I knew you shouldn't have gone home today." By that time, I was dead tired and would have gladly taken a hospital bed again, just to rest for a little bit. Butch was still at a sale when I got home from the hospital the second time.

Mary Walsh had given me a baby shower before I left work at the state hospital, so we had pretty much everything we needed for the new baby. And I have to say, having Tony and Helen around was a huge help. They were only in grade school, just under ten and eleven years old, but they were great with Janet. It wasn't long before they were fighting over who was going to feed her or change her. All she had to do was make a sound, and the kids would jump to see what she needed. Unfortunately,

I can't say the same for Butch. He never held any of the kids when they were babies. Janet was no exception.

After he quit CF&I, Butch continued to go to the livestock sales every day. He would leave early in the morning and come home late at night. Most of the time he would take the livestock he bought to Louie Chantila's stockyard in Blende, and then when he was ready to sell them he would take them back and try to get more money than he paid for them. It seemed as if he always had money to buy more livestock, but he wouldn't give me more than ten dollars a month for groceries. I was on a six-month maternity leave from the hospital and only about three months into my leave when I turned in my resignation there. More out of spite than anything else—since I told Butch I was going to quit, I did.

I was plenty mad at him for quitting his job, and I stayed mad. When the Fourth of July came around he wanted to go to his folks' house. Janet was born in May, so she wasn't more than a couple of months old, and I'm not sure they had even seen her yet.

"I'm not going," I told him.

"For Christ's sake, it's a holiday. Let's take the baby over there and get something to eat."

"If you can only visit your parents on holidays, I'm not going with you."

"What are you talking about?"

"We could take the baby over there for a visit anytime. But you won't."

"What the hell difference does that make?"

"I'm staying home with Janet, and I'm going to paint."

"To hell with you then…" He finished his thoughts in Italian as he walked out the door.

Anytime I wanted to go visit his folks, he had some excuse why we couldn't go. He simply didn't believe in going over just for a visit, so I decided I wasn't going to go at all. He never went to visit his brothers and sisters. If he spent time with his family, it wasn't to visit, it usually had something to do with farming. He didn't believe in them coming to our house either. This time I was the one who made up an excuse not to go. If he was going to quit his job and do his own thing, I was going to do my own thing too.

I took some time to enjoy doing some things with the kids. I remember one time setting out for a camping trip with Zelma, her daughter and grandson, and me and my two daughters. Zelma's daughter, Kitty, was the same age as Helen, and Zelma's grandson was the same age as Janet. The plans went out the window as we drove along the highway, and we stopped where we thought we'd find some fun thing to do instead. We ended up driving through four states and back again, laughing the entire way.

In August when Janet was about three months old, we heard that President John F. Kennedy was coming to Pueblo. The neighbor Shirley McIntire and I planned it all out so that we could take the kids and go see the president at the Pueblo airport. Shirley had kids in school that were about the same age as Tony and Helen. We actually got acquainted through the kids.

Shirley and I packed up the kids and headed out early that morning. We didn't want to miss the president. I think we got to the airport at about ten in the morning. We had to be there early enough to get close enough to see him. It seemed as if everyone in Pueblo was there that day, except for Butch, of course. He never wanted to do anything with us; he was off chasing livestock somewhere. Shirley's husband worked the day shift, so he couldn't go either.

It was so hot out there on the mesa, and it was ungodly crowded. It was more crowded than the fair or any other place I'd ever been, and you know the airport was a pretty big place. There was no place to sit;

you could only stand. It was tiresome because I had to hold Janet the whole time. We spent the day out in the hot sun with hundreds, maybe thousands, of other people waiting for a peek at the handsome face of President Kennedy.

When the president finally got there, he walked down the roadway and shook hands with the people that were nearest to the fence that separated us from the airport roadway. I don't remember a lot of police cars or security or anything. We got close enough to see him up close but not close enough to shake his hand.

It was the only time I ever saw a president come to Pueblo. He was there to kick off the construction of the Pueblo dam and reservoir. He gave a speech at one of the high school stadiums following the approval of the Fryingpan-Arkansas Reclamation Project, or Fry-Ark, which was basically a project designed to bring more water to Pueblo, Canyon City, and the surrounding towns. The project wouldn't be completed for another twenty years.

The president really wasn't at the airport for very long, but it felt as if we were there all day in the hot sun. By the time I got home I was completely exhausted. But I would do it again. That was a big event for us. I'm not all that political, but I liked Kennedy. He gave us all hope.

Tony, Helen, and Janet on the side of the farmhouse

15

Most mornings Butch was either outside or already gone before the kids and I got up. Most evenings he came home anywhere from eight to eleven o'clock. It didn't seem like he had a consistent schedule. Every once in a while he would be home for breakfast and would have something to eat with the kids before they left for school.

"Butch, before you take off, I need some money to go get formula and some groceries."

He took out his wallet and quickly pulled a ten-dollar bill out of one of the folds and tossed it on the table.

"I'm gonna need at least twice that," I said, noticing that he had already put his wallet back in his pocket.

"That's all I got." He turned and started to walk out of the kitchen.

I followed behind him as he walked into the back porch. "But you have enough money to go buy pigs and cattle?" I retorted. Standing there in the doorway, I watched him grab his cowboy hat, put it on his head, and make some sort of gesture with his hand as if he was throwing something that only he could see up into the air. "Eh" was all I heard him say.

I couldn't stand not having any money or even enough money to go buy groceries. So after the kids were off to school, I dropped Janet off with her grandpa and went out to the state hospital to talk to Chorney about getting my job back.

She was in her office when I got there, but there was no warm welcome. She told me I could come back to work, but since I had quit, I would be starting back at beginner's wages. There was no way I was going to agree to that.

Chorney's office was on the hospital grounds on Thirteenth street. I drove around the hospital grounds to the Colorado state employee's union office on Seventeenth street and marched right in to talk to a union rep. A nice gentleman named Doug was more than happy to hear my grievance. It all just spilled out of me.

"I've been in the union for eight years now. I got my LPN license here at the hospital, and I've been employed here for the past eight years. Just recently I took a four-month leave of absence to have a baby, and then I quit during my leave. But my husband has quit his job too, so now I need to go back to work because we don't have an income."

"Did you quit before your leave of absence was over?"

"Yes. And I just spoke with the head of nurses, and she told me that I could come back to work, but it would have to be at beginner's wages. That just doesn't sound right to me."

"No, it doesn't, does it? I can take care of this. Let me get some information from you."

I was a little surprised at how easy it was to convince Doug that it wasn't right but even more surprised when he called me back within the same week. He told me that since my leave of absence wasn't up yet, I could start back at the same wage I was getting when I started my leave. I don't know how much he argued with them, but I was sure glad that he was the one doing the arguing. He gave me a start date and asked if it was okay. This gave me the impression that he might negotiate further for me. So I asked if he could get me on the graveyard shift. I don't know if they make union reps like that anymore. He got me everything I wanted.

I left Janet with Butch while I worked nights. Butch said she cried all night. That was hard for me to believe because she was really good when I was around. I think she had the same personality as Mama— calm, happy, quiet. But I knew it was true because Helen told me that Butch would wake her up in the middle of the night, and she would have to walk the floors with Janet until she went back to sleep.

Janet was walking, talking, and potty trained before she was a year old, but she was tiny. She was still wearing six-month dresses and sleeping in one of Helen's doll cribs at one. In fact, Daddy said she was more like a doll than a baby. Mama never really got to see her because her eyesight was pretty much gone by the time Janet was born. She said once in a while she could make out her form if I dressed Janet in bright colors.

I went over there at least three times a week to help Daddy clean house, cook, and care for Mama even after I started working at the hospital again. Daddy had taken over the cooking when Mama lost her eyesight, so I liked to give him a break and cook the noon meal for them when I was there.

Daddy set up a card table in the front room in front of the couch for Mama to eat her meals. Janet had to do whatever her grandma did. She would sit up there at the card table with her grandma and eat whatever her grandma ate. I usually made them some sort of finger foods to eat. Janet also had to wear an apron like the one Grandma wore when she ate, and she had to have medicine when Grandma took her medicine. Daddy got some baby vitamins for Janet so she could take medicine with Grandma. She was just a baby. She had no idea her grandma was sick.

I would sweep and mop the floors, clean the bedroom and bathroom if needed, or wash windows in the summer. But none of it was ever a chore. Janet and I enjoyed our visits. Before we left, I would put on a pot roast or something that Daddy could finish preparing for the evening meal. Because of her diabetes we had to make sure Mama had three meals a day.

One day while I was helping Daddy around the house, he picked Janet up and sat her on his lap to try to settle her down from a coughing spell.

"This baby's got whooping cough," he announced to me.

"I took her to the doctor, and they told me it was a cold and allergies. We're going to see a specialist tomorrow."

"Well, they're gonna tell you she's got whooping cough." He was certain of it, and he was right.

When the specialist saw her, he put her in the hospital immediately. I couldn't get ahold of Butch while he was at the sales, so I made arrangements for Helen and Tony to stay at the McIntires' and called work to take some time off. They didn't believe me when I told them that my one-year-old had the whooping cough. I offered to let them talk to the doctor or bring in a signed note from him if they needed it. Eventually they found out that she was indeed in the hospital, in an oxygen tent, and would be there for four to five days, and they sure did apologize. I even took some extra time off work to stay home with Janet after she got out of the hospital, and they didn't complain.

Janet was the first of many babies to go into the hospital with whooping cough that year. In fact there was an epidemic with the babies because they had mixed the polio shot with the whooping cough shot, and the polio shot voided the whooping cough vaccination. No one knew that was what was happening at first. But they figured it out, and they stopped giving the immunization shots that way. There were at least a half dozen other babies in that one hospital in oxygen tents by the time we left.

We couldn't get Janet to eat while she was in the hospital. She would nibble at stuff, but she wouldn't eat. Then, when they released her, I took her over to see her grandpa, and the first thing she did when she got inside his house was to get up to the kitchen table and ask for something to eat. Of course, Grandpa gave her anything she wanted to eat or drink, including coffee. He fed all the grandkids coffee from the time they were just tiny babies.

* * * * *

In the spring of 1964 Mama was taken to the hospital for congestive heart failure. When they finally released her from the hospital, she looked at Daddy and said, "I never want to go back to that place again. Just take me home, and let me die at home." The timbre of her voice might have been frail, but her words were unmistakably decisive. Daddy's love for her was unwavering, so I know he probably agreed with her. She repeated her wishes to us kids as well. No one argued with her.

That spring my sister Sarah came down from Washington State to stay with Mama and Daddy and help out. She was still there when Mother's Day rolled around. For Mother's Day I got Mama a short, blue-and-white, flowered housecoat that snapped down the front that she could wear over her nightgown since she didn't really wear clothes anymore. I was glad to be able to spend part of the day with her.

On the day after Mother's Day, Sarah made breakfast, and they all enjoyed some coffee, fried eggs, biscuits, and bacon together. Then Mama felt her way back to the bedroom to rest. Daddy followed her into their room. "Can I get you anything?" he asked.

"I'd really like a cup of coffee," she said.

He went and got her a cup of hot coffee and came back into the bedroom and sat down on the bed next to her. Daddy's jet-black hair had long ago turned gray, but his frame was still sturdy. So I imagine he sat down gently so Mama wouldn't spill her coffee. She had lost some weight and wasn't as strong as she used to be. Her long, black braids had been cut from her head many years ago, and the white locks of hair on her head now barely reached her shoulders.

Daddy said she gulped down a cup of scolding hot coffee and then lay back down on the bed and she was gone. That moment in time was theirs and theirs alone.

When the phone rang that Monday morning and I heard Sarah's voice, somehow I just knew what had happened as soon as my sister spoke my name.

"Bernice, Mama's gone."

"I'll be right there," I said and hung up the phone.

I couldn't control the sorrow that poured out. The kids were still there in the kitchen. They had just finished breakfast. I had never cried in front of the kids before. Tony got up and ran outside and got Butch. I met him coming to the house as I was leaving. I told him what had happened, and I left. The twenty-minute drive to Mama and Daddy's house was blurred with tears and filled with the deepest sadness I had ever felt.

When I got there, Daddy, Elva, Zelma, Sarah, and Pearl were all standing outside on the side of the house where the propane tank was, by the door that went to the downstairs. I parked under the big tree in that front yard. It had started to spout enough green leaves that it stood out against the sepia tones of the house, the dry earth, and the dark-colored cars covered with brown dust. It seemed to sway in a light breeze while everything else seemed so still.

I wasn't surprised that everyone had gotten there before me. I had to drive in from the country. Pearl practically lived next door, and Zelma and Elva lived close by as well. I got out of the car and walked over to where my sisters were standing.

"Is Mama still here?" I asked.

"Yes, she's in the bedroom," Pearl replied.

I heard the kitchen door snap into its frame behind me when I closed it. Then the house was quiet. I could smell the bacon that had been cooked for breakfast and the coffee that was sitting on the stove. For some reason I glanced over at the old grandfather clock that sat on the shelf in the kitchen. It no longer worked, but they kept it there on the shelf nonetheless. The floor creaked as I walked across the kitchen linoleum to the front room. The gas heater in the front room hissed at me softly as if to shush me. I paused a moment to study the living room, taking a snapshot in my mind.

To my left next to the front window sat Mama's gate leg table with Daddy's cribbage board and cards sitting there on top of it, waiting for a game. I remembered when Mama told us she wanted a table like that. Sarah and I searched all over for one and finally found it down on Union Street at a secondhand store. We got it for her for Mother's Day, but Daddy was the one that always used it for playing cribbage with the guys. It was never really used for anything else. On the opposite wall, across the room from the table, was a cupboard with glass doors and dishes in it. There wasn't much cupboard space in the kitchen, so a lot of Mama's dishes were kept there. In the middle of the room, Mama's sturdy wooden rocker with leather seat and back coverings and Daddy's recliner of the same color sat still and empty. There was an old-fashioned couch on the right side of the room under a window that looked out to the prairie. The fact that the old couch had seen better days was evident by the dull maroon color and worn-out flowers that adorned it. There was a buffet for storing tableware next to the couch. The picture of the *Titanic* hung above it, and the picture of my grandma and grandpa Knox hung above the *Titanic*—as they always did in every house we lived in when I was growing up. A picture of my brother Sonny in his service uniform was added to the mix after we lost him to the war. Mama kept her blue Willow dishes stored in the bottom of the buffet.

I remembered Mama saying that she always wanted blue Willow dishes, and I remembered when Daddy bought them for her. When he had the money, he always tried to get her the things that she really wanted. She didn't use them every day, but she got them out for holidays. I wondered if they would ever be used again.

I continued into the hallway, and I could see into the bedroom where my mother lay in the bed. I went in. I tucked the covers around her snuggly, and I kissed her gently on the forehead and told her good-bye.

I was so shaken that I walked outside and took out a cigarette and lit it without even thinking. I never smoked at Mama and Daddy's house. Daddy was right there smoking too. It was the first time I ever smoked in front of him.

"We called Dr. Smith," Sarah started.

"He didn't seem surprised at all," Elva added.

"He's on his way over, and he said he would call the mortuary," Zelma added.

When the people from the mortuary came, they asked us to stay outside. But we watched as they brought her out of the house and took her away.

I sensed that a part of me had been removed. I couldn't trace it to a specific part, but I could feel something missing. I felt dazed and in a state of shock, but I could tell from my sisters' examples that we needed to hold it together for Daddy. I stayed there with them for most of the day.

Within the week, the funeral was scheduled, and all of my brothers and sisters were there. We paid for a guard to accompany David; my brother Charles was there—I hardly ever saw him; and my brother Aubrey even showed up from California. Daddy really broke down when Aubrey got there. It was the first time I ever saw Daddy cry. Aubrey hadn't made it up for Arthur's funeral in '58, so it had been more than six years since we had seen him. Daddy and Aubrey kind of clashed sometimes. When Aubrey went to California and changed his name to Scott Ericson, he cut off all communication with the family. I don't know the entire story there. Mama used to say that Aubrey and Daddy didn't get along too well because they were too much alike. But I don't know about that either. Zelma might have talked to Scott once in a while. It seemed as if she always kept in touch with everyone. But I knew for sure that Scott and my brother Ellis stayed in touch, because I knew Ellis talked him into coming to Mama's funeral. I think Daddy wished Scott could have been there before Mama died.

After the service we went back to Daddy's house. There was so much family the house wouldn't fit us all. Everyone brought food—even people from the state hospital came and brought food. There was so much of it. The food went inside, and we spent most of our time outside.

There were lots of pictures taken that day. It was the first time in a long time that all my brothers and sisters (except Sonny and Arthur, who were with Mama) were gathered together in one place. We all stayed until dark. Those of us who lived locally were the last to leave. Pearl and Zelma put up the family that came in from out of town. Butch didn't like people staying at our house.

They gave me five days off from work with pay, and I took it, plus another week on top of that.

Mama and Daddy, June 1964

16

About six months after I went back to work, Butch went back to work too. He got a job at the fire station. I imagine his experience in the service was what got him the job because as long as I'd known him he either worked at the steel mill or on a farm, which really didn't provide any experience for being a fireman. He was in the army from 1942 through 1945, during World War II. I knew he was in New Guinea in the South Pacific, and I knew he took a piece of shrapnel in the leg, but he didn't really talk much about it. When he did talk about being in the army, he talked about driving a two-and-a-half-ton truck, transporting equipment, food, and people around. So my guess was that the truck driving for the army helped get him hired at the fire station. Either that or he just knew somebody.

He didn't give up the livestock sales when he got the job. If there was a sale going on somewhere, he would spend his days off there. It seemed like they were all over the place: Pueblo, Rocky Ford, LaJunta, Fowler, Lamar. He continued to go with Louie Chantalia. I never did like that guy. Louie used to be a neighbor to my sister Pearl. She told me that he used to run around on his wife and beat her up. Butch and Louie spent most of their time out at Louie's place because that's where they kept the cows they bought and sold. I was glad that he rarely came to our house, and when he did, I was glad that he usually stayed outside with Butch. I don't think I ever met his wife.

Another thing that kept Butch busy was his pigs. He started bringing pigs home back when we were truck farming. He penned them in out behind the barn. He started out with little pigs. Then he would let them breed so he could sell the babies. Eventually we had a whole slew of them. He didn't have to buy food for them because he had agreements with a bunch of restaurants in town. He would pick up their garbage (we always called it slop) and bring it home for the pigs to eat. It was a win-win situation; it helped Butch feed his pigs, and it helped the restaurants cut down on their garbage bill. He seemed to enjoy caring for the pigs, but I didn't mess with them. When Butch wasn't home, Tony took care of them. Quite often Butch and Tony would fish silverware out of the slop and bring it into the house. I would scrub it up and sterilize it. When I got all I could use, I started saving sets for the kids. I swear the restaurants must have all used the same silverware because I had no problem at all getting several matching sets.

As far as I can remember, Butch wasn't around most of the time. Not even for a meal. On the rare occasion that he did eat with us, there was usually less talking at the table because the kids weren't as relaxed. But Butch was never very talkative either. He might ask if Tony did his chores but not much else that I remember. I would always cross my fingers and hope the chores were all done.

I came to realize that I was married to someone that I didn't have much in common with. We just didn't have anything to talk about really. Besides that, it seemed like the less we saw of each other and the less we talked, the better we got along.

He was nothing like I expected him to be when I was dating him. Back then we were affectionate and communicated, and he wrote me love letters when I was away from him. I thought he would be more like Daddy—where family always came first and was the focus of your life. But Butch wasn't that way. He claimed us as his and always told me that I could never leave him, but it never came across as a message of love. It felt more like he was telling me I was weak and incompetent without him.

It wasn't a smooth relationship. If I wanted to do something that he didn't like, then all hell broke loose. It had always been like that. But he was becoming increasingly obsessive and jealous too. He wanted to know where I was and who I was with every moment of the day. After Mama died, I still went over to clean and cook for Daddy. When I did, Butch thought I was going out with someone else. If I was late coming home from work or if I left early to go to work, he would accuse me of running off to meet up with some man.

One time, Lefty, a guy we knew from back when Butch and I were dating, came out to the house to deliver gas. We had a big gas tank that we used to gas up the truck and tractor. I was outside hanging clothes when he arrived, and we started talking. When I told Butch about him being there, he had a fit. I remember him drilling me about it. "Why were you talking to him? Did you invite him in the house? What did he say to you?" I answered his questions, but I also got mad that he was even questioning me. That, of course, made him madder, so I eventually just shut up and let him yell and get it all out of his system. It was useless to argue with him anyway, and I knew it. I might as well have argued with the wall.

One time when we were arguing (I forget what it was about), I got so mad at him that I threw a plate of food at him. It missed and hit the wall, but for some reason it satisfied me. Maybe because it shut him up, and he got up and walked out. I don't know why I stayed there so long. Sometimes I wonder. I guess I was just going along taking whatever life dished out. But I shouldn't have let it go on, especially when he started beating on Tony. There weren't any domestic violence and child abuse laws back then like there are now. It just wasn't recognized as such. If it were, Butch would have definitely been in jail.

I remember Tony skipping school once. I feverishly prayed that I would find him before his dad did. I searched high and low but came up empty-handed. I have no idea where Butch found him, but he brought him home black and blue. I couldn't even touch Tony. I wanted to take him to the doctor, but he begged me not to. He said it would only make it worse. I have no idea what Butch said to him, but it was obvious that he beat the crap out of him. At times like that, I wouldn't talk to Butch for months. It was all I could do to even look at him.

No matter how much we fought, there were still nights when Butch would come home late at night and decide that he had to satisfy his needs. It didn't happen that often, but it only took once. A few months after Mama died, probably around the beginning of the school year in 1964, I missed my period. I told Butch I was pregnant, and his first remark was "Who's the father?" Which was the same thing he said the last two times I was pregnant. So I had my response down pat. "Of course you are—who do you think?"

I convinced Dr. Smith to put down a due date that was one month later than my actual due date so that I could work longer. Since I had no complications, he saw nothing wrong with it. The policy at the state hospital didn't allow anyone to work past their seventh month. Then you were given a four-month leave of absence—unpaid.

By early May 1965 I was overdue. I asked Dr. Smith to induce labor because I didn't want my baby to be born on the same day that Mama died. It just didn't feel right to even think about having a child born on that day. He understood because he had been her doctor too, for many years.

We decided to induce labor the next Saturday. So I got up early, took the kids to the McIntires', and drove myself to the hospital. After I got checked in, they gave me an IV and broke my water. Then Dr. Smith told me to get up as soon as he left the room. I did exactly what he told me, but nothing more happened. So I spent the night there, and the next day we tried again. They gave me another IV, and this time they went in and ruptured the membrane. I could tell this child was going to be a stubborn one—like me. The baby was supposed to be born on Saturday, but it turned out to be Sunday, which was okay because it wasn't the same day that Mama died. But it was Mother's Day.

I don't know where Butch was for sure. He worked twenty-four hours on and twenty-four hours off at the fire station, but he didn't show up Saturday or Mother's Day either. He finally came to see me on Monday.

"Did you see the baby?" I asked when he entered my room.

He nodded. "Mm-hmm."

"I named her Deborah Sue."

"Hmm." He nodded again. Then after a pregnant pause, he said, "Louie brought me by, so I'm gonna take your car home for you."

"That's fine. I should be able to go home on Wednesday. You gonna pick me and the baby up?"

"Yeah, I'll come and get you."

I said, "Okay," and that was about it. He came and got me on Wednesday when he said he would. Just like before, he didn't seem too interested in the new baby. Helen was a little more excited about her new baby sister than Tony, and Janet was almost three and was absolutely fascinated with the new baby.

Things were fairly quiet as I settled into a routine with the kids and finished out my maternity leave. When I got back to work, I changed to the day shift so that I could take the psych tech class that the hospital was offering. Mrs. Reddinger, who lived across the street from North Mesa Elementary School took care of the little ones while I was at work and Tony and Helen were at school.

I had been working with psychiatric patients for almost ten years now, and things were changing. We were still doing hydrotherapy, but I don't remember if we were still doing insulin shock therapy. The biggest change was how tranquilizers had come into play. Melleril and Thorazine were the big ones. With the help of tranquilizers we were able to send patients to nursing homes or out on field trips. There were no cuffs anymore. Restraints had all went by the wayside. In fact, I think straitjackets were outlawed. I guess it was a gradual change, but it made everything different. A lot of the patients were like mummies because of the drugs. Some of them overdosed because the doctors hadn't figured out the right dosages.

Things were changing outside the hospital too. It just didn't seem as safe a world as the one I grew up in and loved. I think a lot of things changed in the sixties.

17

I told everyone I knew that a reporter from the *Pueblo Chieftain* was coming out to take pictures of me and Debbie Sue and interview us. They were doing an article on all the mothers who had a baby born on Mother's Day the year before. It was a total surprise when they contacted me. But they always printed the local births in the paper, and we were listed in the phone book, so I'm sure that's how they tracked us down.

The morning they were coming to the house I woke with anticipation. I got Helen and Tony off to school and excitedly got the house in shipshape. Then I bathed Debbie and Janet and dressed them in matching blue-striped sailor outfits. I pulled Janet's hair back in a ponytail and combed Debbie's the best I could. She barely had enough hair on her head to style, and the curls usually ended up getting their way in the end. They both looked adorable. I put on my favorite yellow Beeline dress. It had a tie in the front that sort of matched the nautical theme.

I told the girls that it was going to be a very special picture day. When the man and woman from the paper showed up, the girls were exceptionally well behaved. Janet and Debbie got along pretty well most of the time anyway because Janet would give in when her little sister wanted or needed anything. She never fussed with her. I couldn't say the same for Tony and Helen. They were always fussing and fighting with each other.

The girls sat in the middle of the front room floor and played with a little rubber elephant while I talked to the reporters.

"Did you know your daughter was going to be born on Mother's Day?"

"Well, I guess I didn't think about it. In fact, I don't think it dawned on me until a day or two after the fact."

"There's usually a lot going on at a time like that, isn't there?"

"There certainly is. When you're having a baby, you just don't think about what day it is," I said, remembering full well that my main concern when I went into the hospital to give birth was that my child not be born on the day my mother died. I was thinking about what day it was all right—I just wasn't thinking about it being Mother's Day. But that's not what I told them.

We chatted a little longer, and then they positioned us on the couch for some pictures. I asked if they would mind sending me copies of the pictures, and they were kind enough to send me an 8 x 10 and other various-sized prints in the mail a few weeks later.

On Mother's Day, when I picked up the Sunday paper off the front porch and leafed through it, I quickly found our picture on the front of one of the inside sections. The one that made it into the paper was of Janet and me sitting on the couch with Debbie standing in front of me. I was reaching for Debbie as she took a baby step and reached for me. The title of the article read, "For Mothers, Every Day Is Others' Day."

For a brief moment, I felt kind of special.

I called my friend Imogene to share my fun news, but I never got around to telling her. She had just come home from the hospital. She had a miscarriage. I was devastated. I could only imagine how she felt. I couldn't help but go see her and make sure she was doing okay. I usually took the kids with me when I went to her house because she had two girls that were about the same age as Helen and Janet. But this time I put Helen and Tony in charge of the little ones and told them that they couldn't come but that I wouldn't be long.

I really wasn't gone very long, and the kids were fine while I was gone. Helen had been babysitting for me since she was twelve (she was thirteen and a half now). Tony had fallen into his dad's footsteps (although I'm not sure it was by choice) and spent a lot of time outside doing chores or just generally playing around out there. Tony was close to being fifteen years old, and his dad had put him in charge of feeding the pigs and taking care of things outside while he was at the fire station. Tony had learned over the years to do exactly what his dad told him. If he made his dad mad, he knew he was in for a beating. I stepped in when I could. In fact, the last time, when Butch accused Tony of stealing money from his folks (Tony's grandparents), he started hitting Tony right in the middle of the front room. The girls were right there, crying, and Butch was hollering. I had no idea what was going on, but as soon as I entered the front room, without even thinking about it, I got right between Tony and his dad and started screaming at Butch to leave him alone. I took a couple of blows in the scuffle, but Butch backed off. Trust me, this was no spanking. He was hitting him with his fists when I stepped in.

When I got home from Imogene's, Helen told me that her dad was looking for me.

"Didn't you tell him I went to Imogene's?"

"Yes, he said he was going to go see if you were there or if you went someplace else."

"What? Like where?"

"I don't know. That's all he said. Then he just left."

About fifteen minutes later I heard Butch's truck pull into the driveway. There were rails around the bed of the truck that went up as high as the top of the cab—like the bed of the truck was fenced in.

When I saw that part of the truck pass by the kitchen windows, I went outside to confront him. I watched him as he got out of the truck. He hitched up his Levis as he tucked in the front part of his shirt that had started to sag. He wore a thick, brown leather belt that had a silver, oval-shaped buckle with a bucking bronco on it. He was stout but not fat and wore his jeans loosely. As he reached in and grabbed his stiff straw cowboy hat off the seat, I noticed the wallet bulging and leaving a faded outline on his back pocket. He put his hat on and shut the truck door. As soon as he turned and saw me coming toward him, I started in on him. I wasn't about to let him speak first.

"Did you actually follow me out to Imogene's?"

He took the toothpick out of his mouth and waved it around in his hand as he yelled back at me. "You left the kids. I figured you were off meeting some guy somewhere. You're always running around. What the hell do you expect me to think?"

"I'm not always running around. I go to work, and I go help Daddy out, but—"

"Nobody goes to their folks' house that often."

"Well, I do."

"Why didn't you take the kids with you tonight? Who you seeing?"

"You know damn well where I went if you were following me."

"You're damn right I do."

"Fine. You want a reason to follow me; I'll give you a reason." I turned and stormed back into the house while he cussed at my back in Italian. I had no idea how I was going to make good on my idle threat. I couldn't count how many times in the past I had told him if he didn't believe that I was going where I said, he should just follow me. Then when he did, I'm not sure why, but I blew up. I was getting fed up with all the accusations. I never went out or did anything that warranted such jealousy and suspicion.

As luck would have it, a few days later some of the gals at work were talking about going out for drinks. When they asked me if I would like to join them, I saw no reason why not to. Normally, I don't think I would have. But I justified it in my head, and if I had it to do over again, I think I would make the same decision. I hadn't been out to a bar since before Tony was born. I was thirty-three years old, had two teenagers and two toddlers at home, and had a full-time job. Plus I sold Beeline clothing on the side, helped take care of my elderly father, and went to church on Sundays. I felt that I deserved an evening out. The problem was I knew Butch would not approve. The thought of that put a nervous knot in the pit of my stomach.

A couple of nights later, I was just about to crawl into bed when I heard Butch come in. I waited for him to wash up and come into the bedroom. I was tucked into the covers, but the lamp on the nightstand was still on. I grabbed the lotion from beside the lamp and rubbed some into my hands. He sat down on the edge of the bed with his back to me and started taking his boots off.

I tried to sound casual when I said, "A few of the girls from work asked me if I wanted to go out for a drink with them some night, and I told them I would." I pushed my thumb hard into the palm of my hand, predicting a harsh response.

"The hell you will," he said, emphasizing each word.

I waited a few moments, but the other shoe didn't drop. So I reached up and turned out the lamp and let him finish undressing in the dark. Since he didn't say anything else, I didn't either. We lay in bed with our backs to each other. I lay there still and awake trying to convince myself that maybe his disapproval wouldn't be that bad this time. When I was confident that he was asleep, I relaxed and drifted off.

I brought it up again several times in the next three weeks. He continued to tell me that I couldn't go, and I continued to tell him that

I was going. There were about five or six of us that were going. I gave him everyone's name. He knew most of them. They were all decent married women who had been in our community for years. But none of them was married to any of his Italian buddies, so they were no good, according to him. He called them all whores in Italian—*puttanas*, I think.

When the day finally came, he not only told me that I wasn't going, he told me that if I did, I would be sorry. Most of the women that were supposed to go had backed out—probably because their husbands wouldn't let them go. I just wasn't changing my mind. Butch knew this when he left for work that morning.

There were only three of us who met out that night—Dorothy, Rayanne, and me. We met at Rayanne's house shortly after dinner. I left Helen, Janet, and Debbie there with Rayanne's kids. Helen was the eldest and would babysit until we got home. Tony didn't want to go. He wanted to spend the night at the fire station, so I dropped him off there—without going in to face Butch before I left.

We really didn't have a plan for the evening other than to have fun, and that's what we did. I wasn't used to drinking, so I didn't drink much. After having a drink and gabbing for a while in one bar, we would leave thinking we were headed back to Rayanne's, but then we would find another place to stop. Since we didn't get out much, I guess we felt as if we had to check out as many places as we could. We didn't talk to any men or any of that nonsense. Most of the men around Pueblo knew Butch anyway and wouldn't mess with me because they knew I was his wife. But we really did have a good time just talking and laughing and playing music on the jukebox.

By the time we finally got back to Rayanne's, the kids were all in bed; even Helen was asleep. So I decided that we would stay the night. Butch and Tony were at the fire station anyway, so we didn't need to rush home to an empty house. But in the morning, after we left Rayanne's, I knew Butch would be home, and I was tentative about facing him. On the way home we stopped by my sister Elva's house for a while to visit. Then we stayed for lunch. I guess I was trying to postpone the inevitable. Finally, sometime that afternoon, I called the house.

"What would happen if I came home?" I asked when I got Butch on the line.

"Nothing, just come home," he assured me.

I found it a little hard to believe that it would be that easy. I knew he was going to be mad at me for defying his wishes and spending some time with my girlfriends. But I had to go home sometime. Although I was leery of it, I finally headed that way.

When I pulled into the driveway, I could see Butch and Tony out by the pigpens. They stopped what they were doing for a moment when they saw us. Things seemed normal enough. I grabbed the baby bag and the baby out of the car, while Helen and Janet got the rest of our stuff and scooted into the house behind me. I had barely gotten in the door when I heard the back door screech open and spring shut, followed by the thud of Butch's cowboy boots closing in behind me. I was standing about three feet from the stove in the middle of the kitchen. Almost instantly he was in front of me. He grabbed Debbie from my arms and tossed her aside as if she were a ragdoll. My eyes followed her as she slid across the floor, barely missing the leg on the kitchen table, and landed against the wall. Helen and I both reached for her. Helen made it; I didn't. Butch brought his fist back and hit me so hard I went sideways into the wall and then straight down. From there he proceeded to beat the living daylights out of me. I remember being on the floor, but I don't remember anything else until the next morning at seven when I heard him leave for work.

Helen remembers the most…

I picked Debbie up off the floor immediately and made sure she wasn't hurt. She was crying like crazy. When I turned around, Janet was pulling on Dad's leg screaming for him not to hurt her mommy. With my free hand I grabbed Janet and pulled her toward me and buried her head in my stomach so she couldn't see. She squeezed me and shook with sobs. Then Tony ran in and yelled at Dad to stop. Dad leaned toward him and pointed his finger in Tony's face. "Do you want to be next?" he shouted at him. I remember looking down at Mom on the floor. She was lying on her side with her knees slightly bent. Her head was right by the wall-heater vent, and her arms were covering her face and head. She wasn't moving. But she wasn't limp. It was like every muscle in her body was tensed up tightly for protection. Everything was happening really fast. The last thing I remember was seeing Dad's scuffed brown cowboy boot striking Mom's head. I remember how Dad's Levis covered his cowboy boots but not the wooden heel. I remember that the heel was worn down on the back outer side and not the inner side. The boots were old and well worn, with a slightly rounded toe.

To this day, I can still see him kicking her in the head. I probably couldn't watch anything after that. The next thing I remember was sitting on the couch downstairs with Mom. I don't remember how we got there, but we sat there for the longest time. Mom didn't talk or sleep. I took care of Janet and Debbie. But mostly we just sat there, huddled together with Mom.

As soon as Butch was gone the next morning, Helen called her aunt Agnes. When she got there, Helen ran up and hurried back down the stairs pulling Agnes by the hand around each bend in the staircase.

Agnes was also a nurse and also taught not to show her emotions, but I could tell by her reaction that she didn't like the way I looked.

"Yegads, Bernice, we need to get you to a doctor." She reached out to touch my face, and I flinched as though she were going to strike me. I was a nervous wreck, but it was also as if I was partially unconscious and unable to think clearly.

She didn't waste another minute. She got Helen and Tony to gather up a change of clothes for themselves and the girls and got us out of there. Before we left, she called Elva and told her to meet us at the hospital. I don't remember much about the ride to the hospital. Maybe I didn't feel like talking, or maybe I couldn't. I'm not sure which, but I'm sure the kids filled her in on what had happened.

The kids went to Frank and Elva's house, and I spent the next ten days in the hospital.

18

The next ten days were pretty blurry for me. I only remember bits and pieces.

I think Agnes or Elva contacted Dr. Smith and told him that I was badly beaten. He probably called ahead to the hospital and told them I was coming so they could admit me right away. But honestly, I don't remember being admitted to the hospital. The next thing I remember was waking up with a start. I felt instantly nervous and jumpy. But when I found myself tucked neatly into crisp white sheets, I knew I was in a hospital bed.

I was in a private room, which I thought was unusual. Normally there were two to four people in one room. It was very quiet and seamlessly still.

Everything in the hospital room was either white or shiny metal, like chrome. Even the floor was shiny. There was nothing distinct about it that I can recall. It was a small room. My bed was centered between a door to the hallway on my left and a large window on my right. I don't recall what could be seen out the window, and I don't think I cared. A door to the bathroom, a sink, and a crucifix occupied the wall opposite the bed. I knew I was at St. Mary Corwin Hospital as soon as I saw the crucifix.

I was so tired. For the most part, all I did was sleep. I soon discovered that three or four days had passed. I don't think they gave me anything to make me sleep, but I guess they could have. I know they woke me up to give me Maalox ever so often. Something was wrong with my stomach. But I don't remember eating, taking any other medication, taking a bath… I don't even remember seeing a doctor the first few days. Dr. Smith told me later that he ordered complete bed rest and no visitors.

I don't know how many days passed before I started staying awake long enough to have a coherent thought. But as I became more lucid, I began to realize what had happened. At first I didn't really believe it. I never thought something like that would happen to me. I had a hard time understanding and accepting the fact that I was hospitalized and had lost contact with reality and my world as I knew it.

I think my saving grace may have been the nuns who came around and checked on me. They asked things like what religion I was, where I went to church, and if I wanted to receive communion while I was there. I don't recall if I answered any of their questions, but they reminded me of Father Murray. I was very close to him while he was giving me catechism lessons, and we had maintained a close relationship after that. Not only was he my priest, he was my friend, my teacher, and my confidant. I don't know if I asked the Sisters to contact him for me or if I called him, but I know, somehow, we got ahold of Father Murray, and he came to see me at least a couple of times, for much-needed visits.

On his first visit I was so glad to see him. I wanted to tell him everything, but my head was full of cobwebs. There was so much I couldn't remember. After the first blow from Butch there were huge blank spots. It was more difficult to explain than I had anticipated. He probably didn't have enough information to go on, so I think that's why he insisted that we set up a meeting for some counseling.

I was reluctant and nervous and fearful. But Father Murray had a way of making me feel better mentally. He made me feel calmer. And for some reason I felt secure and safe in my hospital room. I knew Father Murray would be there by my side when Butch joined us for counseling, so I agreed to the meeting. I don't know which one of us called Butch. I think Father Murray might have called right there from my room.

On the day that Father Murray came back to my hospital room for our meeting/counseling session, we waited for Butch, but he never showed up. Father stood there by my bedside looking down on me. His black priest attire made him stand out against all the whiteness in the room. "Butch has no interest in this marriage, Bernice. You have no recourse but to get a divorce." What he was saying didn't sound or feel real.

The strange thing is I can vaguely recall Butch standing there beside my hospital bed, but I couldn't tell you if it was real or a dream. I don't remember any conversation between us. He just stood there and looked at me. I didn't mention it to Father Murray.

Usually adultery was the only grounds for divorce that the church recognized. But in the state of mind I was in, I accepted Father Murray's advice about getting a divorce without question. The way I saw it, if Father Murray told me it was okay to get a divorce, it was just like the Catholic Church saying it was okay. I trusted him and believed in his authority and guidance.

Although I never mentioned it to Dr. Smith, I think he thought I should get a divorce too. I remember him telling me after I was released from the hospital that when I was admitted, he put the diagnosis as cephalalgia, which basically meant a bad headache. That way there would be nothing on my record about a mental breakdown or psychosis, which was probably what the real diagnosis should have been. Something like that would have been unfavorable for me in a divorce court if it was dug up, and Dr. Smith knew it. He was trying to protect me. In essence, the beating was as hard on me mentally as it was physically. It caused me to go into shock and have a mental breakdown. To this day I cannot think about it or the hospital stay or even talk about it without repercussions in the form of terrible nightmares of Butch chasing me and trying to kill me. The last one I had was so vivid I felt I was awake rather than dreaming. It ended with a gun in my face, and it was about to go off, which jarred me out of my sleep gasping for breath. For some reason, I can't go back to the moment in time when it actually happened. My memory of it is blank. I know what happened even if I don't remember it, and I know it was the wakeup call that I needed to end the marriage.

When the doctor said, "I think I'm going to let you go home tomorrow," I felt ready. I had stayed in bed the whole ten days. I never left the room. But I had started making more contact with people, and I got some of my appetite back. I lost quite a bit of weight during my stay due to a lack of appetite, but in the end I was actually sitting up to eat a meal.

When it was time for me to go home, I called Elva.

"Elva, it's me. How are the kids doing?"

"They're just fine. How are you feeling? The doctor wouldn't let us visit. I've been worried sick about you."

"I need you to do me a favor."

"Are you okay, Bernice? What do you need?"

"I'm all right. I need you to ask Daddy if me and the kids can stay with him for a little while until I can find an apartment."

"Now you know he won't care. And if you need to, you and the girls can stay here."

"I know. I think there's more room at Daddy's. I just need to make sure he won't mind. Okay?"

Elva smoothed the way for me. She also picked me up and took me and the girls to Daddy's house. I vaguely remember something about

Tony refusing to go to Elva's when I went to the hospital. I think he stayed home alone. I'm not sure. But I know it was just the girls and me that went to Daddy's.

When we first got there, Elva came in with me, and we talked with Daddy for a while. Then the girls and I got settled downstairs. The downstairs still looked as it did when we first built the house. The walls to the two small bedrooms still didn't have drywall. The boards in the wall were exposed. The old stove was still down there as well. Mama had some things stored in one of the bedrooms, like her trunk and a couple of dressers. The other bedroom was made up as a guest room. When I saw Mama's trunk sitting there, I realized that she'd had that trunk for as long as I could remember. She kept all sorts of things in it. It had two different layers that you could lift out. But I didn't open it. I knew that my older brothers and sisters had gone through all Mama's keepsakes after she died.

In fact, it still bugged me that they did that. I didn't say anything to anyone at the time. It wouldn't have done any good anyway. They went through everything in the house, every dresser drawer—I mean everything. I don't know if they asked Daddy. If it bothered him too much, I think he would have said something. To this day I remember the one thing that I wanted. There was one photo album that contained pictures of Mama and Daddy and their parents. Elva and I wanted it, but nobody would ever tell us what happened to it, and we never saw it again. Every time Elva and I brought it up, everyone just clammed up and wouldn't say anything. It had been a couple of years since Mama died, and I still missed her.

Once we were settled in, I got busy. It was a little hard to get my bearings. I had filled the prescription Dr. Smith wrote me for Valium. It was supposed to calm my nerves, so I took it regularly as prescribed. When you are on Valium, it's as if everything that is happening is happening to someone else. It's not happening to you, but you are very aware of it. It was strange. I don't remember what day I got out of the hospital, but I know that I went back to psych tech class the next Monday. And by the time I was there, I had already filed for divorce.

I was only allowed to miss three days of the psych tech class. If you missed more than that they dropped you from the class. I think they made an exception for me because I was in the hospital. I'm pretty sure I explained to the teacher exactly what happened. I remember wearing sunglasses for the first week I was back in class. People stared at me, but I didn't care. At least they couldn't see my black eyes. I didn't go back to work for a month, but I was bound and determined to finish the class I had started. The class was held five days a week, and there was only about three months left. If I could pull it off, I could graduate with the rest of the class in October 1966.

It was summer, and the kids were out of school when we moved in with Daddy. I was afraid the little ones were going to be too noisy for Daddy, so I didn't waste any time finding a place for us to live. I think we were only at Daddy's for a couple of weeks before I found this little house with a chopped-up floor plan that included about a half dozen small rooms, over on Cheyenne Street, not too far from the hospital. I think it was a store before it was a home. The main thing was that I could afford it. It was only about $150 a month.

Everything else didn't go quite that smooth.

When I filed for divorce, my attorney told me I should get a restraining order too. So I did. We had our first hearing right away. They told me I could have the house, but I didn't want it, because Butch would get the grounds, which meant I would have to put up with him. I didn't want that. So the judge told us that I could get anything I wanted out of the house in order to get settled in a new place.

When I went to the house to gather up some things, Butch came home while I was there. At first I thought he would stay outside because of the restraining order, and I figured I was okay. But he didn't stay outside.

I heard the familiar sound of him coming in through the back door. My instincts propelled me toward the phone that was sitting on the end table by the front door. It was a big, black, heavy rotary phone. I picked up the receiver, dialed 0 for the operator, and watched as the dial slowly rotated back around to its starting position. I never heard the operator pick up on the other end of the phone before Butch grabbed the phone off the table and heaved it against the opposite wall. I watched as the receiver flew from my hand. Looking down, I saw the phone cord had come out of the wall and exposed wires lay at my feet. I stood still and didn't say a word. He didn't hit me, but he was mad as hell. He was mad about everything, the divorce and me taking things. He didn't want me to take the freezer. For some reason I remember that pretty clearly. He cussed me up one side and down the other. But I still didn't say a word, didn't move a muscle, or look him in the eye. When he finally backed off, I got out of there as fast as I could. At this point, I was deathly afraid of him.

I didn't want him to know where I was living, but the courts made me give him my address. They said I had to because he had a right to see the girls. Mostly Helen went for visitation. Butch said that Debbie was too little and that Janet cried too much. Tony had already decided that he wanted to stay with his dad. I'm sure the promise of a new motorcycle enticed him a little. Tony was just about to turn sixteen. Daddy encouraged me to let Tony live with Butch. He didn't think I could handle Tony. But I didn't have to make that decision. Tony made it for me. He didn't want to live with me, and I didn't fight him on it. In retrospect, I don't know if I should have let Tony go. I often wonder if he would have avoided getting in so much trouble if I had kept him with me.

The next time I went to the farmhouse to get some things I brought my nephew CE, his friend, and Rayanne with me. We didn't have a big truck, so we took a couple of cars and made a few trips. I didn't feel bad about taking things from the house since I had bought most of it. But I didn't take everything either. I left the chrome kitchen table and chair set and took Mama's old wooden table that I had in the basement. I took a couple of beds for the girls and myself and left the bedroom set for Butch and a bed for Tony. I left enough stuff that Butch and Tony could still live there comfortably. However, I did take the freezer, even though I knew Butch didn't want me to. I had three girls to feed and wasn't working, so I felt like I needed it a little more than he did. I think he thought he could deter me from taking it by locking it and taking the key. But I took it any way. He refused to give me the key even after I already had the freezer. CE helped me get it open. We couldn't lock it after that, but at least we had groceries.

When we went in for our interlocutory decree, where we figured out who was going to pay support and who was going to get the kids, Butch threw a curveball by contesting the divorce. Personally, I think it was either because he saw us as a possessions that he didn't want to lose or he didn't want to pay child support. I didn't see any other possible reason. In any case, since he was contesting it, the court ordered us to go to counseling.

I met with the counselor a few times by myself. Apparently Butch did too. Then all three of us met.

Our meeting room was on the fourth floor of one of the Thatcher buildings. It was a huge building downtown with nothing but offices and I think a couple of banks. My attorney's office was in the same building. I liked to be a little early for meetings, so I was there before

Butch or the counselor. The counselor was a woman about my age. She came in just a few minutes after I did. She was dressed in a nice skirt and blouse—a casual outfit, not a business suit. I wore one of my Beeline dresses. She pulled up a chair next to me at one end of the table. It was a pretty good-sized room with a long, sturdy wooden table, with matching dark wood chairs—like a conference room. The furniture was well used but not scratched and scuffed. When Butch showed up, he was wearing his jeans and a short-sleeved cotton shirt with a collar and three buttons down the front. He came in and, without saying a word, went further back in the room and sat at the far end of the table, away from us.

The session started with the counselor asking us some questions. I don't recall exactly what she was asking us about, but she must have been asking some questions about what happened. I definitely remember Butch's response. I think she asked about a half dozen different questions, and he just sat there, kind of slumped over, looking toward the floor, very still, and in a kind of whining voice he said, "I want my family back." That's all he would say.

"Okay, I think that's enough for today. Butch, you can go, and I will call you later," she said, stopping the session short. When Butch was out of the room, she explained, "He isn't ready for this type of counseling, and it really isn't productive for you."

"Should we just keep going with the individual counseling then?" I asked.

"I don't think I need to see you again. I'm going to work on some things with your husband, and we'll take it from there. Okay?"

She never made us meet again.

I was told that it would take about three months to get my divorce, but it wasn't so.

19

When Rayanne asked me to meet her for a drink, I hesitated. The last time I went out with her things turned out horribly wrong. But I realized that things were different now. I wasn't living with Butch. We were separated, and I was trying to get a divorce. I could have friends now, and I had the freedom to spend time with them if I wanted to. So I decided to give it a try.

After dinner I put Helen in charge of the girls and headed up the street to a club that wasn't too far from our house on Cheyenne street to meet Rayanne. It was about dusk when I arrived. The red neon Caravan Night Club sign atop an otherwise indistinct adobe building cast glowing light patterns on a handful of cars that were parked in a gravel parking lot in front. This was the north side of town—the good side of town, on Elizabeth Street, not far from the hospital. I knew that a lot of attorneys and doctors and other upscale folks lived in the area, so I thought it would be a safe place for a woman to walk in alone.

When I opened the door, the lights were just low enough that it was slightly darker than outside. I let my eyes adjust a little, and I noticed the bar was straight across from the door and was pretty well lit, so I headed in that direction. The jukebox was playing Ernest Tubb at a nice moderate level. I looked around for Rayanne. There were a few people sitting at tables off to the left in front of a dance floor and a couple of empty booths off to the right.

Luckily Rayanne came in right behind me. Before now I had only had an occasional drink. I never really liked the taste of alcohol much. But Rayanne liked to drink and seemed comfortable ordering. I ordered the drink my brother Arthur introduced me to—an orange juice with vodka—partly because it was the only drink I knew and partly because if they made it like Arthur made it, I knew I wouldn't taste the alcohol and would be able to drink it.

We sat there and gabbed and had a couple of drinks. I have to say that I enjoyed the Caravan Club. I enjoyed being out. The crowd that gathered there was small and made up of couples around my age, in their thirties or older. Not a lot of young single people and no Italians or Bojons. It seemed like a good class of people. I definitely relaxed into it and returned for drinks with Rayanne several times in the weeks to come.

One night, after we had been there more than a handful of times, a very handsome man, about my age, came up to our booth as if he owned the place. His jawline was as well defined as the crease in his pants. His face looked as smooth as his speech sounded. He introduced himself as the owner, Wayne Sloan, and there was no way to refuse him when he wanted to join us at our booth. He politely asked us about ourselves and listened intently. Then he looked me straight in the eye and asked, "What would you think about coming to work for me here, as a cocktail waitress?"

I was flabbergasted. "I've never worked as a cocktail waitress before. Besides, I already have a job." The words managed to come out without much forethought.

"It's really not that hard. I know you could do it. I could really use someone like you to help me out… just a couple of nights a week."

He had more confidence in me than I had in myself. "Well, I don't know. I'll have to think about it."

I was flattered. But when I left that night, it was still up in the air. I hadn't accepted his offer, but I hadn't flat out refused either. It would definitely be different than being a psych tech nurse, but I wasn't really looking for a second job. I had a lot going on with the divorce. Rayanne thought it would be fun and interesting to work there. She wanted me to take the job and then get her hired too. She worked with me at the hospital, so she really didn't need another job either. But I think Wayne sparked something in both of us. We started going there every other day or so, and about a week later we ran into him again.

"Well, hello there, ladies." I watched the words glide from his mouth. "I'm so glad to see you're back. Bernice, how are you? Have you thought anymore about my offer?"

His words were spoken as a true gentleman would speak to a lady. I couldn't help but smile. "Yes, as a matter of fact I have," I said politely. "I will go to work for you… if you can hire Rayanne too." Rayanne and I looked at each other with girlish smiles.

He gave me one of his charming grins and put his hand out for me to shake. "You've got yourself a deal." He slowly let go of my hand and then placed his hand on Rayanne's shoulder and continued, "But, Rayanne, it's going to be at least a couple of weeks before I can bring you on, okay?"

Rayanne was thrilled. I'm not sure why, but I was kind of nervous about it.

Nonetheless, I started working at the Caravan Club the next Friday night. Throughout the week couples or small groups of people would come in to drink and talk. But on Friday and Saturday nights it got busy. There was a live band and dancing. It was always the same band— but still, they drew a crowd, and the place was always packed. That was probably why Wayne needed extra help. The band played a lot of love songs and fast polkas and some songs that were popular with the crowd, like "Four-Leaf Clover" and "Slow Boat to China." No country-western music and no rock and roll either. It was music that I could listen to, and it didn't drive me crazy like the screaming rock-and-roll stuff that Helen had started listening to.

I was a little uneasy on my first night at work. But Wayne was right; it wasn't really that hard. The bar was about twenty feet long, and at the end of the bar the waitresses went in and out, took orders, and brought folks their drinks. I got the swing of it pretty quickly. Before I knew it, people were buying me drinks. It actually happened quite a lot. Sometimes I would have to turn down drinks. I was just too busy. One drink would be sitting there behind the bar waiting for me to drink it, and then someone would buy me another, and it would sit there until they both went to waste. I never really drank more than a sip or two while I was working. By the time the bar closed, I had collected some pretty decent tips as well.

Eventually Rayanne came to work at the Caravan too. Wayne started her at two nights a week. By then I had worked my way up to four nights a week. One night Wayne waltzed in at the start of my shift and announced, "You're on your own tonight, Bernice."

"What do you mean?"

"I'm putting you behind the bar mixing drinks."

"I don't know how to mix drinks, Wayne."

"If you don't know how to make it, we'll be right here. This guy will show you how." He put his arm around the bartender, and they both stood there smiling at me as if they had just given me some sort of prize.

Thank God it was a weeknight, and there was no band. At first I wasn't sure what to do, but it all just happened pretty naturally. I stood there behind the bar and just talked with the customers and mixed the drink they would ask for. No one asked for anything extravagant. I made it through the night without any problem.

Sometimes, on nights that I didn't have to work at the hospital the next day, Wayne, Rayanne, the bartender, and I would head over to Valencia's after closing up the Caravan. It was the best Mexican restaurant and bar in Pueblo. One of the things that made it the best place to go was a little-known secret about them serving alcohol after hours. And they weren't stingy with their drinks. You got generous drinks and friendly help, and it was all under the covers. We would order drinks in coffee cups and then ask for refills.

Sometimes we would be there for hours, and little by little our booth would fill up and spill over. My nephew CE would show up every once in a while. I'd known CE as long as I could remember. He was Sam and Pearl's son, and he was two years older than me and had always enjoyed calling me Auntie because I was younger. He was always an ornery cuss and liked to drink and raise Cain. But I knew if I ever needed anything, he would be the first person to be there for me. We were close, and we watched out for each other.

Even my brother-in-law Frank, Elva's husband, who was a cop at the time, would stop in to say hi if he saw my car parked out front. I don't think he ever suspected that I was drinking. I would often have a cup of coffee in front of me—spiked with vodka. I didn't worry about Frank knowing I was drinking, because I was convinced that you couldn't smell vodka on your breath or in a drink. I don't know if that's exactly true or not, but that's what I thought.

Occasionally, after being at Valencia's and getting home at four or five in the morning, I would go to work at the hospital at six. But most nights I would try to get about six hours of sleep if I had to work. No matter how much sleep I got, the Valium the doctor had me taking for my nerves was making me sleepy during the day. I would actually find myself nodding off during slow times at the hospital, so I had to mention it to Dr. Smith. In response, he prescribed Ritalin to keep me awake. I don't remember the exact dosage. I think I took the Ritalin once a day and Valium maybe three time a day.

I guess I could have killed myself with the mixture of drugs and alcohol, but at the time I had no idea that something like that was even possible. There weren't any warnings on the bottles about drinking alcohol while taking these drugs, and I never heard about things like that actually happening. The only time I heard about things remotely similar was when it happened within the walls of the state hospital with the Thorazine, Melerell, and Stelazine. When those drugs first came out, the doctors were trying to figure out the right dosage for their psychiatric patients, and there were some overdoses. But I felt that the prescription drugs I was taking were different.

I took other drugs if I needed them too. In fact, anyone who came to work at the hospital with a hangover would go into the medicine room and take a Librium and Darvocet. The Darvocet made the headache go away. I'm not sure what the Librium did, but it was a sure cure for a hangover. At the time, these were not prescription drugs, and they were supplied to the hospital in huge bottles that weren't monitored as strictly as the prescription medication. Officially it was against hospital policy for any employee to take prescription or nonprescription drugs from the medicine room, but everyone took the nonprescription drugs from there when they needed to.

One morning after a night out and a stopover at Valencia's, the phone woke me out of a dead sleep.

"Morning, Bernice. Did I wake you?" I recognized Rayanne's voice, even in a fog.

"That's all right," I gurgled hoarsely.

"How's your car?"

"Fine," I said as I placed my hand on my forehead as if it would help me think. I couldn't recall the drive home.

"Okay, I just wanted to check on you."

"I'm fine," I said. "Call me back later. I've gotta go check on the girls."

I checked on the girls and dozed back off for a little while before the phone woke me again. It was CE.

"Damn, Bernice, you were pretty drunk last night. I wanted to make sure you made it home okay."

"I did, as you can tell," I said a little sarcastically.

"No bruises or broken bones or anything?"

"No," I said, wondering what he was talking about and getting a little frustrated with the inquisition. But I couldn't tell if he was teasing me or being serious.

"You know you hit a telephone pole last night, right?"

"I did not." I feared he was being serious.

"Yes, you did, and you wouldn't let anyone else drive you home afterward."

In total disbelief I let the phone line go silent and stretched the cord as far as it would go as I sought out my car. When I drew back the curtains, there it was, my little blue Comet station wagon parked cockeyed with its crinkled nose turned up at me. I got the car right after I filed for divorce. I hated the Ford Fairlane, so I traded it in for a brand-new Mercury Comet station wagon. It was light blue—not my favorite color, but I liked it, and it was about the same car payment.

"Gads..." I couldn't grasp the memory. Thoughts circled my alcohol-soaked brain. I could have been killed. The kids could've been left without a mother. Then Butch would have to raise them... Then I blurted out, "Butch is going to have a fit when he sees this. What am I going to do?" I suddenly felt desperate. He would use this against me in the divorce proceedings. It would be totally unacceptable, and I would never hear the end of it.

"Hell, Bernice, my dad will fix it, and Butch won't have to know."

"What if he finds out?"

"Tell him I did it."

"I can't do that..." If CE said he was drinking and driving, it wouldn't be as much of a surprise as me saying I was drinking and driving. CE had a reputation with alcohol ever since he was a teenager. I tried to think it all out.

"I'm coming to get the car. I know my dad will fix it if he thinks I did it."

I knew he was protecting me. "You know I totally blacked out. I don't remember how I even got home."

"Well, I'm surprised you did get home. You almost didn't."

"I swear I'll never have another drink of vodka again as long as I live." When I uttered those words, I truly meant them.

I knew Sam Baker could fix my car as good as, or better than, anyone else could. But it was just awful to let CE take the blame. He was living at home at the time because he was going through a divorce too. Sam and Pearl both told me never to let him drive my car again, and by the way they said it, I could tell that they were none too happy with CE.

Sam fixed my car, and as far as I know Butch never knew what happened. As for those of us who did—we kept our mouths shut about it.

20

It had been three months since I filed for divorce. Summer break was almost over, and Helen would be going back to school soon.

I was told that my divorce would be final in ninety days, unless both parties couldn't agree. Well, Butch didn't want a divorce, so the final hearing was continually postponed. He maintained that he wanted to get his family back. It didn't make much sense to me. He never personally asked me about getting back together, unless you counted the episode in our counseling session. I don't think it was making sense to other folks either because I heard that not only was he sent to the hospital for psychiatric evaluation, he was in and out a few times.

I didn't have much contact with him. When he came to get the girls for a visit, he stayed in his truck and honked the horn. We always knew when he was coming. Helen would watch for him, and the girls would be ready when he got there. He was supposed to have the girls every other weekend, but it rarely happened. When he did come and get them, he only kept them a couple of hours. Still, it was hard to let them go, especially the little ones. I knew Helen was there, and I trusted her to watch over her sisters, but it was still unsettling, and I had no way of preventing or supervising his visits.

Butch was paying about sixty dollars a month in child support, which really helped. Plus, I was working two jobs. So I found a better place for me and the girls to live. It was an apartment on Clairmont, closer to Daddy and my sisters, on the south side of Pueblo. It was just a couple of houses down from Bill and Lola (my sister Zelma's son and his wife). Lola agreed to watch the girls while Helen was in school and I was at work. I enrolled Helen at Corwin Junior High, which she wasn't very happy about. She wanted to go back to Pleasant View with classmates that she knew.

The job at the Caravan ended up being too much after I moved, so I quit. I tried working at another club on the south side, closer to the new apartment, but that didn't last long. I just wasn't up for it. I was making a drastic change in my life, and there were times when I got depressed. It wasn't easy. I couldn't help but think, *It wasn't supposed to be like this.*

Rayanne refused to let me sit around at home and mope. She told me that I had to enjoy life. We started going to a nightclub in Colorado Springs on Saturday nights. Sometimes Dorothy and Helen Plant from work would go with us. I slowly started drinking again. I switched to Gin Collins, which wasn't as good as a screwdriver, because I could taste the alcohol. But I never wanted to black out again, so I wouldn't touch vodka.

A lot of military men went to the nightclub in Springs because there was an army base nearby. So we danced a lot and seldom had to buy a drink. There was a local country singer that performed there who I really liked. Her name was Del Ireland. I could walk up to the stage between songs and request Loretta Lynn, Pasty Cline, or just about any song I could think of, and they would usually play it.

When we became regulars, Del and her husband (who also played in the band) started coming over and sitting with us to have a drink and chat during their breaks. She was beautiful, friendly, and talented, and we were the same age—our birthdays were one day apart. We hit it off right away.

She told me she was going to record her song "A Different Place to Cry" and told me that I would be one of the first people to get her record. She sang it at least once every Saturday night. I liked it better than some of the stuff I heard on the radio, and I sang right along with her when she played it.

> My coffee cup is empty, and my cigarettes are gone.
> I've read the paper over twice and played most every song.
> I listened as she closed the door; I heard the table sigh.
> I'm glad she's gone; I hope she finds a different place to cry.

Eventually Rayanne and I started dating a couple of GIs from Fort Collins. I met Bob, who was a rather nice man. He was handsome, well mannered, kind, and good with the girls. Well, the little girls that is. Helen strongly disapproved of me going out with him or anyone for that matter. She didn't really give him a chance. One night she came right out and told him that he shouldn't be going out with me. Despite everything, she still loved her dad and couldn't fathom another man in our lives. I knew how she felt, but we never talked about her dad. The day I filed for divorce I decided that I wasn't going to talk to the kids about their dad, because I didn't think I would be able to say anything nice. So even though I didn't appreciate her behavior, I allowed her to have her own opinion about the situation.

I guess I wasn't too surprised when Helen asked me if her dad and Tony could come over for dinner one night during the holiday season. She was closer to her dad than the little girls were, and I could tell it was something she really wanted. Butch had been quietly out of my life. I thought maybe things had changed. But mostly I think I did it for Helen. Plus it gave me a chance to spend time with Tony and give him his Christmas present.

Our apartment on Claremont was on a corner. I could see when someone drove up and parked on the side street, and I had a clear view if they parked in front of the apartment. I realized I was a little nervous about the visit when I saw Butch drive up and park his truck on the side street, right behind the Comet, and watched him walk to the door. I heard his heavy boots on the front porch and his knuckles on the door. That familiar twisted and tangled feeling in the pit of my stomach returned as if it had never left. Helen jumped up and swung the door open wide. The cold air hit me hard in the face when Butch walked in, and the image burned into my memory. I think he said something like "Thanks for letting me come inside." I didn't have much to say to him. I don't recall much of what happened in the time that he was there. I may have taken an extra Valium to stay calm. We probably ate spaghetti or an Italian dish of some kind and then opened some presents. In the past, Butch never bought Christmas gifts, but I remember that Helen got a new stereo system from him that year. When he left, I locked the door tightly as soon as it closed behind him. It was dark out, so I also closed the curtains. I should have watched him leave.

The next morning when I got in the car to run some errands, I noticed the car was harder to steer than usual. Something didn't seem right. It sounded different too. I stopped at the first service station I saw. They told me that something was wrong with the power steering. From there, I took a detour and headed over to Sam's to have it checked out more thoroughly.

Sam was in the garage when I drove up. He poked his head out from under the hood of a car. He was wiping his hands on a greasy shop rag and walking my way before I was even out of the car.

"Morning, Bernice. What brings you by?"

"My car's driving a little funny Sam. The guys up the street said something's wrong with the power steering. Would you have a minute to take a look at it?"

"Well, I heard it when you drove in. It sounds like it probably is the power steering."

"It was steering pretty hard."

Sam shoved the shop rag halfway into the back pocket of his overalls and opened the hood of my car. I watched as he grabbed a lid off, held it in his hand, and bent into the engine for a closer look.

"The power steering fluid's gone."

"This is a new car. It shouldn't be leaking, should it?"

Sam looked again, rubbed his fingers in a few key places, and then got down on the ground and looked underneath. As he stood back up, he started shaking his head and let out a steamy snort that was visible in the cold winter air. "I don't see anywhere that it's leaking."

We both stood there for a moment. We stared at the engine as if it might provide an answer to our puzzlement.

"Bernice, I think somebody drained it."

"That son of a…" I knew if anyone drained it, it had to be Butch.

"I've got some in the shop. I can fill it up for you. I don't think it's a leak, so you should be okay."

Right about then CE came out of the house to say good morning, carrying a cup of hot coffee to keep his hands warm. I told him what was going on. He invited me in to warm up. What I really needed was to cool down.

That afternoon I called Butch and confronted him about it. He denied having anything to do with it. When I hung up from talking to him, I called my attorney and told him what I thought had happened. But I didn't have any proof that Butch did anything, so there wasn't much we could do.

* * * * *

When I picked up the phone at the nurses station, I was surprised to hear Helen's voice.

"Mom!"

"Helen?" I could hear Janet crying in the background.

"Janet fell on the fireplace and cut her head open. It's bleeding really bad!"

"Okay, I'll be right there. Put a cold wet cloth on it, okay?" I tried to sound calm, but I could feel my heart racing and the adrenaline flushing through me.

"Okay, hurry, Mom."

As soon as the phone was on the hook, I pulled the hospital keys out of my pocket and laid them on the desk. Rayanne and one of the guys we worked with were standing right behind me. I turned and walked past them saying, "I've got to go. My daughter fell and got hurt. I've got to take her to the hospital."

I checked the time as I punched out. Fifteen minutes later I turned the corner and pulled up in front of our apartment—record time. I hit the brakes hard, slammed it into park, and jumped out of the car in one continuous motion.

When I opened the front door, Helen had Janet in her lap sitting on the couch rocking her back and forth, holding a blood-soaked hand towel to her head. Janet was quiet, but her eyes found me almost immediately.

"She was walking on the hearth, and her foot slipped off the edge," Helen explained.

When I pulled back the towel, I saw that it was a fairly deep cut that would need stitches. I grabbed a blanket from the back of the couch and wrapped it around Janet and cradled her in my arms. She was small and light for a four-year-old.

"It's gonna be okay," I said, looking at Helen. I could tell she was scared and a little nervous. "I'm going to take her to the emergency room. You stay here with Debbie. Okay?"

"But, Mom..." The phone rang and Helen did a teenage slump toward the phone, acting as if I had just scolded her.

"We'll be back as quick as we can," I said, walking toward the door.

"Hello... Yeah, she's here... Mom, it's Rayanne."

"Go ahead and tell her what happened and let her know I'm on my way to the hospital. I'll call her later."

I laid Janet on the seat beside me, and we drove to the hospital. She needed a few stitches but didn't have a concussion or anything serious. Initially I panicked when Helen had called me on the phone, but I calmed down after I saw that Janet was okay and after the doctor confirmed it. Helen had been wonderful with her, calming her down and doing exactly what was needed to slow the bleeding. When I got back home, I made sure Helen was okay too. I was proud of the way she handled the situation, and I made sure she knew it. As I tucked the little ones in that night, I realized how important my kids were to me. They were my life. I would have been lost without them.

As I walked back out into the front room and stood there looking at the fireplace, I realized that an apartment wasn't a good place for the kids. They didn't have any place to play. They needed a yard. Besides, I never liked apartments anyway. It seemed like there was no privacy.

The very next morning I went in search of a house and found one for rent out in Blende, on Holly Street. It was in the country, with a fenced yard, even closer to Daddy, Pearl, and Elva. It was about seven miles from our farm, so Helen would be able to go back to Pleasant View Junior High. I even stopped by Mrs. Reddinger's to see if she would watch the little ones again. This time it was exciting news when I told the girls that we would be moving again.

Once we got unpacked and settled into our new home, Frank and Elva came over for a visit. They brought a German shepherd police dog as a housewarming present. Elva said the dog had been trained as a police dog, but for some reason it didn't make the cut for the department, so Frank brought it home. Frank and Elva both thought I needed a good watchdog, and they were probably right.

"Her name is Candy," Elva announced.

They had just picked her up from the vet before they brought her over. She had just been spayed, so she was very calm—drowsy I guess. Frank brought in her dog bed and set it up alongside the food and water that he brought. He showed me where she had surgery and relayed the vet's directions for care. Candy settled into her bed and didn't move the rest of the night.

I never cared that much for dogs. In fact, I was afraid of them. When I was little, a dog bit me on the ankle while I was riding Arthur's bike. It was a big dog that bit me, so I was even more afraid of big dogs like Candy. But as I sat there looking at her sleep, it seemed to me that there was something different about Candy. She needed my care right now, and perhaps I needed her too. We developed a trust between us right away. I took care of her while she recuperated from her surgery, and after that she took care of me and the girls. She followed me around like a shadow. I even took her in the car with me. She was gentle with the little ones, and they loved her. Janet and Debbie used to squeeze her so tight I thought they might hurt her. They also climbed on her back and put sunglasses on her and played with her as if she were another little person. But if anyone came into the yard or near the house, she snarled and barked like the police dog that she was. Candy protected us and our home with conviction and without hesitation.

Tony came over one night to show us a scooter that his dad had bought him, and he couldn't get inside the gate until one of us went out to get Candy. The house was fenced in the front and on the side. There was an area in the front of the house between the fence and the street where you could park half a dozen cars. That's where I parked. I knew Frank and Elva thought I needed a watchdog because we thought Butch was messing with my car. Nonetheless, the Comet was still vulnerable because it was on the other side of the fence from Candy, and there was not much I could do about that.

One morning I got in the car to take the kids to the sitter, and I knew, again, that something was wrong with the steering. Joe Tucci, a friend of Butch's, had a garage less than two blocks away, so I stopped there. He knew exactly what had happened. He didn't sugarcoat it.

"Looks like Butch cut the power steering line," he said flatly.

I couldn't believe it. Was he trying to kill me?

"You can't drive it like this. You might as well leave it here. I'll get her fixed for ya."

I really didn't have much choice in the matter. So I walked the kids home and went back later for the car. When I came back, Joe greeted me as if he had been eagerly awaiting my arrival.

"You know I chewed that son of a bitch out. I don't know what the hell he's thinking. He coulda killed you and those babies." He finished his rant in Italian using some of the words I recognized from Butch cursing at me.

I thanked him, but before I could finish, he started ranting again.

"You know that son of a bitch denies it, though. He won't admit nothing…"

And once again, when I told my attorney, he told me that we really didn't have any proof.

I think Butch wanted me to know that he was doing these things. He wanted me to continue to feel threatened by him and to feel as if I was still under his control. He said something once that made me believe he was watching me and that when he wasn't, someone else was. I don't think he sat and watched our house, but I think he drove by quite a bit. I truly believed I was being watched and that someone kept him informed about my coming and going. He always seemed to know where I was and what I did.

One day Rayanne got this crazy notion that we should test the waters and see if people even cared about such stuff. So we went out to this club that was run by some Italian folks that knew Butch, and we waltzed in and asked if we could apply for jobs as waitresses. We didn't expect to get hired; we just wanted to see what they would do. Of course they refused to hire me. They said there would be nothing but trouble with Butch. I laughed about it with Rayanne. But it really bothered me that he had that effect on people—and by extension, me.

The fact of the matter was he could cause trouble, and he did.

On one of my days off, Bob, the GI I met in Springs, was visiting. By now we had been going out for about six months. I had invited him over for dinner. I needed something from the store, and Bob volunteered to go down to the market for me. Janet wanted to go too, so I let her. I completely trusted him with the girls, even though Helen still had issues with him.

I was shocked when several minutes later Candy started going nuts and I saw Butch parked out front in his truck with Janet squatting in the front seat crying. Butch knew better than to get out of the truck and try to bring Janet to our door because Candy would have bitten his hand off the minute he touched the gate. So he lifted her out of the truck. I was already outside coming to get her when he shut the truck door and yelled something that I could barely hear over the dog barking about "Keeping that son of a bitch away from my babies."

I calmed Janet down and asked her what happened. She told me that her dad told her not to tell me. But she was so scared that she told me everything anyway. The people in the market corroborated her story and filled in some details.

Bob and Janet had walked into the market hand in hand, and out of nowhere Butch appeared and punched Bob square in the nose. Bob's nose started bleeding profusely. The folks who worked at the market backed Butch down and urged Bob toward the exit. Janet stood there immobilized. She started crying and wet her pants before her dad whisked her away to his truck.

I found Bob at one of the bars not far from the market. He wasn't 100 percent sure who had punched him in the face until I told him. I apologized, but it really didn't do me much good. The relationship pretty much ended right there.

Everyone knew Butch was sabotaging my car, scaring off any man who might be interested in a relationship with me, and basically spying on me. There just didn't seem to be anything we could do about it.

"Bernice, you need to get out of town—for your own safety and that of your children," my attorney told me.

"I think getting out of town is a good idea if you don't want to have another nervous breakdown," Dr. Smith advised.

"Well, if you leave here, you make sure you come say good-bye before you go," Daddy said.

"I don't know who we're gonna get to clean Daddy's house if you leave," Pearl worried.

"You know I'll come see you wherever you are," CE promised.

"I know someone who is a professional packer. You get the U-Haul, and we'll help you pack," Elva said.

"I want out of here too," Helen Plant told me. "How about if I go with you?"

I had to get away from him. I was beginning to realize that I could never completely trust Butch again. But until the divorce was final,

I had to be available for court. So when my attorney told me that we would have to play dirty to get the divorce finalized, I didn't feel bad about it one bit. Besides, my attorney did all the dirty work. Somehow he talked Butch's attorney into withholding the court date for the final hearing from Butch. If Butch didn't know the date, he wouldn't show up, and the judge would sign the papers. That same day I could leave town freely. At least, that was the plan.

21

The courtroom was empty except for me, my attorney, and the judge. They pulled it off. Butch didn't know the court date, so he didn't show up to contest the divorce, and the final decree was granted on the grounds of mental and physical cruelty.

I gave notice at work immediately and decided to cash out my pension. After fourteen years at the hospital I would have enough to start over and be comfortable doing it. Little did I know that getting my pension cashed out was going to take a few weeks. So I headed down to Minnequa Bank and applied for a loan. This way I could go ahead with my plans and not have to wait for the pension money. Once the money situation was straightened out, I met up with Elva's friend and took a crash course in how to pack a U-Haul. I had moved enough in my life already that packing wasn't anything new to me. But he was a professional packer who knew a few tricks for making the most of every available space. Every box was tightly filled. The washer and dryer were loaded into the trailer and then they were stuffed with toys, pillows, and odds and ends. Every drawer was filled; every nook and cranny of that U-Haul trailer was occupied. We didn't have to leave one thing behind.

I laid the backseat of the station wagon down and covered it with pillows and blankets for the kids and Candy. I had a cooler on the floor behind the seat with sandwich makings, snacks, and enough room left on top to add a bucket of Kentucky Fried Chicken if we had the opportunity. The thermoses were handy—ready to be filled with hot coffee and ice-cold lemonade right before we left. The little yellow, plastic potty-chair that we had used to potty train the girls was tucked away on the floor behind the seat on the other side in case Janet or Debbie needed to go potty and couldn't wait for me to find a rest stop.

I felt ready, but I had agreed to wait for my friend Helen Plant and her sister Kathy. So the kids and I settled in at Elva's house to wait. It was nice that the kids could spend some time with their cousins before we left, and Helen had a girlfriend that lived across the street that she got to spend time with as well.

Two days before our scheduled departure, I stood alone in Elva's living room. Elva had left to go visit Frank in the hospital. He had injured his leg on the job. The kids were playing outside, getting that last little adventure in before it got dark and I called them in. Frank and Elva lived on Brookfield Street among a series of one-story stucco houses with lawns sprinkled with an occasional bicycle or odd toy. I gazed out the picture window to see my light-blue Comet station wagon with the bright-orange U-Haul trailer attached. It looked so out of place parked next to a sidewalk decorated with a hopscotch pattern and a tricycle.

I was a little antsy. I wanted to start a new life. I saw new possibilities and felt as though the future would be so much better than the past. I poured another cup of coffee, lit a cigarette, and sat down at the dining room table to study the map and verify the directions I had written down to get from Pueblo to Randle, Washington.

The sound of the doorbell chiming jolted me back to my current location. I suspected the kids were playing with it. When I opened the door, I was surprised to see a young man on the other side of the screen that I didn't recognize. His face was pimply, but he was dressed nice and would have looked well groomed in his suit jacket and a crisply pressed white shirt if his hair wasn't dangling down past his collar.

"Hello, ma'am." He gave me a friendly smile but didn't wait for a reply. "Does Frank Bensik live here?"

"Yes, but he's not here right now. I'm his sister-in-law. Can I help you?"

"Yes, are you Bernice Thomas?"

I nodded, wondering how he knew my name.

"Well, I have this…" He held an envelope up and pointed it at me. When I opened the screen door and took it, his demeanor suddenly changed. His tone was brusque. "You've been served," he said as he turned and walked away.

Looking down at the envelope, I released the screen door and listened to it sigh before clicking shut. For a long quiet moment I didn't breathe. The envelope reminded me of the familiar paperwork that I had been receiving from the Pueblo County Courthouse regarding my divorce. My hand started to tremble. "What now?" I asked myself. I forced myself to open the envelope. Inside was a court order that stated that I couldn't leave Pueblo County with my three minor daughters.

I stood there shaking my head. How could he have found out I was leaving? My nerves went into overdrive, and my thoughts raced. By now he had to know that the divorce went through. He was probably furious and had come looking for me. He probably watched as we packed the U-Haul. My cigarette had smoldered to a long line of ashes, so I grabbed another and lit it as I paced the front room, not focusing on anything but the thoughts in my head. What was I supposed to do now?

"I'll be damned if he's going to continue to control me!" I told myself as I picked up the phone and dialed Helen Plant's number.

"Helen, hi, it's Bernice."

"Hi. I was just going to call you. Are you ready?" she said excitedly.

"I just got served with papers that say I can't leave Pueblo County with the girls."

"What?"

"I can't wait until tomorrow night to leave. I'm leaving first thing in the morning. Daddy's gonna be here at seven to say good-bye, and as soon as he leaves, I'm leaving."

"I'm still packing. I don't know if I can be ready by morning."

"I'll meet you in Cheyenne, Wyoming. There's a rest area just past the state line. We'll wait for you there. I can't wait around and see what he pulls next. I've gotta get out of here."

"What happens if they catch you leaving?"

"I don't know... I just hope I don't have to find out."

I tried to get ahold of my attorney but had no luck. After the kids were asleep, Elva helped me gather up all our stuff so we would be ready first thing in the morning. I barely slept. During the wee hours of the morning I drank coffee with Elva and Daddy and said my good-byes. We carried the girls out and laid them in the back of the station wagon, and Helen and Candy crawled in next to them and went back to sleep. I was on the road by six in the morning.

I was scared stiff. I gripped the wheel tightly and kept my eyes peeled for cops. I just wanted to hurry up and get out of Colorado. But I did the speed limit—no slower and no faster, which was seventy or eighty miles per hour depending on where we were on the freeway. I didn't turn on the radio, because the kids were sleeping. I just drove in the tense silent dawn, alone with my thoughts, fears, and hopes.

We made it to Denver in an hour and a half. Debbie was the first to stir, and she came up behind me and put her arms around my neck to give me a good-morning hug and then another. I felt the tension in my jaw slacken as I smiled at her through the rearview mirror. I told her, "Good morning. Mommy's driving now. Sit back please." She turned and sat down hard on her bottom in disappointment. Her sleeping sisters and Candy were all that were left for her, so she engaged them with good-morning hugs and kisses, and it wasn't long until she had hugged and kissed everyone awake, including Candy. Helen crawled over the seat and sat up front with me. Before long she was crawling back and forth to help one of the girls go potty or get a drink. She basically took care of the girls while I drove. I had to focus on making sure we didn't get pulled over before we got out of Colorado, and I had to act like I wasn't a nervous wreck so that the girls wouldn't be scared.

Within three hours we were out of Colorado, and I let the tension go.

When we hit Cheyenne, Wyoming, I easily found the rest area and knew instantly that Helen Plant wouldn't have any trouble finding us. There were a couple of fast-food restaurants just off the exit, so we stopped for breakfast. Then we drove on to the rest area, which was really more like a park. There was a play area with swings, a slide, and picnic tables. So we just parked and waited. The kids ran around and played. At lunchtime we got out the cooler, made some sandwiches, and had a picnic. With the worst behind us I could tell this wasn't going to be a bad trip.

When Helen Plant drove up in her big blue Mercury, we gathered up our stuff and took off again. We stopped at another rest area that night and slept in our cars. The next day we were in Washington. When we pulled off for gas near Randle, Helen Plant started questioning my directions because it felt as if we had been driving such a long time. I'm sure we were all just getting tired.

It wasn't long after that we drove into my sister Sarah's driveway in Randle, where we rested for the night before heading to Tacoma the next morning. Sarah helped us find a place to rent not too far from Fort Lewis and showed us around. Once settled in, it was easy for me to find a job at a local nursing home. It wasn't exactly what I wanted, so within two months I found something that I thought I was more suited for, working at Western State Hospital.

I was excited to go to work at the hospital, but I was also quickly disappointed. They didn't have psych techs at Western State or any nurses who were trained for mental-health care. It was like a step back in time to when I first started at Colorado State Hospital. They didn't evaluate the patients; provide follow-up care; or try to get patients out, rehabilitated, and back out into the community. The facility was run so differently. They didn't take the patients on outings. They didn't have bowling and swimming on the grounds. They didn't even have a basic group meeting with the patients to let them express themselves so we (the caregivers) knew what kinds of things bothered them that we could adjust in the ward or activities they might be interested in that could make their stay more enjoyable. It was such a disappointment after going through so many changes and advancements in Colorado. But I needed a job, so I stuck it out in hopes that I might see that improvement sometime down the line.

Unfortunately, that summer Helen had an emergency appendectomy that set me back a little financially. Then, Helen Plant decided to up and leave without telling me. I just came home one day, and she and her sister Kathy were gone. No note, no nothing. Just packed their clothes, raided the fridge, and left. So I was forced to find a cheaper, smaller place. The upside was that I found a place that was about a block from a grade school where Janet could start kindergarten.

I worked the graveyard shift at Western State and then got a job waiting tables at a local restaurant a couple of nights a week to make ends meet. Debbie stayed home with me during the day while Janet and Helen went to school. Helen didn't complain about going to another new school. She always did real well in school—always had good grades. I gave her my tips for babysitting the girls a couple of nights a week while I worked at the restaurant. She bought me my first set of china with the money she earned. It was a set that had light-green-and-yellow pattern around the edges—a complete set, service for eight. She was such a good girl. I'm not sure what I would have done without her.

I tried to do fun things with the girls as much as we could. We found this private club that held family dances with live country music, and the girls and I would go out dancing. It was only a dollar for the entire family. There was no alcohol in the club, although some people drank outside. I wasn't drinking much. I had also gotten off the Ritalin and Valium. When I left Pueblo, Dr. Smith gave me something other than Valium to keep me calm. It didn't have the side effects Valium had. I don't remember what it was, but the doctor in Washington had never heard of it, so I wasn't able to renew the prescription. I didn't feel as if I needed to either. I felt much calmer now.

Even though we had moved away from the majority of our family, Sarah and her daughters lived near and came to visit quite a bit. We went to visit them too. Then CE and his little brother Sammy, who was twenty-one and had just bought his first car, came up to visit from Pueblo and ended up staying with us. They helped out with anything we needed help with around the house. They both enjoyed drinking a few beers and having fun. I would have a beer with them and laugh and be silly. Every time we had a few beers in us, Sammy would break out singing.

> They're gonna put me in the movies.
> They're gonna make a big star out of me.
> I'll play the part about a man who's sad and lonely,
> And all I gotta do is act naturally.

Everybody else would join in and sing with him. Sometimes he'd pick up one of the kids and make them dance with him. About four months into their stay CE met a gal and moved in with her, and Sammy went back to Colorado. We still stayed close, regardless of the distance between us.

It was hard supporting three kids on my own, so I decided to get in touch with my attorney to see if I could get child support again. That wasn't going to happen as long as I lived out of the state. I think I was told that the only way to get child support was to come back to Colorado and fight it out in court, because Butch wasn't going to pay if he couldn't see the kids.

It was frustrating. We had food on the table and a roof over our heads, but we were barely getting by. I just wasn't making it on my income. The attorney said I had to come back to Colorado; he didn't say I had to come back to Pueblo. Maybe I could keep my distance from Butch, keep myself safe, and get some child support for the kids. I had to at least try.

So after school was out for the year, I told the kids we were moving back to Colorado, and I told Helen she could pick where we lived, as long as it was in Colorado and wasn't Pueblo. I think we opened the Atlas to the two-page spread for Colorado, Helen closed her eyes, and tapped a pointed finger on Grand Junction. And so it was.

Before we headed back, I decided to put a happy ending on our adventure to Washington. I used my tips to save up what I could for the trip back. I was pretty confident that we had it covered as long as nothing went wrong. So I splurged and took the kids on a mini-vacation to Canada, where we stayed at a bed-and-breakfast, did some sightseeing, had breakfast there, and let them wait on us—it was a treat.

Then I put my U-Haul packing skills to the test. I rented the same size trailer as we used to get to Washington. But we had accumulated more furniture, and I'm not sure what else. The U-Haul was packed as full as I could get it. The back of the Comet tilted toward the ground, and Sarah's husband, Alden, warned us that we would never make it. But we did. Elva had a friend in Grand Junction and had us all set up with a place to live before we even got there. My sisters, bless their hearts, were nothing short of a true blessing in my life.

22

The whole reason I came back to Colorado was to get child support, which also meant I had to let Butch have visitation. I still didn't trust him, but I did what I felt I had to do. I called my attorney and let him know I was back. He said he would let me know when they had a court date. I also called Tony and told him where we were so we could set up a time to see each other.

We spent the first week getting unpacked. Then I took out the Grand Junction phone book and looked up nursing homes to start a job search. For my first stop I parked on the street in front of a series of long, one-story brick buildings, skirted with manicured lawns and shrubbery. Beside the entrance a large sign announced the nursing home as Teller Arms. When I entered the building, the entryway reflected light off shiny, white floors, and wide hallways led in either direction. I found the office of the administrator around the corner from the main entryway, walked in, and asked if they were accepting applications. The woman at the desk wore no makeup and dressed conservatively, not businesslike but not casual either. She looked as if she belonged behind her desk—it just fit her well. She was very friendly, as if she enjoyed the job she was doing. She took my application and asked me to wait a few minutes while the administrator reviewed it. The administrator just happened to be her husband, Mr. Shoeman. He checked my references and, finding everything in good standing, came out and asked me a few questions. He wore a gray suit with a plain tie. His initial approach to questioning me was very businesslike, and then he became more talkative and friendly. He introduced me to his wife, and we talked on a more personal level. It didn't bother me as much as I thought it would to tell him I was divorced. Divorce was quickly becoming more widespread than I ever thought it would be. I also told him that I had three kids at home and had just moved to town. The next thing I knew he asked me when I could start. We worked out a start date, and they gave me a tour of the facilities. There were three wings—I would work all three of them. I was beginning to realize that finding a job as a nurse was easy, no matter where I decided to settle down.

On my first days off I went to Pueblo to see Tony. I also wanted to check up on Daddy to see how he was doing, so I had Tony meet me there. A year makes a lot of difference in kids. Tony drove up on his motorcycle, sporting a pompadour haircut. He looked and acted more grown up than I had remembered him. But he was still my little boy, and I did not refrain from giving him a hug and a kiss. We visited for a while, and I told him about our trip to the beach to see the ocean and about how I wanted to bring him back a live crab but Helen had a fit because she was scared to death of it. He seemed to get a kick out of that. We had a good visit, and he spent a lot of time playing with Janet and Debbie.

I had given Daddy $1,000 when I left Pueblo and asked him to keep it for Tony. I told Tony to call his grandpa if he decided he wanted to join us in Washington. Tony didn't know about the money, and he never called his grandpa to ask about coming to Washington, so Daddy gave the money back to me. I quickly tucked it away in my bank account and planned to use it as a down payment on a house.

Less than a month after our visit to Pueblo, Tony showed up on my doorstep in Grand Junction—a strapping seventeen-year-old on a motorcycle ready to take on the world. First stop, Mom's house. I was glad to see him but learned that he had dropped out of high school and had run away from his dad's house.

"You need to call your dad and tell him where you're at" was my first advice.

"I'm not calling him," he said, turning away.

"Why not? What happened?"

"It's the same as it's always been Mom. I'm not going back there."

I didn't want to push him into leaving my house too. He was obviously distraught, but I couldn't get him to talk about it. So I fed him some dinner, fixed him a place to sleep, and let it go for the night. The next morning I insisted he call his dad. From just listening to Tony's side of the conversation, I could tell it didn't go well. Tony didn't say much after he told his dad where he was. His posture changed, and he started looking down and nervously kicking the ground as he mumbled a few words here and there. When he got off the phone, he told me that his dad threatened to kill himself if Tony didn't come back home. That was a lot of weight for a young man to bear, and I think Tony believed his dad would do it. I tried to talk to him about it. I tried to make him understand that it was an idle threat. Tony knew he was welcome to stay with us, but as the week passed, I could see it eating at him. He hopped on his motorcycle and headed back to Pueblo. Butch's threat worked, and unfortunately for Tony, it wouldn't be the last time he would use it.

Our court date, to work out support and visitation, came quickly. It was summer, so Butch would get to spend one month with the girls. I had to agree to bring the girls to Pueblo. I didn't really want to see Butch, so I arranged for Frank and Elva to keep the girls at their house and let Butch pick them up from there.

During the month the girls were gone I tried to keep myself busy around the house if I wasn't at work. I had Candy, so I was never alone, and I checked on the girls regularly. Butch came to see them a total of three times during the entire month, without ever taking them to his house. It irked me a little to think that he cared so little about spending time with his kids. But mostly, I was okay with it. I had never seen him raise a hand toward the girls, but all the same, it eased my mind to know that they spent most of their time at Frank and Elva's playing with their cousins.

Eventually, I found a house to buy. The address, 1111 Ute Avenue, was on a busy one-way street not too far from a grade school. There were two bedrooms, a small front yard, and a huge backyard with gravel that opened up onto an alley. It would be low maintenance, and it was in my price range, I think around $20,000. I put $500 down and moved in. The three girls shared a room. Janet and Debbie had bunk beds. But the kids quite often came in and slept with me; even Helen did once in a while. And of course Candy was right there beside my bed every night.

Debbie wasn't in school yet, so I got her set up with a sitter. I put Janet in school at St. Joseph's, and Helen went to the public high school.

A few months after school started, I got a collect call from Tony.

"Mom, my motorcycle broke down."

"Where are you?"

"I'm in LA, and I don't have any money to get it fixed."

"Good God, Tony, what are you doing in LA?"

"I had to get out of there, Mom. I couldn't take it anymore."

"Does your dad know where you are?"

"No. And I don't want him to know."

I knew Butch had some relatives in California, but it took me a few minutes to realize that my brother Aubrey (who now went by the name of Scott) and his wife, Renee, also lived somewhere in California. "Let me make a few phone calls. Where can I reach you?"

After making a few phone calls I finally got Scott and Renee's number. They lived in Riverside, which wasn't far from LA. I hadn't talked to Scott since Mama died—six years ago. Nonetheless, my brother didn't hesitate to go get Tony and take him home with him.

Tony had been gone from his dad's house for three days, and Butch hadn't bothered to call me to tell me that he had run away again. So I called him, and I chewed him up one side and down the other.

"Do you know where your son is?" I didn't wait for an answer. "He's in California. His motorcycle is broken down, and he's stranded. Thank God he called me. Why in the hell didn't you call me when he left there? Don't you think I have a right to know when he runs away or is missing? You should have called me. After three days you should have called the police. What if something had happened to him? What were you planning to do? Anything? You should have the common decency to at least call me when my son runs away."

I didn't even say good-bye. I just said my piece and hung up.

I called the next day to talk to Scott and Tony. Things seemed to be going well. It sounded as if Tony had opened up a little to Scott, and they were talking. Scott thought it might be best if Tony didn't go back to Butch's house, at least not right away. He didn't have much trouble convincing me, but I had to tell him about how Butch threatened Tony the last time he ran away. We decided that I should tell Butch rather than having Tony call. This time when I called Butch I was a little more civil. It took a lot of talking because once Butch found out where he was, he wanted to send the police out to pick him up and bring him back.

"Look, this is the second time he's run away, and he will do it again. If you force him to come back, the next time he probably won't tell anybody where he's at. At least he's with family, and we know he's safe."

He finally agreed.

So things settled down a little. I settled into work, Helen and Janet settled into school, and Debbie was doing well with the new sitter. We had a routine started and some normalcy in our lives.

Then suddenly, and sadly, a dear member of our family left us. It started out just like any other day. But this day, when the girls and I left the house to run some errands, we left Candy at home. She was normally always by my side. She followed me around, and we usually took her with us in the car—but not this day.

After leaving the house I realized I had forgotten something and turned around and went back. Traffic was heavy, so I couldn't get into the left lane on our one-way street to turn into the driveway. I parked the car across the street, and Helen ran in to get whatever it was that I had forgotten. As soon as she opened the front door of the house, Candy bolted out and headed for the car. I yelled and Helen yelled at her, but she didn't stop on her own. A passing car stopped her. I barely noticed the oncoming traffic as I jumped from the car and went to her. She was lying very still. There was no blood, and she was breathing. I thought she might be all right. But she wouldn't get up, so I picked her up and put her in the back of the station wagon. Helen and the girls cried all the way to the vet's. Candy was bleeding to death—internally. There was nothing the vet could do for her, except put her down.

Candy just wanted to be by my side. That's all she ever wanted. She was a damn good dog. I trusted her with the kids, and she was our protector. I remember one time when we were in Washington and I was at work, Helen called and told me she was hearing noises outside the house. I called the police to have them go check it out. They called me back when they got to the house and told me that Candy wouldn't let them anywhere near the house and that I had nothing to worry about—the kids were safe. But now, she was gone.

I knew we would all miss her, but I stayed strong for the girls. My training at the state hospital was ingrained in me. There was no need to break down emotionally in front of others, especially my kids. A good nurse didn't show her emotions, and as much as I loved that dog, I didn't show mine. Life had to go on. And it did.

Between work and taking care of the kids, my time was pretty occupied. Teller Arms was a great place to work. The nurses and administration were friendly and easygoing. The only thing that was a little unusual for me was the religious restriction they had on pork. I think they were Seventh Day Adventists, if I remember right. Pork wasn't served there, and they frowned on you even bringing it into the facility. They were very strict about it. But they weren't strictly one denomination. They had various church services for the residents.

Other than the pork thing, they were pretty relaxed. If I didn't have a babysitter, they had no problem with me bringing the little girls in with me for a shift. The patients loved it. The girls made fast friends with one of the residents. He was about my age, with jet-black hair slicked back and long sideburns that framed a slender face. He had lived a normal life until an accident with heavy machinery on a construction site left him a quadriplegic. He could move his arms a little at the shoulders, just enough to move the wheels on the wheelchair. He wore braces on his hands to eat because he couldn't move his fingers much. Basically, he was paralyzed from the neck down. He would watch the girls for me when I brought them in, and in return, I would take him home for dinner every once in a while. He loved my spaghetti. The girls would dance around and sing, "Joe Connetti loves spaghetti." He especially liked it with spare ribs in it. Every once in a while I would sneak some in to him, keeping it in my dishes and not advertising that there was pork on the premises.

I hadn't been working there long before I discovered that the state was offering to pay college tuition for waivered LPNs to get a state nursing license. I had heard for years that they might outlaw waivered LPNs and make everyone take nursing training and pass state exams to be a licensed nurse, so I jumped at the opportunity to get on board. The classes I needed were offered at Mesa College. The state paid for the classes and even paid us to take the class. We were supposed to work sixteen hours a week, and the state made up the difference so that we got a full forty-hour week on our paychecks. But Teller Arms was short on nurses, so I always worked more than sixteen hours a week. We just never let the state know about it. It was a year-long course. I found it pretty easy because a lot of it was a repeat of what I already learned in psych tech nurses' training at the state hospital. I finished up with straight As, made the dean's list, and got my licensed renewed so that it didn't say "waivered" anymore. I kept the same license number, but the license now read "Graduate LPN."

Tony had been living with Scott and Rene all this time, and I had stopped receiving distressed phone calls from him. Instead, I received a phone call from him one day about him wanting to join the marines. While he lived with Scott and Rene, he worked construction with Scott building swimming pools. They hit it off better than I ever expected. I think Tony was way better off there than he was with his dad. Tony always spoke highly of Scott. He respected Scott and looked up to him. I think Scott influenced him to join the marines, and I gave him my blessing.

Basic training lasted about three months, and of course, Tony wanted us to come down when he graduated—all of us, including Butch. Unfortunately, Butch wanted to come to Junction and drive to California with us. We hadn't talked much in the past couple of years. After Tony moved in with Scott, we had a couple of civil conversations about visitation mostly. Call me crazy, but I agreed to letting him join us for the trip, on the condition that he pay for half the gas.

We were both proud of Tony, and having that in common actually created friendliness between us. We were both focused on celebrating an achievement in our son's life. The ceremony was like nothing I had ever seen before. They marched in and did a demonstration with guns, and then a speaker addressed the crowd and the graduates. There were so many graduating marines that I couldn't really see Tony among them. After the ceremony, we finally found him. He looked and acted so different. As soon as he saw us, he removed a white hat with a shiny black bill from his head with a white-gloved hand, and the serious look on his face broke away as he smiled. He had an unforgettable smile with beautiful, straight white teeth. I always saw a little mischief curled into the corners of his smile. His hair was so short there was barely any there, which was a big change from the Elvis Presley hairdo he used to have. He didn't look as skinny as before, and his attitude was more respectful.

When we met up, we headed out to the huge, flat parking lot where the Comet sat among hundreds of other cars. The girls were having a great time. One of the patients at Teller Arms made them matching dresses, and they looked so cute. I wore one of my Beeline suits and a red wig. Butch wore a suit jacket, white shirt, and slacks. We were quite the sight after the graduation, all dressed up standing in the parking lot at the back of the station wagon eating cold chicken and potato salad from a packed cooler. I kicked my heels off, felt the warm pavement on my feet, and relaxed with my family.

After the graduation ceremony we went back to Scott and Rene's house. They invited us to postpone our trip home for a couple of days and visit. Scott and Butch seemed to get along well. But I'm pretty sure Butch put a bug in Scott's ear and told him he never wanted a divorce and wanted his family back. The next afternoon, the four of us were sitting in Scott's living room having a drink, and Scott started trying to convince me that Butch and I were a good-looking couple. He asked why we didn't get married again. Butch was all for it. I wasn't. Rene didn't say much. Scott didn't know anything about the way Butch had treated me while we were married or about the beating, and I didn't take advantage of the opportunity and tell him. Maybe I didn't want to ruin the nice time we were having together as a family by bringing all that up. I just told him I didn't think it was a good idea.

A few drinks later, I found myself warming up to Butch. Both men started putting some pressure on me to get my family back together. They ushered me and Renee downtown and conveniently drove by the justice of the peace. Butch urged Scott to pull over so we could go in. I felt myself submitting to the pressure. I know my reluctance was evident to Butch and Scott because they rushed us through the process of getting a license. Still, to this day, I have no idea why I let them talk me into remarrying him. I think I do things sometimes without thinking it through. I have no idea what I was thinking at the time.

Tony's graduation from boot camp, with
Scott, Renee, Butch, Tony, and me

23

Butch wanted to live in Pueblo, and I wanted to stay in Grand Junction. I don't think he liked my house on Ute, because he contacted a real estate agent in Junction and bought a house across town that was big enough for all of us. It had three bedrooms, a bathroom, kitchen, dining room, and living room upstairs and two bedrooms, a full kitchen, and living room downstairs. I loved all the room we had. It was perched on a hill on Lilac Lane, with a long driveway and front lawn that went from the corner halfway up the block before you hit the front porch.

Lilac Lane sounded like such a pleasant place to live. I love lilacs—the delicate fragrance, the soft violet puffs of petals, and the heart-shaped green leaves. But I don't remember any lilacs in that giant yard or on the lane.

I rented out my house on Ute. Butch went back to Pueblo while the girls and I moved into the new house. I'm not sure if I told the kids that we got remarried or not. I think they just thought their dad was visiting because he was only home for about two or three days a month.

His short visits worked for me, but I started having some health problems, and my doctor wanted to do surgery. I asked Butch to stay and take care of the girls for a couple of weeks while I was in the hospital. He agreed to stay, so I agreed to have the surgery. I needed A and P repair, a common surgery for a fallen uterus.

While I was in the hospital, recovering from surgery, Butch called.

"Hey, Red, I've gotta go back to Pueblo tonight."

"I thought you were going to stay at least until I got home."

"I have some things I need to take care of."

"But you told me that you would stay with the girls."

"Ah, they'll be fine. They don't need me."

There was nothing I could do to make him stay.

The next day Helen called.

"Mom..." she sobbed into the phone.

"Helen? What's wrong?" I tried to sit up a little in my hospital bed but couldn't.

"I wrecked the car."

"Are you all right?" I wasn't concerned about the car as much as I was about her. The Comet had already been through hell, and I knew it was a tough little car. But Helen sounded so shaken up.

"Yeah, but the car is smashed in on the side," she said between sobs.

"Were the girls with you? Are they all right?"

"They're okay... We're all okay." She slowed down just a little.

"It's okay." I breathed a little sigh of relief. "Where are you?"

"The lady that hit me... but it's not her fault. I turned in front of her. She's the nurse at my school. I'm at her house."

Junction was a relatively small town. I was glad she was with someone she knew. I reassured her that I wasn't concerned about the car and told her to come up to the hospital so that I could see her and the girls and make sure they were okay. There was only minor damage to the Comet. It was still drivable. But I didn't want the girls to be alone at home until Helen settled down. When Helen got there, we got a phonebook and called the insurance company to arrange to get estimates and repairs. They stayed for quite a while, until Janet and Debbie got restless and tired.

It was my second ten-day stay in a hospital, but I was a lot more lucid this time. I lay there in my hospital bed and seethed. I was mad at Butch for not keeping his end of the bargain and being there for me and the girls when we needed him. I don't know why I ever thought he would be.

On my first morning home after surgery, I woke up and tried to get out of bed to walk to the bathroom and couldn't move my legs forward to walk. I found that I could move my legs backward, and I had to pee, so I walked backward to the bathroom and then immediately got to the phone to call the doctor. He told me to take some more pain medicine and go back to bed. I don't know what the problem was, but when I woke up the next time, I could walk, slowly. That was the strangest thing—having to walk backward. But it wasn't my biggest hurdle.

Debbie wasn't in school yet, and rather than taking her to the sitters, I spent the day taking care of her as much as resting. Plus, I ran Helen and Janet back and forth to school. Between the surgery and the meds, I really wasn't feeling well yet. I ended up getting into a fender bender on one of my trips to pick up Janet. My little Comet station wagon was taking a beating. I felt like I had gotten one too. This was one time I have to admit that it was truly hard being a single mother—and I wasn't even single at the time!

I mustered up some strength from somewhere inside me and made it through. But the easygoing feeling of living alone that I had felt for the past year or two was gone. I was angry again and on edge. The stress was back. Butch and I didn't think of being a family in the same way. I felt that family was there for you. He supported us by providing the house that we lived in. But he just wasn't there for us.

After recuperating from surgery I went back to work. I loved working at Teller Arms, but a nurse I knew went to work at the VA hospital in town and told me how great the benefits were. They had

Federal Blue Cross, which covered just about everything. Helen needed braces, so I decided to see if I could get hired there and take advantage of the benefits.

It wasn't a bad place to work, but I preferred Teller Arms. The hospital was more clinical. The nursing home was clinical in a way, but there was more care for the patient as a person. That was what I was drawn to. I realized that I had gotten pretty attached to the people I worked with at the nursing home, as well as the patients.

After about four months, I left the VA hospital and returned to Teller Arms. I just didn't like working at the hospital. I think I was getting restless again. I didn't appreciate my marriage. I wanted to relax and enjoy my life and my kids, as well as my job. I didn't mind working hard, but I just wasn't at ease with things.

Then one day out of the blue, I got a phone call from a patient that I cared for at the VA hospital.

"Mom, it's for you," Helen said.

"Who is it?"

"I don't know, some guy," Helen retorted with typical teenage sarcasm.

"Hello."

"Hello, Bernice. I don't know if you remember this old guy from the VA hospital that fell off his barstool and broke his leg…"

I remembered him well. He always had saltwater taffy and always offered me some. He was a little flirtatious too. At the time he was just another patient to me, and I assumed he flirted and shared his candy with all the nurses. His name was Alvin Drake, but he asked to be called Al.

"Al?"

"You do remember. I conned one of the nurses into giving me your phone number. I hope you don't mind?"

He was still a patient there when I left the hospital. "No," I heard myself say.

"Well… how are you? Where did you run off to?"

"Oh, I changed jobs. I went back to the nursing home I was working at before. How are you doing?"

"I'm good. The leg is still casted, and I'm on crutches, but they sprang me. So I'm getting around. I was wondering if you would like to come down and have a drink with me. I'm here in town at a lounge down on Twelfth Street."

I'm not sure what came over me, but I agreed to meet him for a drink. I knew I was married, but I didn't feel like I was. Butch was gone more than he was home, and Al was kind and friendly and easy to talk to, so I allowed myself the chance to get out and relax a little.

He was tall, handsome, and unmistakable, sitting at a table in the lounge with his crutches propped on the chair next to him. When he saw me, a smile came over him, and I couldn't restrain one in return. We had a couple of beers and got to know each other a little. We both liked camping, the outdoors, and being a little adventurous. He liked to tell stories, and he made me laugh. I had almost forgotten what it was like to laugh out loud. He was genuinely interested in me and obviously attracted to me, and I simply enjoyed his company.

He lived in Green River, Utah, but from then on, every time he was in town he called me, and we got together. I told him that I was married but not living with my husband. He didn't seem to mind. He still wanted to see me. Eventually I invited him over to the house so that we didn't have to go meet in a bar somewhere. This went on for a while. Then one night I invited him to spend the night so he didn't have to go find a hotel room. We were getting closer, but I didn't feel right having sex with him. Fortunately, I was able to talk to him about it—we talked about just about everything. He understood. He slept on the outside of the covers, and I slept on the inside of the covers, but even that bothered me because I was still married. I was having feelings for another man.

The next time Butch called to tell me he was coming home for the weekend, I decided that when he got here, I was going to tell him that I wanted a divorce. Coincidently, Al was planning on being in town that same weekend. So it was definitely time to make a decision about the man I wanted in my life.

When I told Butch I wanted a divorce, he threatened me, of course. Helen says she remembers him holding a knife to my throat. But to tell you the truth, I don't remember that. I was deathly afraid of knives, and Butch knew it. When we lived on the farm in Pueblo, I would hide all the knives at night before I went to bed. I didn't do that in our house on Lilac Lane—maybe I should have. If he actually did hold a knife to my throat, it was probably so traumatic for me that I blocked it out of my memory. But I do remember fleeing from the house with the girls and going to a motel until he left town. I also remember calling Al and telling him what I did and telling him where we were.

Butch didn't fight me on the divorce. I moved out, filed for divorce, and got the final papers within ninety days. It was so much easier than the first time—I didn't even need to have a reason to get a divorce; they were handing them out like candy.

The next thing I knew, Daddy told me that he read in the *Pueblo Chieftain* that Butch was remarried.

It's funny—that didn't bother me a bit. It made me think that things would be okay and that maybe things were going to start going my way finally. Whether the lilacs were there or not, the faint scent of them seemed to be in the air.

24

The first time Al called me was in the fall of 1970. Before Christmas came that year I moved out of Butch's house on Lilac Lane. I still owned my house on Ute and planned to move back in there. The problem was that I had rented it to a friend from work and didn't want to just kick her out. So I gave her time to find another place to live and rented a small apartment a block or two from my house while I waited.

Helen was in her senior year of high school, and she would be eighteen in January. We were always fairly close, but now she wouldn't talk to me. I think it was because I was moving again and leaving her dad, but it could have also been because I was seeing Al. She didn't want to have anything to do with him; she wasn't even civil to him.

She always thought highly of her dad. We definitely couldn't talk about him without it turning into an argument. One day she asked me something about him. I don't recall what it was, but I remember that I didn't want to argue about it. I told her to call him and ask him about it. He wouldn't take a collect call from her. I thought that might give her some indication about his nature, but for some reason, she sided with her dad. She was being a typical teenager with strong opinions about how things should be, and I think she was trying to assert herself and become an adult.

Butch and I couldn't have a decent conversation about what was going on with her. He told me that Helen wanted to stay in the house on Lilac Lane when I moved. Butch never really lived there; he only visited. So I knew she wouldn't be living with him; she would be on her own. Sometimes, when kids are that age, you just have to deal with what they want. So that's what I tried to do. Mama and Daddy let me move out when I was sixteen. I got my own apartment and a job. I know things are different now, but years ago there was nothing wrong with kids moving out and living alone before they were eighteen. Now, a teenager can blame their parents for so many things that just weren't heard of back then. I suppose, at the time, I didn't see anything wrong with her being on her own at her age. Maybe it was because of the way I was raised. My brothers and sisters and I had all moved out of our parents' house before we were eighteen.

Between me checking in on her, Butch's visits, and the real estate lady occasionally showing the house, I thought she would be okay by herself. She was a straight-A student and a member of the honor society and would be graduating in a little more than six months. I trusted her. She didn't date much. Al tried once to get her tied up with Dennis, his nephew, but she wouldn't have anything to do with him. For the most part Helen hung out with a few girlfriends and basically stayed out of trouble. I don't think she was into pot like a lot of the kids her age who were turning into hippies.

Then one day I got a phone call that made me question my initial instincts.

"Bernice, this is Judy Butler."

Why is the real estate lady calling me? I wondered.

"I'm calling to let you know that Helen had a bunch of kids at the house partying last night when I went there to show the house," she said.

"Oh, well, thanks for letting me know. I'll talk to her."

"I need to be able to keep the house in order until I get it sold. I talked to Butch, and Helen can stay with me until she finds her own apartment."

"Well, I don't know about that. I'll talk to Butch and Helen about it, and we'll see."

"If you want to talk to Helen, you can call her here."

That struck a nerve. I felt as if this woman thought she had some control when it came to Helen. "Of course I want to talk to her. Put her on the phone."

"She's not here right now. But I'll tell her to give you a call."

The gall of that woman… Why hadn't Butch called me instead?

I tried to get ahold of Butch but couldn't, so I headed straight over to the house to assess the situation. Helen wasn't there. The downstairs was kind of a mess, but it didn't look like a house that had been partied in. There were dirty clothes on the floor, the beds weren't made, and there were dirty dishes in the sink. But I didn't find any alcohol bottles or evidence of pot—really no signs of a party in my opinion. I didn't accuse anyone of lying about what had happened, but I seriously wondered if there really was a party there.

Judy lived out toward Clifton, not in Grand Junction. I didn't have any interest in going to that woman's house, but I did want to talk to Helen. Every time I called Judy's number, I was told that Helen would have to call me back. With a teenager, you worry and wonder what's going on. I wasn't getting much information from Judy, just basic, nonresponsive answers. "She's not here right now… Yes, she's doing fine… I can't make her call you back, but I'll tell her you called."

Judy had sold us the house on Lilac Lane when Butch and I remarried, and now she was taking care of the sale while we were getting a divorce. I wondered if she and Butch were having an affair, but I didn't know. I don't know what anyone would ever see in her. I never saw her and thought she looked good. She was a tall, big-boned woman. She seemed like a country girl—no makeup, very plain. She didn't wear flattering clothes; they were clean, but she didn't look dressed up. Her hair seemed combed, but it didn't look done. She didn't stand out—even her personality was nondistinct. Her demeanor wasn't abrupt, but she wasn't overly friendly either. She wasn't what I expected a real estate agent dealing with the public to look or act like. I think I expected her to look more presentable and be friendlier.

As the months passed, Helen did call me back, occasionally. She didn't want to talk much. I would ask how she was doing and how things were in school. I assumed Judy was making sure she made it to school, but I should have checked on that. With only two or three months left before graduation, Helen told me that she quit school.

"I think that's a very foolish thing to do. You're on the honor roll. You're doing so well. You're forfeiting a huge achievement in your life. You only have a couple of months left…"

As I laid the phone in its cradle, I knew that my words hadn't reached her. She wasn't going back.

I stood still and silent in my tiny one-bedroom apartment gazing at the wall-to-wall furniture. I wished Helen could come live with us, but the space barely held all our belongings. If I had never remarried Butch, maybe none of this would have happened. Maybe I would have met Al, and Helen would have still been with me, and maybe things would have been different.

25

Al continued to live in Green River, Utah, after I moved. He wanted to move to Grand Junction, but he could never find any kind of work in town. So he stayed with his friend Sam Holland and did odd jobs for the owner of Ray's Tavern and another guy who had a farm. He took care of the animals, put up fences, and picked up whatever odd jobs he could find. However, he regularly rode the bus from Green River to Junction to visit us on the weekends.

Over the Christmas and New Year holidays Al spent more time with us. He watched the girls during the day while I was at work. He was a fun-loving man who was always thinking up things to keep the kids entertained and happy. One night, when I got home after work, I found that Al and the girls had spent the afternoon crafting a mannequin that looked strangely like me. It startled me and at the same time made me laugh. They took a mop, hung one of my nurse's uniforms on it with a hanger, and then perched the Styrofoam head that held my red wig on the top of the mop handle. They painted a face on it with lipstick and markers and left it standing in the front room for me to see when I got home. I'm sure they had fun making it, but I was a little peeved that they used my good wig on the mop. I could never get rid of the face they painted on that Styrofoam head. From that day on when I would brush or style my wig, that face stared at me and made me smile. It was a constant reminder of fun times and the laughter that Al brought into our lives. Al's visits were always a treat. He was good with the girls and tried his best to lighten my spirit when he noticed the holidays might be difficult for me that year.

I guess I didn't hide it very well. The Christmas that we spent in the tiny rented apartment was my worst Christmas ever. Christmas is my favorite holiday—I love everything about it, but this one has always stood out as the worst one I can remember. I'm pretty sure it's because it was the first time ever that I didn't have all my kids with me on Christmas.

For most of the Christmas holiday it was just me, the girls, Al, and a cranky old Chihuahua that Tony asked me to watch after Candy died. I got the dog for Tony when he was younger, before he started school, because some doctor told me that a Chihuahua would help relieve his asthma. We named him Smokey Joe Mouse. He had been in the family for fifteen years at this point, and I found it hard to say no. But Smokey was old and always jumping on the girls legs or snapping at them. They were little and just wanted to play.

We managed to squeeze a Christmas tree into the room that the bunk beds were in. After adding presents, the place was so crowded we could hardly move around. I remember it snowed that year, and we let the girls play outside as much as they wanted to.

On Christmas Eve I prepared our traditional Italian meal (which was usually homemade ravioli or lasagna). But Helen didn't join us, and Tony was in the marines, so there was more than enough food for me, Al, and the girls. Nonetheless, I went right back to work in my tiny kitchen on Christmas morning to cook a Christmas ham (Helen's favorite). I put one of my best table clothes on the maple dining room table that was adjusted down to its smallest size, set out the good dishes, and prepared for Helen to join us for an early dinner.

The girls both got talking baby dolls for Christmas, the first of their kind. So they were wound up. It was noisy and crowded, but during the three or four hours that Helen spent with us, it felt like home. It wasn't where we were or what surrounded us; it was having all my girls with me that made it feel normal for a short while. But when the real estate lady picked Helen up, I really wanted her to stay. It was hard to say good-bye. I realized that I just wasn't used to Helen not being home.

After the first of the year things started looking up. The renters were finally out, and we moved back into the house on Ute, and Al spent even more time with us.

Al didn't drive, but he knew a lot of interesting places to go because he was born and raised in Utah and knew Colorado as well. He told me about working in the uranium mines and took us out to see some of them. We would spend a sunny spring day driving to some remote location in the hills, then stop to see the mines, have a picnic lunch, and let the girls run around and climb the hills. We couldn't go into any of the mines because they were halfway boarded up, but we would peek inside and listen to Al's stories and imagine what it was like when the mines were thriving. Al was interesting and entertaining. It was refreshing to simply relax and enjoy a day spending time together.

Once, he led us up a remote mountainside, and the girls and I hiked behind him as he kicked tumbleweeds to the side and cast a tall shadow our way. I watched the girls as they followed. His large heavy boots crunched the dirt and made small puffs of dust rise. They skipped and jumped to try to land in the same spots as Al's big boots. We all walked in his shadow as he gazed ahead. He smiled back at us and told stories about cowboy outlaws who hid out in "the hole in the wall" that we were visiting that day.

He also wanted us to meet and spend time with his family and friends. He had a brother, Jack, who lived in Junction. Jack and his wife had a teenage girl about Helen's age and two boys a little older than Janet and Debbie. He introduced us to his good friend Johnny Newman in Moab, Utah. Johnny played the guitar and sang for us every time we visited. Janet was enchanted by Johnny's musical ability, and Johnny noticed it and took the time to show her some chords on the guitar.

Surprisingly, Al even knew about some of my family and took an interest in them. He was never jealous about the friends I had or the time I spent with my family or friends. He knew the sheriff in Price, Utah, and the sheriff knew my brother Scott, or Stormy, as they used to call him. I don't know where Scott got that nickname because he was fifteen years older than me, but I long remember people calling him Stormy. Al knew about Scott rolling dice and getting into trouble. The sheriff talked about the great drawings of the Salt Lake City prison that Scott created. They still hung in the prison, and the sheriff still talked about them—and Stormy. I was glad Al knew some of my family. I was also glad that we could easily talk about family—all of it, good or bad.

Al liked to talk, and he liked to tell stories. He was always telling us about the different things he had done, like breaking horses and herding cows in southern Utah on some celebrity's ranch. He told us about rabbit hunting the day before a big rabbit fry and not getting any rabbits. So they rounded up a bunch of cats and fried them up for the folks who showed up. Surprisingly, no one knew the difference. It sounds awful, but the girls and I teased him about it. Any time after that, when we had rabbit for dinner, one of us always asked if it was really rabbit.

The time spent with Al helped me relax and enjoy my life. I felt loved and respected by him. Plus, we had fun. I learned to laugh again.

26

Despite being happier with my life, some things didn't change. Butch and I couldn't stop fighting. Our fights centered around me trying to collect child support and him trying to take the girls. Knowing how he was with money, I thought he wanted to get out of paying child support, but I also knew that he was madder than hell that his girls were at my house with Al.

Years later, Tony told me that his dad contracted somebody out to kill Al. I don't know if it's true or not, but I do know that Butch had some shady friends and talked about the Mafia while we were married. I ignored him at the time because it didn't make sense to me. He used to say that he could get so-and-so who was in the Mafia to do things for him, and I didn't see why he thought they would just do things for him. I guess it could have been true, because at that time, we had an Italian sheriff, Italian cops, and Italian firemen. There were so many Italians that were high up that if there was a Mafia, you wouldn't know who to trust and who not to trust. The Italians were very clannish. If one Italian did something, another Italian would not turn on him. I knew that for a fact.

I remember hearing about a local woman whose husband was a cop. She got tired of him beating her up, but when she reported it to the police, no one would believe her, because he was one of them. When she turned him in, they just laughed at her. Then, when he wouldn't let her leave him, she hired someone to kill him. She had the hired killer come to the house and hide outside around the time her husband was expected home—this was in the country out on the mesa. He used a shotgun and actually succeeded in killing her husband. Turns out, the guy she hired was just a teenager. She got arrested for the contract and was sent to prison with a longer sentence than the killer. She also had a son who was only four or five years old at the time. She didn't see him again until he was eighteen. It was a testament to how those Italians all stuck together, and they didn't care. She literally couldn't get any help. They actually wrote a book about it, and many years later they made it into movie called *Cries Unheard* starring Jaclyn Smith.

I could relate to her. At times, I remember being so afraid of Butch that I would jump at my own shadow. But after our first divorce and after I moved to Washington State, I realized that I was stronger than I thought, and I wasn't afraid anymore.

I remembered when I was in downtown Tacoma picking up a typewriter. I left Janet and Debbie in the car while I ran into the store. When I came out, three colored guys were sitting on my car. Without hesitation I walked right up and yelled at them to get their butts off my car. I don't know exactly what I said, but I know they jumped up and left. As soon as they did, I realized how stupid it was for me to do that. They could have grabbed me, killed me, beat me up, anything... There were three of them. I just reacted. I wanted them away from my kids and my car, and my instincts just kicked in.

I realized that I was scared most of my life, but I was proud. I didn't let people know I was scared. After the incident in Tacoma, I realized that I wasn't afraid anymore—maybe I was just scared so much that I couldn't be scared anymore. I also noticed that after that incident in Tacoma, I stopped hiding all the knives every night before I went to bed.

Although I was hesitant, I don't think I was afraid of getting married again. Al and I started talking about it. I loved spending time with him. We liked the same things, we were happy, and he was so good with the girls. We talked about going to Moab and getting Johnny to stand up for us in front of a judge.

I didn't want a church wedding, and I didn't want any more kids. In a loving, teasing kind of way, Al called me Mother Nun (or none), because I wouldn't have sex with him before we were married.

As part of planning to get married, I went to see Dr. Morasco about birth control. He was the same doctor that did my A and P repair. He was a surgeon, but he was also my primary care doctor. We became friends while I worked at Teller Arms. His mother was a patient there, and he had some other patients there as well. I liked the way he treated his patients. He would come in and do charts and go over things, and then he would say, "Do you have a cigarette?" and we would sit there at the nurses station and add cigarette butts to the ashtray and talk. He was never rushed or too busy to discuss a patient or just chat with a friend.

He was a little hesitant about giving me birth control pills because he was a Catholic. But he did. And as it turned out, I was allergic to the birth control pills he prescribed. He said I would be allergic to all of them. It was awful. I bloated and itched all over. He didn't have to convince me to stop taking them. But then he wouldn't do an IUD because of my previous surgery. Al was with me and heard all this. So he asked for a vasectomy as the only other alternative. But Dr. Morasco wouldn't do that either. He referred us to another doctor.

Al and I got married May 17, 1971, in Moab, in front of a judge, with Johnny and his wife as our witnesses—just as we planned.

Al moved into the house on Ute with us but couldn't find any kind of work in Junction. So after a while he went back to Green River to make some money. He would work a few days and come back when he wasn't working. It wasn't long at all before we knew I was pregnant.

I knew from experience that I would have to take a leave of absence from my job at Teller Arms well before I was ready to deliver the baby, so we planned to move to Green River when I left work. Al would support us as best he could with his part-time odd jobs. They all paid under the table, so he would be able to add us to his welfare claim as well. We figured that would be enough to get by until after the baby was born and I could get back to work.

Green River was only about one hundred miles from Grand Junction, a little over an hour drive, so I kept Dr. Morasco as my doctor through the pregnancy. I scolded him when I found out I was pregnant. "You wouldn't give me anything to keep me from getting pregnant, so it's your fault," I told him. He just laughed at me.

We scheduled a C-section for February 21, 1972. He told me that I would have to come up to Junction a week before that, and if I had one single pain I was supposed to call and get to the hospital immediately. Because I was a nurse, and knew the risks of having a child at the age of 40, he gave me some slack. Plus, we were friends and he knew I would tell him if there were any problems.

I was awake for the C-section. He talked me through the entire process as he was doing it. He was a great doctor. As soon as the baby was delivered, he said everything was fine, and a few minutes later I was holding my son, who I would finally get to name after my father.

Al got a vasectomy while I was in the hospital having Eddie.

This was Al's first child, and he was so happy to be a father. Every time Eddie woke up in the middle of the night, Al got up with us and stayed up until I went back to bed. He changed diapers, bathed his son, played with him, nicknamed him. I loved that. Butch never was a hands-on caregiver—this was so different. Despite some financial challenges in our life, it felt right with Al, like nothing could prevent us from being happy.

The house we lived in was spacious but didn't have a bathroom. This was 1972, so it was unusual to have an outhouse and a portable tub that we filled with water warmed from the stove for baths. But the kids had a huge playhouse out back, acres of land to explore, and a new baby brother to dote over.

We asked Helen to come and help me out after I first got home from the hospital. I'm not sure how she felt about our home, but she still didn't like Al much, and I don't think it was easy for her. For one, I wasn't easy on her.

"Helen, you can't lay a baby down in the crib like that. You need to make sure his head is away from the bars."

"I did. His head was up here. He must have moved."

"He's too young to move around like that."

"Mom, I swear…"

She had been my right-hand babysitter for years. After doubting her, I ended up eating my words when I laid Eddie in the crib and found that he *had* wiggled around enough to end up with his head by the bars. After she went back to Junction we didn't talk again until later that summer when I got an invitation to her wedding. It was an invitation for me—Al wasn't included. I told her I couldn't go unless Al could come with me. She refused to have Al at her wedding. Between a rock and a hard place, with no extra cash to spend on a trip, plus the fact that I didn't really like the guy she was marrying, I missed my daughter's wedding.

I realized quickly that I needed to get back to work so that we would have more money. But the state of Utah wouldn't give me a nursing license based on my training and licensing in Colorado. They said, ironically, that I didn't have enough maternity hours and would have to go back to school. The nearest nursing school was in Helper, which was about an hour's drive north. Al and I decided to find a place in Helper so I could start taking the nursing classes that I needed.

Al found a decent job on an oil rig in Green River that helped us finance the move to Helper. We found a cute little house, and I got the girls and myself enrolled in school. I applied for tuition assistance at the local Catholic school and was able to get tuition waived for both Janet and Debbie.

But it still wasn't easy. Eventually Al convinced me that I needed to get the child support that Butch was supposed to be paying me all these past years. It made sense to me. So with the support of my husband, who found me an attorney, I took Butch back to court… again.

27

I saw Helen and her dad in the hallway before I entered the courtroom. I said hi to Helen, didn't say a word to Butch, and went into the courtroom. I figured that Butch had probably come down to Junction from Pueblo and stayed with Helen the night before. He probably asked her to go with him to court. I had come down the night before too and stayed at Al's brother Jack's house. Eddie was a little over a year old, and they hadn't gotten to spend much time with their new nephew, so Francie agreed to watch the kids for me while I went to the child support hearing.

It was a small courtroom, with dark wood benches arranged in a U shape facing the judge's bench. I walked down the aisle in the middle and sat in the first row. Helen, her dad, and her dad's new girlfriend came in behind me and sat on the opposite side of the aisle. My attorney stood at a table in front of me.

They announced our case, and Butch's attorney asked Butch to take the stand. He asked Butch about his job at the fire department and a few questions about the farm where he still lived. Then he asked him what he knew about Al Drake. I thought this line of questioning a little odd at first. This was supposed to be a hearing strictly to get Butch to pay back child support and start paying it monthly.

"I know he shouldn't be around my little girls. I know he cut up my little girl's doll buggy when he got mad."

"Do you think he's dangerous?"

"Yes, he's a good-for-nothing alcoholic."

There was no way Butch could have known about the doll buggy. Helen must have heard about this incident when she was in Green River helping me with Eddie last year. The buggy had gotten in Al's way, and he ended up ruining it, but the girls and I weren't there. So it was something he told us about after it happened. I figured Helen must have told her dad some version of the story. I'm not sure how he knew Al was an alcoholic. The way it was coming out made it sound like Butch was this great, stable person and Al was mean and awful—how ironic.

Then Butch's girlfriend was called to the stand. She was taller than Butch and thin, with short, dark hair. I didn't take my eyes off her, but she never looked at me once. She stayed very focused on the attorney. She also made Butch sound like this great guy. She said she would watch Debbie and Janet while Butch was working. Then she swore she would raise the girls just as if they were her own—even though she and Butch weren't married.

What did all this have to do with child support? I couldn't make sense of it.

Now it was my turn. I stood at the side of the judge's huge desk and swore to tell the truth before I was seated. He sat up higher than me. I watched Butch's girlfriend sitting there, relaxed and assured. I cussed her in my head. Then I looked at Butch and felt nothing but disgust, like a bad taste in my mouth.

The first thing his attorney asked me was about the doll buggy.

"Yes, that happened. We had gone somewhere, and when we got back, Al explained to me that he had gotten mad. It was in his way. He apologized and said he would get her another one. I never saw it happen, though, and neither did the kids."

"Is he an alcoholic?"

"Well, yes. I guess that's what his medical records say. He goes to a couple of different rehab places to try to stop."

My attorney finally asked some questions about support. I was confident that there was no way that Butch could get out of paying child support after this.

But my attorney and I weren't prepared for any of the things that were off the topic of child support. The incident with the doll buggy and the alcoholism seemed to prove to everyone that Al was a dangerous man. I could see that everyone was thinking that the girls shouldn't be around him. But in my eyes, he wasn't a bad man at all. He couldn't apologize enough for the doll buggy, he never acted out in front of me or the kids, and he wasn't always drunk as they were trying to imply. I wished I had told my attorney about how Butch beat Tony and me and about how he threw his infant daughter up against the wall—now that was a dangerous man. But I didn't. Butch's violent behavior never came up. They only saw our most recent divorce papers, which showed what was what was known as a no-fault divorce because I hadn't stated any reason for the divorce when I filed those papers—I didn't have to.

This was supposed to be a court hearing for child support—custody had already been settled. But something was going very wrong. Butch's attorney railroaded the entire hearing into proving that Al was a bad and dangerous person. In those days, if you were labeled an alcoholic, you were automatically worthless. The general picture that came to a lot of people's minds when you said *alcoholic* was one of a bum—unemployed, with no home, drinking out of a paper bag on the streets. Al didn't go to a treatment center, if there was even one around. He didn't have a counselor or belong to a program. As far as I know there was no real place for treatment except the state hospital. The rehab he went to was usually at someone's house. But I think it was hit and miss with that method, depending on the group. In some cases, I know the group meetings involved drinking beer.

I knew I was married to an alcoholic. I knew that his medical charts identified him as one when I cared for him at the VA hospital. But I never really looked at him that way, or maybe I looked past it because of the happiness he had brought to our lives. He drank yes but not every day. He often went weeks without a single beer. I didn't see him as someone who couldn't be without it. But being a nurse, I knew that you didn't have to drink every day to be an alcoholic. I also knew Al couldn't have just one. If he started drinking, he had to get drunk. It was the truth. But it wasn't as they portrayed it. Al was actually what I would call a happy drunk. He was never mean to me or the kids like Butch was. But as it turned out, Al was labeled an alcoholic, and in 1973, domestic violence didn't even have a name, let alone a legal identity or a label to hang on a man like Butch.

After the questioning, the judge looked directly at me and asked, "Are the girls here in town with you?"

"Yes, but I didn't bring them to court with me."

"We will recess until 2:00 p.m. At that time you are to bring the two minor children back to court with you. Custody is hereby granted to Mr. Thomas. However, Mr. Thomas, you are ordered to pay $3,000 in back child support to Mrs. Drake. Until the back child support is paid you will be held in county jail. Bailiff, please place Mr. Thomas under arrest."

The judge dismissed the court and got up and left.

The bailiff cuffed Butch right there in the courtroom. His back was to me, so I couldn't see his face or his reaction as they took him away. I got no satisfaction from this at all. I had other things on my mind. First and foremost, there was no way I was going to let that SOB take the girls. The judge in the black robe may have some authority, but he definitely wasn't right in the decision he had just made.

By the time I got back to Jack and Francie's to pick up the kids, I had already made up my mind that there was no way I was going back to that courtroom. So I called my attorney.

"I'm not bringing the girls back. There's no way that I am turning over my kids for Butch to raise."

"You have no choice," he told me.

"I'm leaving town, and I will not be back in that courtroom this afternoon—period."

"You know I have to tell the judge what you're doing?"

"That's fine. By that time, I'll be out of the state," I said, ending our conversation.

Helen was expecting me back that afternoon with the girls just like everyone else was. According to her, when I didn't show up, Butch's attorney talked him into filing kidnapping charges against me, and the judge also charged me with contempt of court because I didn't obey his orders.

Later, Helen told me that she sat with her dad in a meeting with his attorney before the custody hearing. His attorney told him that if he got custody, he wouldn't have to pay child support. Butch said no, he didn't want custody, because he worked two days on and two days off at the fire station. He admitted that he couldn't take care of the girls. He hadn't even seen them in the last two years. But before the hearing started, Helen said the attorney had convinced Butch that it was the only way to get out of paying support, so he finally agreed.

The way it turned out, Butch got custody *and* he had to pay back child support. But I couldn't go get the check, because if I went back, I would be arrested. I found out much later that the check was returned to Butch because I never went to claim it.

28

I hired an attorney in Utah and started the process of fighting the charges. I even met with the governor of Utah at one point to try to plead my case. Unfortunately, he told me he wouldn't deny extradition if they came to get me. So I had to trust in my attorney.

Then one warm spring afternoon, I was home alone with Eddie (just a toddler). The other kids were at school. I was finishing up some household chores—cleaning up the kitchen and finishing the laundry while Eddie played on the floor next to me. I heard the sound of tires on gravel and realized someone was pulling into our driveway. As I looked out the window, I saw two uniformed officers getting out of the car and walking to my door. I dried my hands on a kitchen towel, picked up the baby, and walked to the door with him on my hip.

I don't know why, but I thought, *I wonder what they're doing here.*

"Good afternoon, ma'am. Are you Bernice Drake?"

"Yes."

I don't remember what they said after that, but by the time they were done saying it, I was crying. They were there to take me in and turn me over to the Colorado police for kidnapping and contempt of court.

"Can I call my attorney?"

"Yes, ma'am, you can."

Between sobs and sniffles I jumped his butt for not telling me that all this was going to take place. He was supposed to be on my side. He could have at least given me the opportunity to prepare myself. I was livid and also disarmed. All I got from him was some dumb excuse that really didn't sound like anything more than a dumb excuse.

Later, after Al talked to my attorney, he told me that the reason the attorney didn't tell me was because he figured I would run. He knew my history, and he knew my brother Scott (Stormy).

After talking to my attorney on the phone, I asked the officers if they would let me take my son across the street before they took me in. They agreed. In fact they were actually kind of nice. They let me pack a diaper bag and walk over there by myself while they waited in my driveway.

I had met the neighbor across the street and knew that her husband was on the state patrol. We had visited a few times, but the kids had never stayed there before or anything like that. It was hard to ask a neighbor that you know only this well to take your child, to say, "Please care for him. I don't know what to expect next." If you haven't done it, you can't imagine what it was like.

I could see her modest clothes, a soiled apron, and an inexpensive haircut as she stood in her doorway, concern on her face. I could feel that her heart was in the right place.

"Do you want me to go pick up the girls from school too?"

Her children went to the public school, but the neighbors to the left of her, who had a little more income, had children who attended the Catholic school that Debbie and Janet attended. She knew this.

I couldn't stop crying. "Yes, could you please?" I asked as I handed my son to her in the doorway.

It was all I could do to keep from doubling over as I walked back across the street to where the police officers were waiting for me. Without a word they opened the door of the police car and motioned me in.

After a silent fifteen-minute drive we arrived at the police station where I was held until Colorado authorities arrived to take me back to Colorado.

They didn't fingerprint me, didn't take my picture—nothing. They were actually pretty kind. They sat me down and let me use the phone. I called and left word at Ray's Tavern in Green River for Al because I knew he would probably stop there while he waited for the bus to return home. Then I called the college and talked to one of the instructors for the class to let them know I wasn't going to be in class. The two nursing program teachers actually came down to see me. They talked to me and tried to calm me down. I was crying and upset when I talked to them on the phone. When they arrived at the jailhouse shortly after that, I was in a small ten-by-ten cell with three cement walls, one wall of metal bars with a metal-bar door, a cot, a toilet, and a sink.

The short visit didn't calm me down. I couldn't eat the sandwich and chips the police officer brought. I was worried sick about the kids and what would happen to me. I cried for most of the next four or five hours in isolation. I've never cried easily. I was taught to control my emotions. But this time there was no stopping it. I had no control as it poured out of me. I never want to go through something like that again. It was the worst thing that ever happened to me. I was devastated. But I'll tell you what. By the time the Colorado cops came to get me, I was getting mad, and I knew I had to be stronger than I had ever been before.

The Colorado cops weren't as nice, and the closer we got to Colorado, the madder I got. When we reached the jailhouse in Grand Junction, one of the cops waited with me just outside a doorway, while the other cop checked me in. I couldn't see whom he was talking to, but I could hear them. I heard some woman say, "I don't feel sorry for her. She had plenty of time to take care of this." I was fuming.

Then they brought me to another room and took my picture, took my fingerprints, and asked for my watch.

"Why can't I keep my watch?" I asked.

"You could break the crystal and try to kill yourself."

"Maybe you better take my glasses too. I might break them and try to cut my wrist."

"No, we don't need your glasses."

Idiots... I thought.

They took me back and put me in a dorm-like room. It had no furniture. There were about six or eight other women in the room. I expected another cell but was relieved that I didn't have to be isolated. The women there weren't thugs and hardened criminals; they seemed fairly normal. A few of them talked to me and asked why I was there. They were friendly.

"Bernice Drake." A woman officer had opened the door, stepped inside, and called my name.

"I'm Bernice," I said, walking over to her.

"I need you to sign this and come with me."

The paper was consent to draw blood. I told her no.

"We need to check for drugs and alcohol, and we need some information for your file."

"Anything you want to know about me you can ask my doctor. You will not draw my blood."

"It's routine. Everyone does it."

"I don't care what it is. You will not draw my blood."

She shook her head at me and then turned and left the room.

Not only was I mad that I was there, I had made up my mind that I was not going to cooperate with the Colorado police.

They brought in dinner on individual trays. We were expected to sit on the floor and eat. I still couldn't eat. One of the other girls asked if she could have my dinner, and I gave it to her.

Sometime that evening I asked to make a phone call. I called Jack and Francie (Al's brother and his wife). Francie said she would call my friend and coworker from Teller Arms, Mike Kent, and they would try to post bail.

The next time someone came into the room looking for me, they told me that I was scheduled for a bail hearing in the morning.

When it came time to go to bed, we were given a roll, like a sleeping bag. I was expected to roll it out on the floor and go to sleep. I had a restless night. My mind wouldn't shut off. What was actually one day and night seemed like months.

I refused breakfast.

In court they assigned me a public defender. My bail was set at $1,000. Francie and Mike each put up fifty dollars to pay the bail bonds. I had a court date. The public defender made arrangements with the court so I could go back home to Utah and then come back to Colorado without being arrested again. The judge let me know that he was not removing the warrant for my arrest on contempt of court charges. If at any time in the next seven years I was found in the state of Colorado, and it wasn't for a court hearing, I would be arrested.

All three kids were still at the neighbor's the next day when Al and I got back home. It was a relief to be home and know the kids were fine. The neighbors were really good people. The welfare authorities went looking for the kids after they were notified that I was in the Colorado jail. The police in Utah, my neighbor the state patrolman, and his wife were all questioned about their whereabouts, and they all said they didn't know where the kids were.

One of the first things I did after I got home, besides smothering my kids with hugs and kisses, was call Daddy. I told him everything. Then I told him I was thinking of calling Ellis and fleeing to Texas.

"You don't want to go to Texas, Bernice. Why don't you call Sarah? Maybe she'll watch the kids for you while you take care of the court hearings. Her kids are grown, her husband's overseas, and she's not working. The kids'll be safe, and you can pick up where you left off after everything's all said and done."

He's such a kind and wise man.

Sarah agreed to take the three kids and keep them at her home in Washington so they would be safe while I fought the kidnapping charges. Sarah was a very caring, loving, helpful sister. Like most of my family, Sarah had an undeniable soft spot for babies, and I trusted her completely with mine. Sarah decided to become a nurse after Marjorie's first baby was born. The baby was what they called a Thalidomide baby—badly deformed. Marjorie let Sarah take the baby home with her, where Sarah cared for the child until it died. The child lived only a few months. After that, Sarah decided that if she had known more, she could have helped the baby more—so she started studying to be a nurse when she was in her forties.

Al, Eddie, and I on Eddie's first birthday

29

Late that afternoon, I sat with Al at the kitchen table. Eddie was in his diaper and T-shirt on the gold-and-brown linoleum floor beside us playing with some Tupperware. The girls were outside in the backyard. I could see Janet climbing a tree by the garage and Debbie below her in the dirt with a Barbie doll. The kids were fine, but I was exhausted. I looked down at Al's big hand on mine in the middle of the table and felt the tiredness seep in and weigh me down.

"Don't worry, B. We'll find a decent attorney this time. We'll work this out. But right now, I think you need something to eat." I tried my best to give him a smile. I remembered that I hadn't eaten since before I'd been arrested. I felt like maybe I could finally eat something.

Al liked to cook and was always concocting something interesting that the kids would like. He introduced them to corn cakes (pancakes with corn in them); SOS (shit on a shingle, but just SOS for the kids), which was hamburger gravy over toast; and just plain boiled rice eaten with milk and sugar like hot cereal. It didn't matter what he cooked for me that night. He knew I enjoyed a chili pepper with most any meal.

As Al moved around the kitchen, he teased me about how hot the chili peppers were and how they would fire me up for the battle ahead. He had several pet names for me, and one of them was "red-headed Mexican" because I liked hot peppers. I knew he was trying to lift my spirits. I began recalling the last two days and filled him in on every little detail. Then we talked about me taking the kids to Washington. Eddie didn't have to go, but Al was working, so we decided it would be better to keep all the kids together. Hopefully they wouldn't have to be gone too long. We had a nice dinner with the girls and went to bed early.

I was rested and motivated in the morning. I had become a skilled packer and mover. It didn't take me long at all to get the car loaded and the kids ready for what would become a very familiar drive to Washington State.

As far as the courts or anyone else knew, the kids were in Utah. Only my family knew they were going to Washington, because family members were the only ones I knew I could trust. I refused to bring the kids back to court the first time, and I wouldn't hesitate to do it again. Taking them to Washington was the only way I knew to ensure their safety. But I knew that as soon as the kids were safe and settled in with their aunt Sarah, I would have to hightail it back for the hearing in Colorado.

When I got back from Washington, Al and I found a couple of attorneys that we hoped would be better than the last one. I met with them several times. I had one attorney for the contempt charges and another, a criminal attorney, for the kidnapping charges. But I only went to court one time, and that was an arraignment. My sisters Zelma and Pearl drove down from Pueblo to be with me for moral support. Frank wouldn't let Elva come. We were all wearing our nicest dresses and holding our heads high. Pearl always kept her hair neat and short— off her shoulders—and carried herself with confidence and certainty. Zelma was nothing but serious. There was no weakness among the three of us. It was a very simple procedure in which the judge told me what I was charged with. I pleaded not guilty, and he set a court date.

When I got home that night, I was fired up again. This should have never happened. I started drafting a letter to the governor of

Colorado and the state's prosecuting attorney in Denver. I named the attorney that represented Butch when he got custody of the girls, listed the name of my attorney at that time, as well as the name of the judge, and wrote that I thought they were corrupt and probably bought off. I told him that we went in for a simple child support hearing, but the judge awarded custody of my children to a man whom I divorced on the grounds of physical and mental cruelty. I also got a statement from Jack and Francie (Al's brother and sister-in-law) that backed me up in my belief. Basically, I told them the whole thing was fixed and that these men needed to be barred from practicing law. I didn't hold back.

Then I called the school and made an appointment. I had already taken the girls to Washington, but I hadn't withdrawn them from school. I told the nuns what was happening, and they were very sympathetic. Since it was around the middle of the school year, I would need paperwork to transfer the girls to a new school. Janet was in the fifth grade, and Debbie was in the second grade. The girls both did really well in school, so they passed them onto the next grade and told me I shouldn't enroll them in school in Washington until the beginning of the next school year. They also offered to change the names on the school records so that the girls would be harder to find. They suggested that the girls go with the last name of Drake instead of Thomas, and I agreed. The state of Colorado was looking for the girls because I still didn't have custody. So all the school records at this school and the next would be under different names, Jan Drake and Deb Drake, this way it would be harder to track the girls down. I really believe that they thought I was a good mother and doing the right thing. They just wanted to help me. There are parts of the church that will go all out for you if they think you've been wronged. I told them about the divorce and the fighting and about me refusing to turn the kids over. I told them that I didn't think Butch was a good father, but I didn't tell them about the beatings—at least I don't remember telling them that—it was never easy for me to talk about, or fully remember. After that, the sisters came to see me quite often to see how things were going.

I can't even begin to guess how many times I drove back and forth from Utah to Washington. It was a sixteen- to twenty-hour drive depending on how often I stopped to get gas, stretch my legs, or go to the bathroom. I would leave Price, Utah, and drive straight through to Randle, Washington, every chance I got—without stopping to sleep. I cherished every moment I got to spend with the kids.

This was probably hard on my relationship with Al. We gave up the house we were renting in Price shortly after the kids went to Washington. I stayed in a motel room and worked at the hospital in Price. Ironically, I was assigned to private duty for a judge who had suffered a heart attack. He needed twenty-four-hour care and could afford a private room with nursing around the clock. I wish I could have talked to him about my case, but I couldn't. Al went back home—to Green River—which I really believe was his home. We spent time together when we could, but it wasn't too often, because I also worked at a restaurant as a waitress. But one good thing about Al was that I think he knew my kids were my priority, and making sure my kids were safe was my focus—second only to just getting by.

Eventually Al got us a place in Green River so that we could spend more time together, and it was also closer to Colorado. It was just a couple of rooms—just big enough for the two of us and Eddie and Sarah. Eddie wasn't off the bottle yet when I left him with Sarah, and she was trying to wean him off of it. It wasn't easy for her because Janet wouldn't let Eddie cry. Sarah said it was harder on Janet than Eddie. So she took the girls to her daughter Marie's house in Puyallup for the summer and brought Eddie with her down to Utah. Marie had three kids that the girls would enjoy spending the summer with, and Sarah thought it might be easier for me to have Eddie with me. She also took Eddie to Pueblo to spend time with Daddy—his namesake. I couldn't thank her enough. I needed my kids just as much as they needed me. The law wasn't looking for Eddie, just the girls. This way Al got to see his son too.

As the months passed, I waited, but I never heard back from the governor or the attorney general. Still, I want to believe that the letter I sent did something for me. They might not have been able to respond because I was facing the criminal charges of kidnapping, but I think something happened. On one of my last meetings with my criminal attorney, he told me the trial for the kidnapping charges had been canceled. When he told me this, I was at his office because we were supposed to go to court that day.

"There's good news and bad news," he said.

I braced myself.

"You weren't given custody of the girls, but the state has agreed to defer prosecution of the kidnapping charges for one year. So you're going to be on probation for one year. You can move to Washington, but you have to meet with a probation officer."

I remembered telling him in passing that I would like to move to Washington. "Okay," I said, knowing full well that he wasn't done talking. I hoped he would hurry up and spill the rest of the story.

"You also have to get a job and stay off of welfare. If you go on welfare, they will pick you up and take the girls."

I got it—loud and clear. I didn't think it was a problem at all! I slowly nodded, waiting for more.

"You'll also need to stay out of the state of Colorado for the next seven years so they don't arrest you for the contempt charges."

I was speechless, relieved and elated all at the same time. "Thank you" was all I could say.

He smiled at me and nodded. "Do you have enough money to get to Washington?"

"I'll manage." I smiled back. I didn't even have $150 to my name, but I had no doubt that I would make it.

"You know, you could probably get custody of the girls if you would divorce Al."

Those are the last words I remember him saying.

30

I drove up to Ray's Tavern to meet Al and tell him what had happened. Green River was barely a town. The main street had a drugstore, a bank, a gas station, and Ray's Tavern. There were small houses scattered on the side streets. It was quiet, and the tavern looked idle and uninhabited in the broad daylight of Utah's desert sun. I parked my car right in front, where I knew Al would see it. Inside, the tavern was dark and soundless with only a couple of guys sitting at the bar with a few barstools between them. Ray Sherril, the owner, was behind the bar—as usual.

"Well, hello there, Bernice. I know someone who's going to be happy to see you," he said cheerfully.

I smiled back at him, and as I reached the bar, he asked, "What can I get for you?"

"How about a red beer?"

"Coors draft, right?" he said as he turned and grabbed a glass.

I nodded.

"Al tells me you been wrangling with the law a bit. Everything okay?"

"Everything turned out okay." I didn't feel like saying much more.

"Glad to hear it," he said, handing me a beer with tomato juice in a tall glass.

"What time does Al usually show up here?"

"Well, if he stops in after work, he should be here in the next half hour or so."

"How about some change for the jukebox?" I asked, pushing a five-dollar bill toward him to pay for the drink and get some change.

"Sure." He quickly returned with my change and some quarters for the jukebox.

I took my time thumbing through the songs on the jukebox and picking out a few that I liked. Then I went over and sat down in one of the booths and lit a cigarette. I had been here a few times with Al. We even brought the kids in a couple of times to get something to eat. I suppose if Butch would have known about that he would have brought it up in court too. Fact was, this was where most people in town came to have a meal out. We could get a burger and fries for the kids, some deep-fried gizzards for us, and not spend a lot of money. Al and I didn't go out of town to the fancier restaurants; we couldn't afford it. But we liked to go out once in a while, and this was where we went. They served beer and wine at the fancy restaurants too—but without the stigma of a tavern.

I looked around at the guys at the bar and then over at the pool table. I tried to remember what it was like the times we brought the kids in. The place was never loud or rowdy. Maybe a laugh rose up over the jukebox, or maybe someone broke the balls on the pool table. The people who came here were just regular small-town folks. Everybody knew each other. The people here were Al's friends, and they were great to us.

I shook my head, tapped the ashes off the end of my cigarette, and decided I wasn't going to be judgmental. I hadn't done a damn thing wrong by bringing the kids in here. It wasn't against the law. And I hadn't done a damn thing wrong when I married Al either. He had a hard time finding a job for a while, but he was working steady on the oil rig now.

I loved Al. I really didn't see him as a bad husband or father. He was my friend and companion. I knew the attorneys and judge were trying to tell me that he was unfit. But up to this point, I hadn't seen the alcohol as a problem. He wasn't sloppy drunk every night of the week, though he did like to have a few beers. As I studied the glass of beer and tomato juice in front of me I realized, I enjoyed playing rummy or cribbage in the evening, having a beer with him, relaxing, and talking. I trusted him and felt okay leaving the kids in his care. I loved his playful teasing with me and the girls and the way he had engaged with our son and was developing a relationship with him.

When Al came in, he spotted me immediately and came over and gave me a kiss and a careful hug that told me he didn't want to get me dirty. His clothes were dusty, and his hands and face slightly darkened by the day's work. I watched him slide his tall frame into the booth across from me.

"What happened, B? Is it all over? Is everything all right?" As he spoke, he motioned to Ray to bring him a beer.

"Well, I don't have custody of the girls yet, but I can move to Washington with them. They put me on probation for a year. As long as I can stay off of welfare, I can keep the girls. But I can't go back to Colorado for seven years, because they're not dropping the contempt charges, and they could still arrest me for that."

"Well, that's something. Did you get child support?"

"No."

"That don't sound right." He slicked his hair straight back and then positioned his big hand on top of mine where it rested next to my drink.

"If I'm not allowed in Colorado, Butch can't see the kids. So I guess they figure if he doesn't get to see the kids, I don't get support."

"Do you have to move to Washington? Can't we stay here?"

"I can't stay here. Who knows if they'll come over here and arrest me again, like they did before."

"That's a hell of a deal, ain't it? I sure as hell don't want that to happen." Al nodded at Ray as he set a glass of beer in front of him.

"Me either. I think there's a better chance that Washington won't know about the charges."

"Yeah," he sighed. He picked up his beer and took a long drink off of it.

"The girls are already up there," I said softly. "Plus you know I've been taking my things up there little by little every time I've gone to see them."

"Yeah, I know you gotta be with your kids, B. It's just… I got a good job going here with the oil rig."

There was a big difference between Al and me. Even though my roots were in Pueblo, I had never stayed put for very long. Al, on the other hand, was born and raised in Green River, Utah, and had spent most of his life there. He felt at home there, and at this time in his life, being in his early fifties, I knew it was hard for him to fully uproot. I could see it in his demeanor and hear it in his voice.

"I know," I said, letting my thoughts go unspoken. I wondered if I should tell him that the attorney told me I should divorce him. A split second later it came out. "My attorney said I could probably get custody if I divorced you."

"What?" He looked hurt.

"You know what they said in the custody hearing. They're still hanging that over my head."

"Goddamn it, B. You know I'd never hurt those kids. I love them as much as you do. I'm sorry. This is all my fault. You go ahead and divorce me if you have to, but don't take Moggie from me." He was

253

being strong, but I could tell this was hard for him. Eddie (Moggie) was his only child.

"We both know it's just paperwork. We could still be together, as long as we're out from under their watchful eyes."

"But you're gonna move to Washington."

"You can come up later if you want."

"Yeah, I don't want to leave right now. What's a guy like me supposed to do up there?"

We didn't make any promises, and we didn't consider it a separation, but Al wasn't going with me.

Sarah flew back to Washington with Eddie while I gathered the last of my belongings and prepared for the final drive up with my stuff. Sarah gave me her gas card to use. Being the loving sister that she was, she also found me a house to rent in Tacoma, just off Canyon Road, not far from her daughter Marie. And she paid the first month's rent for me.

I filed for a divorce from Al before I left, but I didn't think I would follow through with it. I didn't want to be forced to divorce him.

When I arrived in Tacoma, I was able to pick up the kids at Marie's and go straight to our new home. I had stored most of my things at Sarah's, and she and Marie had already brought them over. That night, we managed to make up the beds but didn't unpack much else. Eddie fussed when I tried to put him down. He wanted to sleep with Janet. I knew it was because I had been gone so much. He had gotten used to sleeping with his sister rather than me. So I had Janet come and get in bed with me and Eddie. Then Debbie came bouncing in too, and we all snuggled into one bed. When your baby doesn't want to sleep with you, it kind of hurts. But honestly, I was happier than I had been in months—grateful to have their warm little bodies next to me. I totally relaxed into much-needed deep sleep.

Having my kids back gave me a renewed sense of strength and the motivation to once again get my life in order. It didn't matter that I was flat broke. I applied for food stamps and went to the food bank to feed the kids. Foods stamps were not considered welfare, so it was allowed under the terms of my probation. Then, taking all the kids with me, I stopped in at a nursing home in Puyallup at the foot of the hill near the fairgrounds. It reminded me of Teller Arms in Grand Junction.

It was never hard to find a job in nursing. They hired me on the spot as a nurse's aide because my Utah and Colorado nursing licenses were not applicable in the state of Washington. I would have to apply for a new license. Being a nurse's aide didn't pay much, but it was a job and would keep me off welfare.

Al would occasionally send me a money order for twenty-five dollars or so. We wrote letters back and forth, but neither one of us had a phone. I couldn't really afford to pay a babysitter, but I had to. I worked days; it was summer, and the girls weren't back in school yet. Marie watched the girls for a little while, but I think she had something wrong with her legs and couldn't keep after an active toddler like Eddie.

It wasn't long after I started work that the director of nurses called me into the nurse's station and sat me down for a talk.

"Bernice, I know you have your nursing license in two states, you have ample experience in nursing, and you are a great asset for us here. We are really shorthanded. I need to put you to work as an LPN," she said.

"I've applied for my license, but they told me it takes at least six weeks."

"I'm going to call the Department of Licensing and see what we can do about that. You sit right here in case they need to talk to you."

I watched her slender fingers dial the number. Then she sat up straight in her chair, delicately adjusted her golden wire-framed glasses, smoothed her white skirt over her white-stockinged knees, and looked directly into my eyes, as if I was the one she was going to have the conversation with. Everything about her seemed very pleasant as she spoke on the phone, asked me questions, and very professionally took care of business. I found it amazing how she went to bat for me. Maybe she saw something in me that the court system and the lawyers couldn't. The next day I was working as a licensed practical nurse and getting better pay, even though my license was still being processed.

After being in our new house for a couple of months, things were put away and organized. I visited my probation officer every month, but she then told me I could just call in. The last letter I got from Al sounded as if he missed us, especially Eddie, and was planning on taking the train up to be with us. I was glad Al was coming up. I missed him too.

The kids were elated when Al showed up, especially Janet. She didn't like the babysitter I had hired. She thought she was too old to have a babysitter. She had just started sixth grade and wasn't twelve years old quite yet. Maybe she felt like the caregiver for her little brother and sister while I was gone. But I knew she wasn't old enough yet to be left alone with Debbie, who was a feisty eight-year-old, and Eddie, who was just a toddler. When Al joined us, Janet was happy to see the babysitter go. She didn't really consider Al a babysitter. We referred to him as their stepdad and Eddie's dad, but the girls never called him Dad. They called him Al.

Al was getting social security disability checks, and he added me and the three kids to his social security claim when he came to Washington. It was helpful to have that money going directly into my checking account each month. He didn't mind watching the kids while I worked, but he also tried to find work—something to keep him busy. He seemed to drink more when he wasn't working—not just in the evening, but sometimes during the day too.

On one of my days off we drove to Yakima to meet Al's aunt Gladys. She lived in a small tidy house, decorated with doilies and splashes of flower-patterned furniture, dishes, and knickknacks. She lived across from a park, so we let Janet and Debbie run across the street to play. With the front door open, the fresh air replaced the stale, and Al, Eddie, Gladys, and I enjoyed a quiet visit. She was a wonderful, gracious, and happy woman. With her white hair styled neatly atop her head, she stood tall—taller than me. She wore a smile with a sparkle in her eyes as she moved slowly but comfortably around her kitchen serving us cold drinks to soothe the heat of a summer's day in Eastern Washington.

Aunt Gladys had lived in Yakima all her life. She knew people and encouraged Al to come back and do odd jobs for her and her friends. So he did. He started going pretty frequently in fact—either taking the train or hitchhiking if he didn't have any money. Sometimes he would be gone for two or three weeks at a time. Sometimes he would drink up all the money he earned. Sometimes he would mail some of it home. One time he mailed a check and got back home before the check got there—I remember because he told me it was coming, and then after it arrived, he told me that he cashed it and bought some beer.

I enjoyed a cold beer too, especially in the summer, but I didn't drink to the degree that Al did. It seemed that he was at a point in his life where he would do anything to get some more alcohol in him. I don't think he was happy being up in Washington, struggling to find work and not having any friends around. He didn't mistreat me or the kids, but the drinking and wasting money on alcohol was starting to get to me.

31

A couple of letters from Tony were forwarded to me at my new address. I didn't get a lot of details, but he was discharged from the marines after hitting an officer and was traveling around a bit, seeing the country. Since I couldn't afford a phone yet, I sent him my new address and gave him Marie's phone number in case he needed to get ahold of me. By the time fall rolled around he called and left word at Marie's for me to get ahold of him.

He said he was stranded in San Francisco and wanted to know if I could come and get him. Of course I didn't have the money to travel, but I borrowed some money from Marie for a bus ticket and sent it to him.

Tony was in his early twenties, and I thought he would be helpful around the house since Al was spending a lot of time doing odd jobs in Yakima and wasn't home much. Our house was small. There were only two bedrooms, but the front room was bigger than usual. There was a large arched wall in the middle of it that I could hang some curtains on to break it into two rooms. This would give the girls a big bedroom to play in, and I could move Eddie's crib into my bedroom and give Tony the other bedroom. The house didn't need much upkeep because it had been pretty well maintained. But there was a big yard that I had trouble keeping mowed. Over the summer we brought one of Marie's Shetland ponies over to eat some of the long grass down in the back.

I figured I could get Tony to keep it mowed, plus he could help with the bills after he got settled in and got a job. But it didn't exactly work out that way.

When I wasn't at work, Tony used my car to go job hunting and then later to go to work. He told me he found some piddly little job but didn't give me any details. He was vague about it, in a way that told me he wanted me to know that he was no longer a child but a grown man. He let me know that he was making enough to pay the utilities and told me not to worry, which kind of reminded me of Butch.

He wasn't home too often when I was home, and he wasn't that helpful around the house. He would usually come home after I was already in bed. We didn't get a chance to talk a whole lot. He hadn't been in Tacoma very long before things took a sour turn.

I thought it was a little unusual when I saw Marie pull into the driveway one evening after dinner. She didn't usually come over when it got late. I instinctively thought something must be wrong. I opened the front door before she reached the steps.

Marie generally looked serious, but I could tell from her tone that she was none too happy at the moment. "You got a call from the police station, and they want you to call them back." She had stopped just short of the steps and didn't look as if she wanted to come in.

"Let me get my purse." I left the door open, but she didn't come in. Janet, Debbie, and Eddie were sprawled out in the front room watching TV. I told Janet I would only be gone for a few minutes and left her in charge. I didn't want the girls to worry. I knew Janet was old enough to realize that my dealing with the police had not been a pleasant thing for any of us in the past. So I was glad she hadn't heard the message Marie delivered. "Lock the door, and don't answer it for anyone until I get home. Understand?"

Janet got up and followed me to the door. I listened to hear the deadbolt shift into place before I turned to Marie, already in her car with the motor running.

When I got in Marie's car, I asked more about the phone call. "Did they say why I needed to call them?"

"They said your car's been impounded, Aunt Bernice." I could hear the irritation in her voice. She looked at me only for a second as she twisted around to look behind her and back up the hill and out of the driveway onto the street.

"Gads! Did they say anything else?"

"Just for you to call—I have the number and a name written down for you."

The drive to Marie's house took all of two minutes. I couldn't imagine how Tony would have let my car get impounded.

It was much worse than I anticipated. When I called the officer back, he told me that Tony and another guy tried to rob a grocery store. They didn't get far before they were caught. The car was impounded, and they were both arrested.

I didn't want to tell Marie what had happened, but I did. She just shook her head and listened without saying much. I didn't know where I was going to find the money to get my car out. I couldn't ask Marie. I still needed to pay her back for the bus fare I borrowed to get Tony up here. I had to have my car to get to work, so I knew I would have to scrimp on something else that month and use what little money I had to get my car back. The entire situation was just maddening.

Marie took me to get my car the next morning, and somebody bailed Tony out—I have no idea who.

Later that day somebody dropped him off at the house. I didn't wait for him to come inside. I wanted to be out of earshot from the kids when I laid into him. The last thing I needed right now was trouble with the law, and I let him know it. I gave him hell for using my car and for thinking he could get away with armed robbery. I told him he could've been killed. I swear something was haywire with the kids in the '70s. Maybe it had something to do with all the drugs they were doing, but I didn't want to believe Tony was into all that.

He left knowing I was mad. He went and stayed somewhere else while he awaited his trial date.

A few short days later I was cleaning his room and found a container under his bed that made me curious. When I pulled it out, I knew immediately that it was marijuana. I had seen bits of pot before but never this much. Smoking marijuana was pretty prevalent, but I think they were cracking down on the people who were selling it. There was enough to fill a small suitcase. I wondered if selling pot was the piddly job that Tony was so vague about.

I knew I should call the cops, but I argued with myself. Tony was already in trouble, and this would only make it worse. There was too much to flush down the toilet. I was still on probation. If the police discovered this in my house, I could lose the girls. I couldn't really confront him about it or ask him to get it out of my house since I didn't know where he was staying or how to get ahold of him. Tony was my son, and I loved him no matter what, but he was heading down the wrong road. How could I best help him change his course and protect myself and the children? I wrestled with it for a couple of days. It tortured me, but I had to do something.

I still had mixed feelings when I finally made the call. I told the police about what I had found, told them it was my son's, and gave them my address. I told them I would not be there but that I wanted it out of my house. Then I took the kids and disappeared for a couple of days. I think we went to Elma to see my sister Agnes and her daughter Jody.

When I came back, the marijuana was gone, and Tony was still gone. I'm not sure what happened between him and the police, but I know something did.

He came back home shortly before his trial date, and he laid into me. I had never seen him so mad. He reminded me of Butch. When he started yelling at me and threatening me, I told Janet to go to the neighbor's house and call the police. He was gone before she got back and before the police arrived. But that wasn't the end of it. I think he came home again while we were gone. We came home one night and found the Christmas tree knocked over and the house a mess—as if he rummaged through everything looking for something. I actually got a little scared of my own son.

At his hearing, the judge brought up a "disagreement" Tony and I had about drugs that were found in the house. I'm not sure how he knew—maybe from the police report when I called and had them remove it from the house. But they didn't bring up any charges for it. The other guy who was involved in the attempted robbery had a wife and baby. Both he and Tony got sentenced to time in the Monroe penitentiary.

I never gave up on Tony while he was in prison. I wanted him to know that I still loved him. I knew he was mad at me. I think somehow he thought I was partially to blame for him being in prison. Once a month or more I wrote him a letter. I don't know when he got over it, but he finally wrote me back, and shortly thereafter, the girls and I went to visit him.

I don't remember what his sentence was for the robbery, but he got out on probation after about a year and a half.

32

When I got my 1975 income tax refund, it was enough for a down payment on a house. I managed to hold on to it until I found a place that I really liked. It reminded me of the old-style houses that I always loved. It was green with white trim—a roomy two-story, four-bedroom home with a covered wraparound front porch and a fenced backyard. The location was perfect—across the street from the Puyallup High School, which had a swimming pool that the girls and Eddie would love, and walking distance to the junior high and elementary schools that Janet and Debbie would attend.

Shortly after the last box was brought in, Al disappeared again. By now I was used to him taking off for weeks at a time. I knew that he was most likely in Yakima at his Aunt Gladys's house, doing odd jobs. I figured that he would come home after getting enough money to keep beer in his belly and bus fare in his pocket. But when the real estate agent paid me a visit and told me that he had left a refund check for an overpayment with my husband, I knew that Al might be gone longer than usual. The refund was a couple hundred dollars that we really could have used to help with the moving expenses and utility hookups and whatnot. But I knew in my gut that I would never see a dime of it. When Al had money like that in his pocket, I figured he would spend the day in a tavern drinking it up, find a place to sleep it off, and do it again the next day. His urge to drink had taken him over. He would yearn for the day's responsibilities to be gone and look forward to the time when he could have a drink. His drinking was worse now than it had ever been before. If he had one, he didn't know how to stop.

I wished he could just quit drinking altogether, but I couldn't make it happen. Only he could. I began to wonder if he was capable of quitting. I realized I had to let go. Even though I was raised to believe that marriage was forever, with Butch I had already proved that it wasn't. It was a commitment that sometimes, for good reasons, you just couldn't keep—even if you still loved the person. So I took the now-familiar steps of filing for divorce.

There was no shame in being a divorcee in the mid-'70s. Nobody cared. Things were looser. Divorce was common. I could get one for any reason or no reason at all. I think that, along with everyone else in this country, my faith in marriage had been broken.

I gave Al's aunt Gladys's address in Yakima as his residence to be sure that he would receive the divorce papers. Al came home about a month after I filed.

When I got home from work, I usually picked Eddie up from the next-door neighbors. Janet and Debbie would either be there or at home. But when I walked in the door, saw Eddie, and smelled something cooking, I knew Al was home. The kids were watching TV, and I found Al in the kitchen.

"I didn't expect to see you," I said, walking into the kitchen and talking to Al's back.

"The kids were hungry, so I thought I wrangle up some grub so you didn't have to. How was work?"

"Didn't you get the divorce paper?" I didn't want to be mean, but I was surprised that he was in my kitchen.

"Yeah." He turned to face me and leaned back on the stove. "I brought 'em with me. You sure this is what you want, B?"

"I can't take the drinking, Al. You disappear and spend all our money on beer. We can't live like that."

"I'm sorry," he said, looking right at me. Then he looked down at the spatula in his hand and turned back to the stove. "I guess I'll get some money up and head back to Green River. Do ya mind if I spend some time with the girls and Moggie before I go?"

"As long as you're not drinking," I said.

I'm not sure why, maybe just out of the kindness of my heart, but I let him stay for a bit that time. He really wasn't a bad man. He just had a bad drinking problem. I had a soft spot in my heart when it came to Al. He came back a few other times after that, and I let him stay then too—as long as he wasn't drinking. But deep down, I knew it couldn't go on this way.

We were pretty settled into our new home, feeling like a part of the community. The girls were in school and making new friends. We befriended the neighbors. I was working at Good Samaritan Hospital. It felt as if my troubles were behind me. But the past isn't something that just disappears. I was about to learn that sometimes it takes some extra effort to actually, really shake free of it.

Before the year was out, I got a call from Helen. I hadn't talked to her much since she had gotten married. It was nice to hear from her, but the reason she called was to plead for her dad. She told me how sorry he was and that he really missed the girls and wanted to see them. I resisted at first, and then I finally just gave in. I wanted her to know that it was okay to forgive and forget and move on. Then she threw the curveball. Butch had booked a flight, and all I had to do was pick him up at the airport. She gave me the date and time. I couldn't find a way to back out of it at that point. I really had no idea when we were talking on the phone that I was agreeing to something that had already been planned out.

I took the kids with me to pick Butch up at the airport because I felt nervous about it. I had to convince myself that this was my chance to let him see that I was making it on my own. I wanted him to know that I didn't need him—despite all the years he spent telling me that I could never make it without him.

I tolerated his visit as best I could. It was my home not his. I wanted him to see that the girls were doing well and so was I. But I wonder if the strength and independence I showed didn't backfire on me, because it didn't take long at all for him to start in about us getting back together.

A couple of days into his visit he brought his cousin over to the house. Butch called his cousin Scange, but his name was John—Giovanni in Italian. He was an older man, very nice, well dressed, handsome, and friendly. He asked Butch and me to join him and his girlfriend for dinner and a drink. I really didn't want to go, but I did—only to find out that Butch had recruited his cousin in his plea-bargaining efforts.

I remember sitting at a table in a quiet nightclub. The seats were overstuffed and covered in red vinyl. John and I were the only two that smoked. He drank Canadian Mist and water. He was smooth and confident yet not cocky like a lot of the Italians I had met in Pueblo—more of a ladies' man. He wore a gray suit jacket with matching trousers, a pressed white shirt unbuttoned at the neck, and dress shoes. The material in the suit kind of shimmered when the light caught it just right. I could tell he wasn't worried at all about money by his generosity when it came to paying for dinner and ordering drinks afterward. He also wore a nice watch and a ring that I imagined were fairly expensive.

Butch sat in between John and me. I sat as far away from Butch as I could.

"Would you like another drink, Bernice?" John asked. He had his arm around his girlfriend, and with the opposite hand he tilted his drink toward me.

"I think I'm fine for now." I realized I had probably been quietly watching John a little more than anything else. I hoped he hadn't noticed.

"It's okay to relax a little. Why don't you two scoot in a little closer to each other and enjoy yourselves?"

I knew what he was up to the minute I heard this, and I wasn't having it. Although I liked the nightclub, the atmosphere, and getting to know Butch's cousin a little, at that point I wanted nothing more than to cut the night short.

I knew I would never go back to Butch. The problem was that I let him stay longer than I should have. I gave him the downstairs bedroom and asked him to pitch in while he was there. He paid for some baseboard heaters to be installed downstairs, and I was grateful for that. But he was relentless in his pursuit of me. I gave in to him once and let him sleep with me, which only made things worse.

Then one night Al showed up. I knew how Butch treated the other men in my life, and I wasn't about to have him and Al punching each other, or worse. Luckily, when Al came to the door, Butch wasn't home.

We stood just inside the entryway. There was a glass door between the front room and the entryway. I closed it and stood in front of the stairs that led to the upstairs bedrooms. Al looked the same. He wore a red plaid shirt and Levis. His hair was slicked straight back, and although the widow's peak seemed a bit deeper, there was no sign of gray in his hair.

"Can't I come in?" he asked, looking at the kids through the glass door to the front room.

"Al, you can't just show up here whenever you feel like it." I hesitated. I know it hurt him. "Butch and I are back together." I said looking away. I cared for him enough to justify hurting him to protect him. But it made me sad when I saw him shrink a little at my words. "Butch isn't here right now, so you can visit for a few minutes if you want," I said, opening the door to the front room.

It wasn't a playful visit with the kids; it was more of a good-bye visit. When he left, I asked him to give me a call before he came to visit his son again. It was sad, but I knew that it would work. Al was nothing like Butch. He actually listened to me.

I thought maybe Butch would leave when his sister called and said that their mother was sick. I stood there and listened to him tell his sister that he wasn't returning. Then he handed me the phone, which irked me. I was stern with Butch when I got off the phone.

He was sitting at the dining room table.

"Your sister thinks I'm keeping you here." He looked up at me but didn't respond, so I continued, "Your mother is sick. She might not make it. You need to go back to Pueblo and be with her and your family."

"Well, she's old. My family is here."

"No, Butch, it's not. We're not married anymore."

"Well then let's get married."

"I'll never remarry you." I felt strong saying it. I wasn't afraid. I walked away.

I could barely believe that the news of his mother falling ill didn't make him want to go back to Pueblo. Unfortunately, it wasn't long before we received news that she passed away. I was never extremely close to Butch's mom, but I went to Pueblo with Butch to pay my respects. After the funeral, I drove home to Washington alone.

I thought that was the end of it with Butch, but it wasn't. A few short weeks later he showed up with his pickup truck packed as if he was here to stay. He continued to try to convince me that we should get remarried. I continued to tell him that I would never remarry him.

But no matter what, he persisted. He got a job at a nearby restaurant washing dishes, and I let him stay through the holiday.

The whole family was there for Christmas, including Tony, Helen, and her husband, Fred. Plus, Butch invited his cousin John over for Christmas Eve dinner. Unfortunately, Tony also started in on me about getting back with his dad. I think Butch put him up to it. I told them both to forget it.

Then one day, shortly after the holidays were over, Janet and her girlfriend got into some teenage mischief. I don't remember what they did, but I got a call from her friend's mother. She didn't call to complain about the girls getting into trouble; she called to complain about the way Butch handled it. I don't remember the details, but I know when I got home from work that night, I hit the ceiling and flat out told Butch to get out. It took a couple of days, but he finally left.

Christmas—Freddy (Helen's husband), Helen, Debbie, Tony, Eddie, Janet, and Butch. Inset top right, John Thomas.

33

B utch left me alone after his extended visit to Puyallup. I never
heard from him or about him again except through the kids. Al
left me alone too. He came to visit Eddie once after our last encounter
in Puyallup. But even after the divorce, he never took us off his Social
Security. In fact it increased. When I noticed the increased deposit, I
actually went down to the bank to make sure it was right.

The bank lobby was small and tidy, with too much orange for my
taste. The bank teller wasn't busy and gave me an enthusiastic hello as
I walked up to the counter.

"Hello. I just want to make sure this deposit is right," I said, showing
the teller my last statement.

"I'll be happy to check that for you," she said as she began tapping
a few keys on a keyboard in front of her computer terminal. "It seems
to be correct."

"Well, it's usually much less than that," I said. "I wonder why it
went up."

"Hang on a second, lemme check something." She turned, walked
away, and came back a few minutes later with a taller, older man that I
assumed was in management.

"Hello, Mrs. Drake, the deposit is correct. Social security benefits
often change after a person is deceased."

I couldn't speak. My eyes dropped to focus on the tie he was wearing. In stark contrast to his white shirt, the wide, gray tie held small, black, triangular shapes, which initially seemed randomly placed but in the end took on a pattern.

"I'm sorry for your loss. Is there anything else we can help you with?"

I searched for concern, noticing he had deep-brown eyes. "No," I said, turning away.

I sat in my car for a few minutes in pure stillness. It was weird to have him, a stranger—I didn't even know his name—tell me Al had passed away. Questions and imagined answers shuffled around in my mind.

I called Jack and Francie as soon as I got home. Al passed away in the VA hospital, the same hospital where I first met him. Jack and Francie were under the impression that the doctor that took care of Al was going to call me. They were surprised that I hadn't called earlier or attended the services, but they knew we were divorced. They were also disappointed in the way Al was cared for. They felt that Al shouldn't have died. He was just at the hospital for an x-ray. They told me that Al looked unkempt with a three-day beard when they went to the viewing. I couldn't imagine Al when he wasn't clean shaven. My heart dropped as I imagined the people at the hospital not caring for him. I imagined those who might have prepared his body for viewing not caring either.

Jack and Francie encouraged me to sue the hospital because Al vomited and asphyxiated during what should have been a normal x-ray procedure. But I understood after talking to the doctor that in no way did he foresee what was going to happen, and he did everything he could to revive Al. A bigger concern for me was Eddie. I told him that his dad got sick and was now in heaven, but he was only seven and didn't really have a reaction. Maybe Al was gone too much before this, or maybe it had been too long since his last visit for Eddie to understand that he was really gone now. I was so sorry that Eddie didn't get a chance to say good-bye to his dad. But the funeral services had long passed by the time we knew.

John, Butch's cousin, kept calling me after Butch left. At first he seemed to just want to check in on me and the kids and see how we were doing. We talked on the phone pretty regularly, and then he started stopping by and asking me out for a drink. I always liked John from the first time I met him. He knew how to treat a woman. He always opened doors for me, the door to the house, the door to the car, any door anywhere. He was a gentleman in other ways as well. I enjoyed spending time with him at home or when he took me out. He introduced me to horse races, which became a fun night out that we both loved. Gradually, surprisingly, I fell in love with him. Even though he was Italian, he was suave and never abusive. Even though he enjoyed a drink, he wasn't an alcoholic.

John worked at Boeing and kept an apartment in Tacoma, and I kept my home in Puyallup—and several homes after that. We were together as a couple for about six years, even though we both agreed that we wouldn't get married. I know he loved me. He told me often, and he treated me and the kids well, as if we were his wife and kids. Unfortunately, about five years into our relationship he was diagnosed with lung cancer. I stayed by his side. I helped him with his recovery after a surgery that claimed a lobe of his lung, and I nursed him back to health after the radiation. While he was in the hospital, I remember him telling the nurses that they could not bathe him—he had his own personal nurse that would do that, and I did. The doctors didn't tell us that most patients only lived about one year after lung surgery.

The day he died, we got up, got dressed, and had coffee with another couple and then went to Olympia, although I don't remember why we went to Olympia. When we got back in town, we stopped at the grocery store. It was so crowded that I just turned around and told John I would do the shopping later. We were about a block from the house, and he was holding my hand as he often did. I remember him giving my hand a squeeze about a block from the house. Then, as I drove into the driveway, I asked him something or started to ask him something, and he wouldn't respond. He was still holding my hand. I honked my horn, and someone came out of the house. I don't remember who it was, but I told them to call 911. I didn't want to let go of his hand, but I made myself get out and go to the passenger side of the car. I opened the door and tried to wake him, but he was unresponsive. The ambulance was there in nothing flat. They took him to the hospital but couldn't revive him.

John was the only man I really truly loved. I probably thought I was in love with Butch and Al, but it just wasn't the same. When you're really truly in love, you know it.

Just keep going…

That's what I did, and that's what I continue to do. It's been a long road, and much of it was not yet paved. Looking back, with today's ethics, morals, and laws some people might question the decisions I made. But I did what I thought was right at the time. It wasn't easy, and I sure wouldn't want to relive it, but I have no regrets.

I've lived and learned.

I know people shunned us for what my brother David did, but I've learned that you can't judge an entire family by the actions of one member. My family was amazing in so many ways. They always stood behind me, supported me, and helped me when I needed it. Unconditional love was what they gave me and taught me to give. They were there to listen, to advise me, to help me figure out what I needed to do. For me, family always came first—and still does.

I've learned that you can't tell anyone who to love or when to love. But I will tell you this—if you find yourself with an abusive spouse, get out as quick as you can. Don't stick it out for sixteen years and keep going back as I did. Even if it is your first love, know that there will be others.

Butch was too damn mean to raise kids. I would kidnap the kids again if I had to—no regrets there. And just so you know, I didn't stay out of Colorado for seven years either. I took the kids with me and went back to visit my family about once a year, usually around Independence Day. I wanted them to know the people I loved and the people who loved us unconditionally. Once I got pulled over in Gunnison on my way out of Colorado, and I about peed myself it scared me so bad. But fear—being afraid—it's no way to live your life.

I figure while I'm here, I have a job to do. Maybe my job was to raise my kids, keep a roof over their heads and food on the table, and make sure they knew I would always love them. Maybe my job was to be a nurse and care for others. I loved everything about my nursing career. I learned so much. I especially enjoyed working in the mental institution and later on working with Alzheimer patients. For these patients I think it was sometimes harder on the families than it was on the patients. These patients really needed someone to show them care. I especially liked the ornery ones. They had a little spunk in them.

Maybe my job was surviving in situations that required the gumption to do what I felt was right so that I could tell my story. Most people know inherently what's right. I listen to my gut and follow my heart—it's a combination of that, will power, and God that's got me this far.

Now my kids are grown, and I have grandkids and great-grandkids. I finally retired from nursing when I was in my seventies. So now, my job is to do what I want to do.

Of course, I always did.

EPILOGUE

This story is a piece of my life. Many years have since passed, as have my parents and all my eleven brothers and sisters. I just had my eighty-first birthday, am an active volunteer in my community in Carnation, Washington, still travel back to Colorado when I can, and enjoy as much time with my family as I can get. My children are grown with families of their own. I have thirteen grandchildren, thirteen great-grandchildren, and a foster child (little Emma).

Tony lives with his wife in Florida. He still rides a motorcycle, but he's stayed out of trouble for the most part. He was able to turn his life around. He's the only one of my kids who followed in my footsteps and went into nursing. We talk on the phone regularly, and I stay in touch with his daughter and her two children who live in Texas.

Helen divorced her first husband. She's been married to her second husband for more than twenty-five years. They have a beautiful home in Olympia and two daughters. Helen homeschooled her daughters, who are now both college graduates. Both girls are grown, and her husband's children are all grown as well. It's only about an hour's drive to Olympia from my house, so I see them often. We always get together on holidays and special occasions. We've maintained a good relationship.

Janet was a lot like Mama when she was younger. Now I think she is more like me than any of my other kids. She's a single mom of two. Bobby, her eldest son, is my first grandson, and his daughter is my first great-grandchild. Bobby died at age twenty-three. This book is dedicated to him. He will always hold a special place in my heart. He had a heart as big as all outdoors and was as ornery as sin. He was living with me in Florida when he passed away. I was in my seventies and ran a day care at my house during the week and worked weekends at a nursing home at that time. He often helped me with the kids. On Sunday, May 4, 2003, I came home from work at eleven in the evening and found him unresponsive in my living room. It took me a long time to recover from this. About a year after Bobby's death, Janet adopted her daughter. I moved back to Washington and helped care for the baby. She is my youngest grandchild, and I still babysit her after school. They both live in Redmond, ten minutes away from me. My great-granddaughter lives in Grays Harbor with her mother, and we see her often.

Debbie is a single mom with three sons. Debbie's youngest is still in school, but the other two are grown. Her eldest is in college and lives nearby. He regularly joins me for breakfast and helps me with chores here on the farm in Carnation. Debbie has always been a mama's girl. She's always lived near me, no matter where I've moved over the years. She would pack up her kids and be right behind me. She lives in Olympia now, which is about an hour away, and probably the furthest away she's been in years. I think we both wish she lived closer. She makes frequent trips to Carnation to visit, and I drive down to Olympia to see her too.

Eddie turned out to be a very caring grown man. In some ways he reminds me of Al. He'll tell you that he's happily married, but he hasn't lived with his wife for probably fifteen years. He has two grown children, a son in Texas and a daughter and two grandchildren in Centralia, Washington. He's currently an ironworker and stays here with me in Carnation when he's not working out of town. He's a very devoted son and very handy when it comes to upkeep here on the farm.

I didn't keep track of Butch over the years. On April 18, 2011, at the age of eighty-nine, he passed away. I know that Helen helped care for him during the last couple of years of his life. But I can't think of a thing more that I want to say about him.

My first family—Mama, Daddy, and all my brothers and sisters have passed from this world but are never forgotten in mine.

Edwin Earl Smith Sr. (Daddy)
November 16, 1891–September 24, 1981
Myrtle Climena Smith (Mama)
June 1, 1893–May 11, 1964

Mama and Daddy were both born in Kansas. They married on December 22, 1911, and had twelve children together. Daddy was a farmer, cattleman, and accomplished blacksmith. However, after moving to Colorado in 1934 and after several years of farming in the Rye area, he moved us to Pueblo where he drove a delivery truck and then became a manager for the Westland Oil Company, until his retirement.

Mama was a schoolteacher until she married Daddy and devoted her life to being a wife and mother. She provided our meals, our clothing, and a loving, nurturing environment for us kids. She was the most wonderful mother I could ever imagine having. Daddy was extremely good to her. Even when he didn't have money, he would save to get her what she wanted, like her blue Willow dishes and her bedroom set. One thing I know for sure is that Mama and Daddy lived for their family and loved each and every one of us with a recognizable unconditional love.

Unfortunately, diabetes complicated Mama's life. On May 11, 1964, she lay down for her final rest.

Daddy stayed strong well into his eighties. In fact, he flew to Washington for a visit when he was in his mid-eighties. Then, just a couple of month before his ninetieth birthday, he passed away quietly at home in the house that he built. His granddaughter and great-granddaughter were staying there with him. At the time he had thirty-two grandchildren, sixty-two great-grandchildren, and eighteen great-great-grandchildren.

Rosella Pearl
January 6, 1913–August 21, 2000

On August 21, 2000, at the age of eighty-seven, Pearl passed away after a lengthy illness. At the time, she had eleven grandchildren, sixteen great-grandchildren, and five great-great-grandchildren. Her husband, Sam, and her sons Don and CE passed on before her, as did one grandson and one great-granddaughter. She will always be remembered for the kindness, strength, unconditional love, and devotion she gave to her family.

Her kids—CE, Sammy, and Phyllis—and I stayed close all through our lives, regardless of the distance between us. Sammy now lives in the house that Daddy built.

Ellis Ulysses
June 18, 1914–February 4, 1991

After World War II, Ellis got married to Edna and lived in Texas. I saw him occasionally when they came to visit Mama and Daddy in Colorado. But it seemed to me that he changed after the war and after getting married. He didn't show as much affection toward his sisters as he did before. Still, I remember him as a gentle, kind, and caring brother.

On February 4, 1991, while I was celebrating my grandson's third birthday, I got a call that Ellis had passed away. He was seventy-seven years old.

Sarah Elizabeth
March 1, 1916–March 14, 1984

Sarah started her nursing career in her forties and stuck with it until retirement age decades later, even though she didn't have to work, because her husband provided for them. I trusted Sarah completely with my children. She stood by me, always stayed in contact, and willingly lent a helping hand when I needed it. There couldn't be a more supportive sister.

On March 14, 1984, at the age of sixty-eight, Sarah passed away.

Aubrey Uriah (Scott)
February 8, 1918–July 29, 1989

He liked gambling, dice mostly, and it caused him some problems. I think after some run-ins with the law over gambling debts, he changed his name to Scott Ericson and made a new life for himself. Personally, I never saw anything but good in Scott. I appreciated his help with my son, who needed an encouraging male influence in his life. I'll never forget how Scott stepped up and provided guidance for my son when he needed it. After suffering from a stroke, Scott passed away at the age of seventy-one.

Zelma Climena
November 5, 1919–August 29, 2006

Zelma was more than a sister; she was a friend.

As we grew older and our hair grew whiter, we continued to enjoy trips together. Be it gathering seashells in the rain on a beach in Florida, a gambling cruise in the Caribbean, or wondering at the green, green growth in the Pacific Northwest, seeing something different brought us joy together. The last time I saw her in Colorado she was in the hospital and wanted to come to Washington with me. I told her next time I would take her. But she didn't leave the hospital. She passed away on August 29, 2006, at the age of eighty-six.

At the time she had nine great-grandchildren and four great-great-grandchildren. Her husband Bill passed before her. Zelma was an LPN who spent years helping those who needed her, including family. Zelma retired from Sangre de Cristo Hospice in 1999 at the age of eighty, having many years as both a dedicated volunteer and employee. Many referred to her as a legend at hospice. At the time of her death she was also an active volunteer at the AARP Pueblo Information Center. She just loved helping others.

Edwin Earl Jr. (Sonny)
July 17, 1921–February 24, 1945

I didn't get nearly enough time to enjoy his company before he went off to war during World War II. He was killed in action in 1945 in Manila on February 24, 1945, one day before Americans recaptured the area. His name has been posted to the Veterans Bridge in Pueblo, Colorado.

Charles J.
April 18, 1923–June 11, 1982

The last time I saw or heard from Charles was when I was living with Butch on the farm in Pueblo, shortly before he moved to Indiana. He died June 11, 1982.

David Grant
June 4, 1927–May 9, 1996

David died alone in a nursing home on May 9, 1996. Despite everything, I loved him.

Agnes Sophia
September 13, 1929–December 16, 1982

When I moved to Washington, we visited Agnes and her youngest daughter, Jody, often. Janet, Debbie, and Jody are still close. Agnes passed away at home on December 16, 1982, at the age of fifty-three. At the time she was working as a nurse at a nursing home in Centralia, Washington. She had three children, eleven grandchildren, and a great-grandson.

I'll never forget her smile.

Arthur Eugene
August 21, 1931–September 3, 1958

Arthur was a good brother who provided endless entertainment during my childhood. Arthur lived in Pueblo for about twenty years before moving to California. He died at the young age of twenty-seven, in Orange, California, on September 3. Although the authorities said it was a suicide, I still have my doubts.

Elva Ruth
February 9, 1935–July 25, 2005

Elva and I were very close. We were married and having kids at the same time. I think we became closer as we became grown women with kids. We spent countless hours at each other's homes and had just as many hours of fun and laughter together. Her husband was a bit like mine. At times he could be mean and controlling, and I would get so mad at him. But I held my tongue. I knew if I opened my mouth it would only make things worse for Elva. But he could also be very fun-loving. I enjoyed numerous Colorado vacations at Frank and Elva's house, with water fights, fireworks, and just plain old-fashioned together-time visiting. Frank used to say that I was nothing but trouble for Elva. But thank God he never stopped me from seeing her. He knew how close we were.

Over the years, I made several trips to Colorado to help Elva battle cancer. Then, on July 25, 2005, at the age of seventy, Elva passed away. At the time her six children had given her sixteen grandchildren and nine great-grandchildren. She was a dearly loved wife, mother, grandmother, and sister.